MW00699301

Saint Paul

Saint Paul

Master of the Spiritual Life "in Christ"

Elliott C. Maloney, OSB

A Michael Glazier Book

LITURGICAL PRESS
Collegeville, Minnesota

www.litpress.org

A Michael Glazier Book published by Liturgical Press

Cover design by Jodi Hendrickson. Detail from *But Now that You Have Been Freed from Sin*, Thomas Ingmire, Copyright 2012, *The Saint John's Bible*, Saint John's University, Collegeville, Minnesota, USA.

1   2   3   4   5   6   7   8   9

Library of Congress Cataloging-in-Publication Data

Maloney, Elliott C.
    Saint Paul, master of the spiritual life "in Christ" / by Elliott C. Maloney, O.S.B.
        pages   cm
    Includes bibliographical references and index.
    ISBN 978-0-8146-8265-4 — ISBN 978-0-8146-8290-6 (ebook)
        1. Bible. Epistles of Paul—Theology.   2. Spiritual life—Christianity.
    3. Catholic Church—Doctrines.   I. Title.
    BS2651.M35   2013
    227'.06—dc23

                                                            2013041490

Contents

Part Two
God's Gift to Humanity "in Christ"

Preface

As far back as 2007, after many years of teaching the New Testament, I began to feel something was missing in the usual approach to Pauline studies in textbooks, college classes, and even seminaries. Although my main scholarly focus was on the Gospel of Mark, I had been teaching surveys on the Pauline corpus for almost thirty years. Even so, I knew that I didn't really have a handle on what the great saint says about the spiritual life in the day-to-day activities and concerns of Christians—about how people should *live* in covenant relationship with God, committed to seeking God's will in every aspect of their lives.

"Spirituality" is a popular topic among Christians and others, but it is often treated as something separate from ordinary life, or as only a part of life on some "higher level" when compared to the ordinary. Furthermore, even Catholic scholarship, notable as it is in Pauline exegesis and theology, can sometimes lack a certain feel for the kind of living Paul wanted for his communities and so miss out on his wisdom for modern-day Christian living.

For Paul, all of a believer's life is the spiritual life; the alternative is a life "according to the flesh," a self-centered life without God, a continual spiritual death. Surely my life in our Benedictine monastery here at Saint Vincent Archabbey had a lot to do with the question of how to live as Paul imagined a Christian would, especially since our Rule depends so heavily upon Scripture for its inspiration as a "school of the Lord's service" (*Rule of St. Benedict*, Prologue). As a matter of fact, now that I look back over more than forty-five years of life as a monk, I wonder why I didn't start asking these kinds of questions much earlier.

Late in 2007, I contracted to teach a course on St. Paul's letters at the Dominican seminary in Ibadan, Nigeria, having already had two very exciting visits to that land of joyful people and painful contradiction. It was then, even before Pope Benedict XVI's announcement of a "Year of St. Paul," that I decided to throw myself fully into research and teaching in preparation for writing this book. In the spring 2008 semester I taught my usual two classes on the Pauline letters: a graduate course here at Saint Vincent Seminary and an undergraduate course at the liberal arts college. I also began teaching an online course for Dominican Institute that I would conclude in person in Nigeria after the spring semester ended.

Following my summer in Nigeria, I was granted a study semester to read at the great library of the Pontifical Biblical Institute in Rome and then at Candler School of Theology at Emory University. I was privileged to give three Bible workshops to many of the spiritual leaders of the Catholic Church in Jamaica, and it was there that I came up with the precise topic and an early sketch of what I felt needed to be covered in my book. Thank you Sr. Bernadette! I spent the end of that semester with beloved friends in Brazil—scholars, monks, and laypeople—who always teach me about authentic Christian living. Returning home to St. Vincent, I taught my two St. Paul courses once more and finally started writing in May of 2008. It was just about three years later when I first submitted the manuscript of this book for publication.

How little I knew of St. Paul, even after teaching him for so long! For three years I pondered his letters, reading and rereading them, reading around them, reading about them in so many excellent publications. I taught, gave Bible studies and retreats, had conversations and spoke to our monastic community about St. Paul. And I wrote—day and night thinking, asking, and dreaming. Yes, a lot of my best work happened while I was asleep!

I was happy about the "Year of St. Paul," since so many fine introductory books on the subject were produced. But this is not an introductory book on the great theologian. I have tried to make this study as accessible as possible to the educated lay reader who has had some introduction to the subject, but I wanted also to help seminarians and theologians to understand St. Paul more clearly, and perhaps even bring something of interest to my peers in biblical scholarship.

In order to begin to understand the subtlety and complexity of the Apostle's ideas, one has to look at multiple texts. Paul was always nuancing his great ideas, applying them, fine tuning them, even rethinking them. I have tried to relate some of this richness by citing many, but by no means all, of the pertinent texts. Lest the reader feel bogged down in detail, I give a summary at the end of the longer sections of the book and have placed a more detailed data set in the Appendix.

I must thank too many people to mention here: my teachers, my students, the great Pauline scholars of yesteryear and of today, along with many insightful writers from all over the world. There are two very important people in the process that I want to name and thank here: my confrere Fr. Campion Gavaler, OSB, whose fine insights helped me to clarify several points, and Pastor David Ackerman, whose careful reading of the text was reassuring, helpful, and very exact. Perhaps most important was the support and patience of my Benedictine community during this long process from my awakening to the fact that I knew Paul so poorly to my discouragement at the sheer size of the work I needed to do. Later setbacks from a couple of unwilling publishers required an update of the manuscript to include several important new books. Because of the loving patience of many friends and confreres, I now feel a greater esteem and empathy with the extraordinary Apostle whom I shall from now on simply call "Paul."

I would be very happy to see much more of an ecumenical dialogue on the question of the spiritual life according to Paul, a conversation that would emphasize our part as members of a believing community, following Christ as model, channeling God's grace and changing our world into "a new creation." There is still much to learn from Paul for our contemporary Christian living and witness.

Introduction
Some Preliminary Considerations

This is a book about the Christian spiritual life as taught by the master, Paul of Tarsus. Throughout the centuries of the Christian movement there have been great teachers, "masters," of the way believers in Jesus Christ are to conduct themselves. Paul of Tarsus was certainly one of the greatest of them. The word "spiritual" in the phrase "spiritual life" reflects Paul's own characterization of human life in its entirety as it is transformed by God's Spirit in Christ. Thus the spiritual life does not mean some "higher" part of the human endeavor in contrast to the "secular" or "ordinary" concerns of daily living. For Paul, spiritual people are those whose whole lives are different because they have rejected a life without God. They have been taught the Gospel of Jesus Christ by the Spirit and are thus able to discern all things differently from those who remain locked in sin, "in the flesh." Thus the whole of life for Christians is affected, from acceptance of the Gospel as its center and its sustenance, to the entire range of generous and selfless activity in community, including the ethical life, the exercise of one's gifts, and every facet of life up to the transformation of life itself in the resurrection.

We need to be aware of some common ways Pauline teaching gets misconstrued. It is natural to think that every culture is basically the same as ours, but we can misunderstand some of Paul's directives because of real cultural disparities between his time and ours that are not readily apparent to us. We can easily import some of our own cultural understandings into Paul's thought in a way that distorts it. Let us note some of these differences in order to clear the way for a more productive examination of the great apostle's theology and spiritual leadership.

Cultural Differences

As is well known, all the instructions we have from the great saint and theologian exist in several letters that address ongoing problems in specific communities. Paul personally brought the Gospel to most of these communities, and their members were well acquainted with his teaching. We, on the other hand, do not know either the extent or the full content of Paul's earlier evangelization of those communities. We can hear only one side of the conversation in Paul's letters, and we are not always sure of the context of his words. This we must try to ascertain by a kind of "reading between the lines," so as to more fully understand the background and thus the fuller meaning of what he says. It is important to keep in mind, then, that Paul and his readers had certain inside information that we do not have.

Paul is sometimes very hard to understand precisely because he was writing to these local communities, two thousand years ago, in Greek, in a profoundly different culture, addressing specific problems that may seem irrelevant today. In addition, he was almost always breaking new ground as he applied the Gospel to new situations and new problems in Gentile, urban, and extra-Palestinian locales. Indeed, Paul was often misunderstood, even by his own communities. No wonder that it is often difficult for us, living in our vastly different age and society, to get to the core of what he meant by the spiritual life.

It is a shame that many Christians do not know Paul's writings. Worse yet, it is a shame that that many good people have a dislike for the great saint because of what they have heard about him, whether from uninformed fellow believers or from confusing passages in the Pauline letters themselves, read out of context in church and left largely unexplained. The biggest problem that people have with Paul, I have found again and again, is an imagined intolerance, especially in his alleged anti-feminism.

As to Paul's alleged intolerance, we should understand that the early Christians shared the general cultural assumptions of their contemporaries in Italy, Greece, Asia Minor, Syria, and Palestine. This Circum-Mediterranean culture was an honor and shame society, very unlike our self-aware, psychologically sophisticated culture with its high regard for individual rights. In Paul's society, any accusation of error or failure of leadership had dire consequences. Hesitation at refuting accusations meant a breach of honor, which would cause a complete loss of face that meant an end to one's credibility and any further leadership. Hence Paul was insistent on maintaining the rectitude of his position, often in the then-current rhetorical style of belittling or caricaturing the arguments of his opponents. This was expected, for Paul received his share of rough handling, although he gave as good as he got.

Other cultural differences abound. For example, in thanking the Philippians for their monetary support, Paul sounds ungrateful when in fact the opposite is true. He says, "Not that I seek the gift, but I seek the profit that accrues to your account" (Phil 4:17). This may seem to us to be saying that he did not really need the gift. It is in fact a way of thanking them, but not in the profuse way that in Paul's culture was really a request for more gifts. There are many of these differences that we are becoming more fully aware of in recent study, and they have given rise to a whole methodology of scriptural interpretation, aptly called the "social-science approach." We shall discuss several other such differences in the course of our study, including differences in the experience of time, the politics and economics of empire, and the use of symbolic thought.

It was a very important consideration for Paul that his churches not act blatantly against the external cultural mores of the day. For much more so than in our culture, any unconventional behavior or dress would not only dishonor the individual himself or herself, but would bring shame to the whole group of which they were a part. Unlike our society, the ancients considered that loss of honor totally invalidated anything an individual *and their group* may have accomplished, no matter what the extenuating circumstances. Thus the stakes were very high when Paul argues that both women and men ought to be properly attired at public worship in accord with normal societal standards of his day. For many modern readers, the manner in which Paul sought to correct the conduct of certain women at public worship in Corinth sounds demeaning and offensive to those women. They think that he manifests the ancient conception that women were inferior to men and thus ought to be completely subject to them in all but a few domestic matters. But nothing could be further from the truth! We shall answer the question of Paul's supposed subordination of women in the one text he himself wrote on the subject (1 Cor 11:2-16) in our discussion on the equality of all believers in chapter 8. As for the other texts that in fact do subordinate women—Paul did not write them!

Pseudonymous Paul

When we consider the Scripture verses that offend modern, gender-aware readers, we first observe that all but one of these passages occur in texts that the majority of scholars now consider to be post-Pauline, that is, not written by the Apostle himself but by his later disciples. Such pseudonymous writing was widely practiced in the ancient world by writers who wanted to carry on the traditions of an important author, seeking to update the thinking of the past or to address important new questions. Pseudonymous writing, the writing of a new text under the name (and authority) of an established author, was common in both Jewish literature (e.g., the Wisdom of Solomon, the Epistle of Jeremiah, the Testament of Moses, etc.) and in certain Hellenistic writings like the Hermetic Corpus and the Sibylline Oracles.

This practice should not be judged by us as forgery. The ancient world regarded the individual identity of an author quite differently from our insistence on the inviolability of intellectual property. As a matter of fact, the vast majority of the Old Testament was written anonymously. It was the influence of the Greek literary tradition that led to the identification of Moses as author of the Pentateuch and David of all the Psalms.

In the New Testament itself, the original copies of the gospels were all anonymous; the names of the Evangelists were added to them only in the second century. The Letter to the Hebrews and the First Letter of John are also anonymous. As the Church became more at home in the Hellenistic culture, the practice of pseudonymous writing was used in the Letters of James, Peter, and Jude, and, as we maintain, for several letters attributed to Paul. Later, Christians in the second and following centuries produced a veritable avalanche of gospels, epistles, and "acts" attributed to well-known figures like Peter, James, Thomas, Barnabas, Mary Magdalene, and even Judas. The confusion that this caused is one of the chief reasons the Church had to establish a "canon" or official list of the twenty-seven specially inspired writings we call the New Testament.[1]

---

[1] For my Catholic readers, I want to point out that the official teaching of the Catholic Church recognizes that what God wanted to reveal in Christ "was faithfully fulfilled by the apostles . . . and others of the apostolic age who, under the inspiration of the same Holy Spirit, committed the message of salvation to writing" (*Dei Verbum*,

Almost any introductory study on Paul's letters will go into the details of this question of authorship, so here we may give just a brief resume of the major points. Of the thirteen New Testament letters attributed to Paul, only seven (Romans, 1–2 Corinthians, Galatians, Philippians, 1 Thessalonians, and Philemon) were surely written (or dictated) by Paul himself. The six other letters, even though they use his name in their introductions, were probably written with the literary convention of a pseudonym. There are two sets of these post-Pauline letters.

First, a triad of "deutero-Pauline" letters (2 Thessalonians, Colossians, and Ephesians) respond to new questions posed by Christians with language different in vocabulary, style, and theology from the seven "proto-Pauline," or clearly authentic letters. They represent a later development of and reaction to the teaching of authentic Paul. Some disciples, probably members of Pauline churches who knew his letters well, decided to invoke his authority to respond to new pressures both from within and without their Christian communities. A majority of scholars think that even if these three writings contain some material from Paul himself, their overall composition and theological tendency is from a later date and by a different author. This is most evident in discrepancies in the writings with Paul's own teaching on eschatology, transformation, reconciliation, mystery, faith, justification, salvation as future, Christology, ecclesiology, and the grace of Christ, not to mention the attitude to slavery and the role of women in the Church.

The second group of pseudonymous writings, the so-called Pastoral Letters (1–2 Timothy and Titus), are even more remote from Paul. A very great majority of scholars think that they reflect a background of a more developed and institutionalized church at the end of the first century, or even at the beginning of the second. By this time Christianity had become more of a successful movement and began

---

2.7; italics added). The 1993 Instruction of the Pontifical Biblical Commission allows for the possibility of pseudonymity in the canon of Sacred Scripture when it holds "the conviction that the writings of the New Testament were a genuine reflection of the apostolic preaching (which does not imply that they were all composed by the apostles themselves)" (III.B.2). Thus the Church recognizes the inspiration of the Holy Spirit in all the canonical writings of Sacred Scripture, regardless of the identity of their inspired human authors and the development of the Church's beliefs and praxis in them.

to avoid conflict with non-Christians by conforming more and more to the ideals of the imperial culture of which they were becoming a part. Some of their teaching actually contradicts that of the proto-Pauline letters. For example, a quite different teaching on the ministries of women appears in 1 Timothy.

Since such is the extent of the doubtfulness of authenticity by a majority of scholars, and since so many of the discrepancies they see occur in the very instructions that we wish to examine in this study, it seems best to concentrate on the seven undisputed Pauline letters only. To be sure, there is important inspired teaching in the disputed letters, too, but that material must wait for another study.

The Methodology of This Book

Having laid out our reasons for considering only the seven undisputed Pauline letters in this study, we may now press on with our inquiry about the spiritual life according to Paul. We shall begin in chapter 1 by presenting the problematic that Paul believed confronted every man and woman, namely, the human condition that works against what thinking people know can be our true greatness. In chapter 2 we consider Paul's belief that the law of the Hebrew religion was inadequate by itself to deal with the human dilemma. Specifically, we will look at the two ways the Pentateuch sets up the problem of human imperfection and separation from God and sums up how God used Israel to commence the great story of salvation. We shall see how, according to Paul, Israel both failed in its mission (not producing righteousness) and succeeded (bringing forth the Messiah).

At this point we shall begin to explain the threefold manner in which Paul explains the present possibility of salvation based on what occurred in the Christ Event (the suffering, death, and resurrection of Christ). First, in chapters 3 and 4 we discuss the rich theological images that Paul presents as his way of explaining the effects of Christ. Next, we identify in chapters 5 and 6 the gift of the Spirit, as Paul speaks of how the Spirit affects the whole of Christian life, that is, "the spiritual life." We then move on to chapters 7 and 8 where we will delineate the various nuances of Paul's most frequent descriptor for the new possibility for humanity: the community "in Christ."

After this exposition of what God has done for humanity in Christ and their present existence as believers—what we may call the Pauline "indicative"—we present the climax of the book in chapter 9, "The Praxis of the Spiritual Life 'in Christ.'" Here we shall examine what Paul wishes for his communities, what he prays for, and what he tells his communities to do. After presenting the data, we shall organize these wishes of Paul in a summary of how he says that Christians ought to live in response to God's offer of salvation for humankind. Our study will then conclude with a description of what an ideal Pauline community of committed Christians might look like today.

Since constraints of space do not allow us to cite all the biblical passages we mention in the course of our investigation, it will be most helpful to read along with a Bible at hand. In the texts we quote, we have used the New Revised Standard Version of the New Testament when the translation is not my own.

Part One
Humanity before Christ

Chapter 1

The Human Condition

Human beings from the beginning of recorded history have felt that there was something drastically wrong with their lives. They know in their hearts that they are made for greatness but somehow, for some reason, many do not live up to what they truly are and what they should be capable of as they live out their days. The course of human history does not seem nearly like what it ought to have been. The ideal of what people *should* be doing too often does not correspond to the reality of what they actually *are* doing.

St. Paul uses several images to explain this human dilemma, depending on what aspect of human potential or failure he wants to emphasize at the moment. He often speaks of "sin" and "death," the result of Adam's rebellion against God's commandment, to underline human bondage to evil. On the other hand, when he wants to convey human weakness and the predisposition to living less than greatly, he uses the language of "the flesh," the realm of the "carnal." Other images are "the old person/self" (*anthrōpos*, what used to be translated as "the old man"), "slavery to the elemental spirits" (*stoicheia*, literally "the elements," the fundamental powers of this world), "the old leaven," and "the corruptible."

In order for us to more easily grasp these images Paul employs to explain the human predicament, it may be helpful to attempt a synthesis in which all these ideas have a place, so that we can more easily get our heads around some of his more difficult explanations. The great Pauline scholars have attempted this many times, and their monumental works have shown us that it is truly impossible to come up with a tight, logical schema that encompasses all of Paul's statements about the human condition and the many nuances he employs to drive his point home. This difficulty stems from the fact that Paul never wrote a full-length treatise on the human condition—or on anything else, for that matter. All we have of his great life and career, apart from the later presentations and updated theology of the post-Pauline letters and the Acts of the Apostles, are the seven letters he wrote over the span of some seven or eight years. Most of the time these letters are but small windows into a lengthy and complicated ministry to six different communities. In addition to this limitation, we also must deal with the fact that the ancient mind was not necessarily given to absolutely logical, abstract thought, the kind we find among philosophers then and the great thinkers of our day. Such consequential thinking is demanded for modern writing, but in Paul's time the impact of a rhetoric that employed concrete images was more crucial for the success of an argument. Thus many times Paul preferred symbolic thinking over abstract logic to convey a complex idea.

Symbolic Thinking

Symbolic thought depends on the familiarity of some concrete image to explain a difficult idea. It moves inductively from things already known to the realm of an unknown or a reality difficult to understand. A good example of such an image is the Greek word *ouranos*, "the sky," the concrete reality of what we see above us. When we moderns want to refer to the realm of the supernatural, we use a different English word, a nebulous abstraction called heaven. How different was the case in the ancient world! *Ouranos* was conceived of as a vast physical vault like a large arched ceiling above the earth upon which the heavenly bodies were affixed. Since it was utterly unattainable to the ancients who had no vehicle that could approach it, it acted as a symbol for all that is unattainable to humanity, and thus the natural place for the abode of the gods, the realm of the supernatural. Mountains were considered sacred because they were closer to the sky. This image of *ouranos* is used for the entirety of the supernatural realities people believed in, and it expressed very well to them the idea of the transcendent. Thus when Paul says, "Our citizenship is in heaven" (Phil 3:20), he does not mean that our real life ought to be somewhere else other than on earth. He is speaking symbolically. He means that our new Christian way of living should be governed by a supernatural character, and not by creaturely laws.

We moderns still understand the meaning and importance of citizenship. When Americans travel to some out-of-the-way place, they are often consoled that their citizenship is in the United States. With passport in pocket, they feel protected by that relatedness. Their citizenship is always in the United States, even though they may actually be in Thailand. What makes our understanding of *ouranos* so difficult, however, is that we have a completely different understanding of "sky." After all, it is a place we've been to and beyond. We know that it is not a physical vault, but an illusion caused by the light of the sun because molecules in the air scatter blue light from the sun more than the red. At night the effect disappears and we are able to look far beyond our atmosphere to the light of the distant stars. Using the sky as a symbolic image is not really very helpful when we want to name the supernatural abode of the gods. So, we often have to translate the word *ouranos* in ancient texts with our more abstract idea of heaven.

In contrast with symbolic thinking, abstract thinking works deductively, usually from nonconcrete ideas or premises, to build up meaning logically. The result of this process is what the Greeks called *theōria*, a stream of reasoning in which all the propositions flow logically, one from the other, and do not contradict each other. This is why we use the word "theoretical" in argumentation in our day. Paul is often accused of being illogical because one cannot always take everything he says and line it up in a system of thought—a *theōria*—but we must remember that Paul was not trying to do that. When using high rhetoric, one often overstates a belief to such an extent that, when taken out of context, one statement may contradict another one from another context. Symbolic thinking is like walking around a great piece of art like a monumental statue, and taking various snapshots from all angles. No photo can do the whole work justice, and by themselves some close-ups can even be misleading.

We propose the following synthesis of Pauline thought on the human condition not because we think that Paul thought with such modern consistency or such modern connotations for many of his ideas, but because we feel that such a presentation, inadequate as it is to his rich thought, can help us better approach the complexity of his ideas. A fuller understanding of what he says on any subject requires each of us to go further into the text and unpack the richness of the images he uses there for ourselves. With this awareness, then, we may proceed to explain Paul's understanding of how we are and how God wants us to be.

Two Biblical Images of the Human Condition

The Bible has many ways of speaking about the human condition, but two powerful images stemming from the creation stories in the Book of Genesis can help us understand the paradox of the human condition in Paul's anthropology—namely, the dilemma of knowing what we should do, but so often not doing it. The first story in the Bible (Gen 1:1–2:4) is a presentation of the origin of humanity in which God creates a totally good world out of chaos and nothingness. Here we see God calling into being the basic realities of the earth, gradually forming it by adding order and many good things. God reaches the culmination of creation by introducing human beings, male and female.

In the second creation narrative (Gen 2:4–3:24) God's finest creatures, both the man and the woman, break trust with their Creator in sin. Within these two different yet complementary creation narratives, I believe we can see the origins of two different ways of understanding evil and the way it affects the lives of humans in Paul's letters. The first way of speaking describes human weakness and fragility as it reaches out for the creative fulfillment that only God can provide. The second employs the well-known experience of human sinfulness as the origin of a broken humanity who "miss the mark" (the Hebrew meaning of "sin") set for them by a loving God. This sets off a tendency toward rebellion toward their Creator and conscious denial of their true greatness as creatures.

This twofold explanation of the human condition plays out in the later Bible stories in two narrative directions. The actors in them, who actually represent all living persons, are presented at times as innocent victims. For example, Job in the Old Testament, or the helpless marginalized persons that Jesus is constantly concerned with in the Gospels. But in other great Bible stories, we are told of sinners like Cain who kills his brother Abel, of the wicked citizens of Sodom and Gomorrah, of King David who seduces Bathsheba and has her husband killed, actors who knowingly do what is expedient for them-selves regardless of the consequences for everyone else. God is able to remedy the situation in both types of human weakness.

This is important to keep in mind because Paul is often character-ized as thinking only in the "sin and redemption" schema of salva-tion. I think, however, that an understanding of Paul as always and only focusing on the sinful nature of humankind can be misleading. It comes more from the interpretation of him by Augustine and Martin Luther than from the great apostle himself. So, while it is true that some of Paul's greatest insights into God's plan for the salvation of humanity flow from the "sin" model, there are other paths he maps out for his believing communities that are full of respect for human nature and the greatness it may attain with God's help.

The Image of Human Weakness: "The Flesh"

The central image by which Paul expresses the incompleteness of human beings and their inability to reach their potential as the image and likeness of God is "the flesh." In Hebrew the root meaning of the word "flesh" is the soft material of the body or the meaty part of an animal. In the Old Testament, flesh becomes an apt symbol for hu-manity in all its fragility and impotent existence. Flesh thus is a neu-tral term that can be used to connote a person's existence as human, as in the saying, "all flesh shall know that I am the LORD, your Savior" (Isa 49:26). This is simply another way of saying "all human beings; all people." Paul can use it this way, e.g., when he says, "If I am to live in the flesh, that means fruitful labor for me" (Phil 1:22). All Paul means here is that he will be able to continue to spread the Gospel if he remains alive. The flesh can even be the locus of our Christian witness: "so that the life of Jesus may be made visible in our mortal flesh" (2 Cor 4:11).

Ancient Hebrew thought is not dualistic, and so flesh is not opposed to "soul" or "spirit" as the material "body" is in Greek philosophy. The latter idea shows itself in modern thought as the body/soul dichotomy and divides the human being into the physical and the nonphysical. Although the Hebrew idea of "flesh" is transitory as belonging only to mortal life, it is not the same as our modern con-notation of "body." In fact, Paul does use the term "body," but for him it is a completely neutral term that encompasses all of one's concrete earthly life, good and bad, as when Paul says, "glorify God in your body" (1 Cor 6:20).

Nevertheless, Paul connects the flesh with imperfect humanity some twenty times out of a total of about sixty uses (almost all of them in Galatians 5–6 and Romans 7–8), especially in the phrase "according to the flesh" or the adjective "fleshly" (frequently translated into English by the word "carnal," from Latin *carnis*, "flesh"). In this usage he draws upon the basic meaning of flesh as the limitedness of the human being but focuses on how it may become closed in on itself, cut off from the source of its spiritual life, closed to the Transcendent: "The mind that is set on the flesh is hostile to God" (Rom 7:7). In this limited context we may understand Paul's use of the term flesh as a kind of shorthand for human weakness when bereft of a saving God.

It is a great misunderstanding of Paul's use of "flesh" to think that it denotes the human body in the sense of the physical. Because of this misconstrual, Christians at least since St. Augustine have reckoned Paul's condemnation of "fleshly" desires as limited to, or even focused primarily on, the human body, especially in its sexual aspects. This is very far from the truth. A simple example from the Letter to the Galatians shows that flesh has a larger meaning that includes all human faculties and activities. When the Galatians make the mistake of seeking to be justified by works of the Mosaic law, Paul says, "Are you so foolish? Having started with the Spirit, are you now ending with the flesh?" (Gal 3:3). Here Paul is pointing out an error in their faith life, not their moral behavior.

In today's existentialist language we might explain flesh as the condition of any human person reacting defensively when left to him or herself and bereft of God's help and encountering the menace of nonbeing and finitude (Gorgulho and Anderson 2006, 72). Such a person lives in a way that safeguards the ego and thereby closes off the higher calling of God's will. When the Corinthians divided into factions and became jealous and quarrelsome, Paul accused them of not acting like "spiritual" people but being "carnal" (fleshly), that is, behaving "according to human inclination" (*kata anthrōpon*), literally, "as a [typical] human being" (1 Cor 3:1, 3).

To sum up, "flesh" portrays the innate powers of humans as weak, their needs and tendencies as subservient, their lives full of anxiety and not truly free as God wishes them to be. As Jerome Murphy-O'Connor points out, being human for Paul means being a creature, but not one fixed in being like an animal whose progression to the fullness of life as God created it is instinctual and "automatic," as it were. The human has the choice to move toward life or death. As transitory, flesh refers to the inclination to the latter. Flesh is corruptible both physically and morally, and points at the frailty of mortal life and the disorientation of humans in their daily living: "To set the mind on the flesh is death, but to set the mind on the Spirit is life and peace" (Rom 8:6). As we shall see, Paul contrasts the realm of flesh with life "according to the Spirit," which is life endowed with God's grace—grace being the special aid necessary for one to live as God created humanity to live.

The Image of Sin and Redemption

Now we may examine Paul's other main image for the human condition, that of "sin." Let us begin with his very Jewish conception of salvation history, that is, of how the eternal plan of God plays out in the great stories of human history in the Old Testament. In this biblical tradition, God created Adam and Eve to begin a great family of human beings who could enjoy a loving relationship with a beneficent God (Gen 1:26-28). This aspect of their being the progenitors of a great clan of humans is very important, because in ancient thinking everyone's personal reality was deeply embedded in their identity as a member of a group. We might say today that their anthropology was preconsciously communal. As I have explained at length elsewhere, it is "a sociological factor so different from our modern psychological independence [our individuality] that without grasping it we cannot appreciate the self-awareness of the early Christians" (Maloney 2004, 88).

In Paul's day people did not think about themselves as individuals, nor did they consider their personal characteristics and limitations as making them "different." All thinking and moral choice was geared to and dictated by one's position in a group, be it family, religion, or clan. The accomplishments and failures of the clan head were visited on all the clan members in a way that identified them and conferred on them their reality as human beings. Paul's explanation of the origin of sin, what we call "original sin," is based upon this presupposition.

In the Genesis story, God gave the humans everything they needed to live a full and happy life, including a helping partnership between men and women. With the command to cultivate the goods of the earth, they were given the human instinct to preserve their life in freedom by enjoying all that God had given them that they might need. Since God wanted the humans to live in peace and without evil, God commanded the humans not to eat of the tree of the knowledge of good and evil. Here the story narrates, using the symbolism of a fruit tree, that God did not include evil in creation. Therefore, God did not need to give them the means to combat evil in their lives. In order to allow the first humans to return creative love in a truly mutual way, however, God gave them the freedom to choose whether or not to comply with this plan.

What happened next was something God did not want. The couple was tempted by what they perceived as their human limitation and succumbed to an altogether alien force for evil (symbolized by the serpent). They broke their trust with God in order to gain for themselves the divine knowledge of good and evil and so "be like God" (the serpent's words in 3:5). This, of course, did not make them like God, but instead destroyed their innocence, making them the slaves of the fear of all the bad things that could harm them and threaten their wellbeing. Protecting their own lives became more important than trusting in God. Thus they commenced a life of misfortune that God spells out in a divine edict, expelling them from Paradise (3:14-24), mandating the pain of childbirth and the subservience of women to their husbands, and the difficulty of their labor for men. Moreover, they bring the catastrophic results of this denial upon all their offspring.

God took a tremendous risk in giving humans the freedom to reject their Creator. The consequences were so terrible that the ancients expressed them as the direct results of a whole cosmic array of supernatural powers ranged against the happiness of humankind. There is a great intuition here, especially in the imagery of the Bible, for no one force can be singled out to account for all the misery present in the world. There are forces of evil too widespread to be allocated to any one person or movement. Rather, they inhere so deeply in the structures of society and in the very fabric of political action that they appear to be supernatural. Even today we find the need to express our wonder at the enormous evil of some megalomaniac leaders and ruthless cartels by calling them "satanic." Paul sometimes uses the powerful symbolism of these familiar evil powers and their ancient names: "elemental spirits" (Gal 4:3, 9), "death, angels, rulers, powers"

(Rom 8:38), and "Satan" (1 Thess 2:18; 1 Cor 5:5; 7:5; 2 Cor 2:11; 11:14; 12:7; Rom 16:20). He uses them to make it clear that God is not evil and that evil is not from God, but that God is striving mightily against evil in a cosmic battle that will not be completed until in Christ "the last enemy, death, is defeated" (1 Cor 15:26).

When Paul really wants to talk about evil, however, when he wants to grapple with this unexplainable mystery that appears to be a powerful reality independent from God and opposed to God's will, he departs from the usual biblical descriptors and speaks about "sin." He intuits that the brokenness of humanity is something that comes from the disorientation of humans themselves, and so prefers to discuss this reality with the image of something very human. The result is the personification of sin as a power that blinds human capacity and acts as a quasi-superhuman force that binds each person. Rather than trying to explain it theoretically (as I have just been doing), he uses the literary device of personification to bring to the imagination the picture of a superhuman power that, contrary to God's intention, enslaves all of humanity. Thus he portrays sin as a force that can, like a human slave master, inhibit and control another's life: "Jews and Greeks, all are under the power of sin" (Rom 3:9). Humanity's own sin, rather than some extrinsic alien power, has harmed human beings more than anything else in life.

Paul elaborates the metaphor when he tells us that sin not only entered the world (which it was not supposed to do) with the transgression of Adam and Eve, but that it spread its result, "death," to every subsequent human (Rom 5:12). Death, which was supposed to be a natural cessation of a normal lifespan, under sin became the crushing object of fear of one's complete annihilation. Paul, then, uses "death" as a symbolic way of talking about all the paralyzing effects of the sin of Adam and Eve that separated them and their offspring from God and brought a great spiritual darkness to humanity. This effect is roughly equivalent to what medieval theology calls "concupiscence." Spiritual death caused even more sin and so increased its power to the point where even God's own law, the Torah, was made the object of sin's power (Rom 7:8).

In what Paul says next, it is important to be aware of the ancient Semitic notion of causality that makes no distinction, as we do, between the active and permissive will of God. Without it one might think that God actually wanted an evil result, rather than just permitting it. Such thinking goes back to the fact that God created everything. In this way God is in some sense responsible for everything that happens, good or bad. Thus when Paul says that God "handed humans over" to the power of sin for a time until God could free them with mercy (Rom 11:32) we would say that because of their evil deed that God allowed because of the freedom God gave them, they are consequently ruled by the sin of their choosing (compare the language of Rom 1:24, 26, 28). Although human sinners are worthy of death (Rom 1:32), God wishes to redeem them from this slavery by creating in them the capacity once again to respond freely in love. As we shall see, this is accomplished by Jesus demonstrating God's own merciful love as the true source of life. Merciful love is the only power God can wield when it comes to human destiny, so greatly does God esteem the free response of men and women. God cannot force us to be truly human, for that is a contradiction. God knows that violence only begets more violence while mercy neutralizes evil and renders it powerless. Tersely put, "Cruciform love . . . does not inflict, but absorbs injustice" (Gorman 2004, 248).

Romans 5:12-21

Paul's main teaching on sin occurs in the Letter to the Romans, where around sixty of his eighty mentions of sin can be found. Just after he outlines (5:1-11) the wonderful effects of the death and resurrection of Jesus Christ, he explains what later theology calls "original sin" in Romans 5:12-21. His argument is difficult to follow because it is both truncated at one point and at the same time distracting in its added details. It is truncated because in 5:12 he says, "Because of this, just as sin came into the world through one person, and death came through sin"—and he doesn't finish the sentence. We would expect a conclusion something like "so also grace came into the world through one man, Christ, the second Adam, to bring life." But in his enthusiasm, Paul skips over the obvious and leaps to the sublime, saying "but the grace is not like the trespass" (Rom 5:15). Before he gets to verse 15, however, he complexifies his argument with a statement on how "death came to all" at the end of verse 12, and then goes on to add a very long parenthesis to clarify in verses 13-14 the difference between "sin" and "transgression" (= sin plus breaking a divine commandment). He goes on in the rest of chapter 5 to compare the wonderful effects of grace over the sad occurrence of what we call "original sin." We will examine these effects of the Christ event in chapters 3 and 4 of this volume. For now, let us get back to verse 12 to see just what he says about Adam's sin.

The first part of verse 12 is easy enough to comprehend: "Therefore, just as sin came into the world through one person, and death came through sin." The initial "therefore" of the verse refers back to the effects of the Christ event listed just before it in verses 1-11. The next words, the conjunctive "just as," as we have said above, set up the missing conclusion, "so also grace came through Christ." Having thus understood these initial words, we are left with a statement: "sin came into the world through one person, and death came through sin, and so death spread to all." Paul means that sin was not meant by God to be part of the world, but that it was the first Adam who allowed it to come in by his rebellion against God's prohibition of the forbidden fruit.

The text goes on to say that along with sin came its partner, "death." Death here is also personified as a power that hangs over humankind from Adam to the present day, a force by which "the many were made sinners" (v. 19). By this word Paul doesn't mean just physical death. Sin kills physically and morally, and so a total death is meant here. Such spiritual death refers primarily to the loss of true human life, a life designed, created, and based on an intimacy with God that we can see in the story of creation (Gen 1:26-29). With every sin one dies a little more, withering up spiritually, as Paul says, "sin exercised dominion in death" (v. 21a), so that the spiritual death of human freedom is also effected. After Adam and before Christ human life was bereft of any hope "that grace might also exercise dominion through justification leading to eternal life" (v. 21b). Although he never explains exactly how, Paul maintains that it was because of Adam's sin that spiritual death spread to all, and that all have sinned (v. 12). As Frank Matera puts it, "Adam's transgression was more than the pattern for future transgressions: it *made* Adam's progeny sinners" and "Paul portrays sin as a cosmic power that rules over Adam's progeny" (Matera 2012, 92).

How Humanity Misses Its Calling to Greatness

Now, according to Paul, even though they had no laws to guide them, primitive (and fallen) humanity was still able to perceive God in creation, "the invisible attributes of eternal power and divinity . . . through the things [God] has made" (Rom 1:20). By this he obviously means the magnificent reality of the universe, but he certainly includes the beneficial effect of human affection that God never took away, even after original sin. In fact, the high moral standards called for by so many pagan philosophers were proof that humanity could still discern what was right and what was wrong. Thus for Paul it is still possible that even people who do not have God's law to guide them can act rightly (Rom 2:14-15). But these exceptions aside— remember that Paul is thinking communally about the whole human race—the reasoning necessary for right behavior was so clouded over by humanity's sinful habits that they could not bring themselves to follow a high ideal: "by their wickedness they suppress the truth" (Rom 1:19).

The truth is that humans are relational beings: they are naturally oriented toward obedience and loyalty to a higher power (Rom 6:16). As we have seen, the way Paul sees it is that human beings were created to be in a loving and obedient relationship with God—nothing less than that. The authenticity and fulfillment of their lives therefore required them to honor this intimacy and thank God for the invitation to share in God's own being. But since their minds were darkened by that first denial of the sovereignty of God, the offspring of Adam and Eve continued to make wrong choices—from Cain's murder of his brother Abel to the petty injustices of the village marketplace where dishonesty became the acceptable norm.

Paul focuses on idolatry as the fundamental error of humanity in Romans 1, just as it is seen in Jewish tradition as the cause of all corruption (see esp. Wis 14:22-31). When people deny that the higher power is their Creator, their first sin is to fill up the void by making false gods (Rom 1:25). Worshipping a creature does two things: first, it fulfills the need to be related to something higher. Second, it inevitably ends up being worship of some aspect of the person's own self, whether symbolized in human or animal form. Thus the truth that God is transcendent and not subject to our bidding is suppressed. The inevitable result is a disordering of a human's proper role as a part of creation, epitomized by Paul in homosexual activity of married heterosexuals (vv. 26-27), but leading to all manner of injustice vis à vis their fellow human beings. Paul lists twenty-one vices to illustrate the way humans who have lost the proper worship of God mistreat their fellows (vv. 29-31). He calls the result of this injustice the wrath of God. He says three times that God "gave them up" (or "handed them over") to evil and that "those who practice such things deserve to die" (v. 32). Since such people cut themselves off from the life-giving unity with God, their whole potential is shut down, they succumb to spiritual death, and they suffer so badly from it all that it appears that God is angry with them.

The Wrath of God

The wrath or anger of God belongs to the great array of symbolic language used in the Bible to explain life's mysteries in a way that moves to action (rhetorical effect). It is in fact part of the symbolic picture of God that includes other human traits like jealousy, sadness, patience, and tenderness. God's wrath is one anthropomorphism stemming from another one: God's jealous love of Israel. These metaphors speak to our deepest human understanding of how a husband can possibly deal with an unfaithful wife that he loves, or how a father can mete out just punishment to a recalcitrant child. Although God's justice is often pictured as very strict, the overall conviction of the Old Testament is that "the LORD is merciful and gracious, slow to anger and abounding in steadfast love" (Ps 103:8; see all of vv. 2-18 and Isa 54:9-10). Unlike pagan gods, God is never simply in a bad mood! God's "wrath" is always shown as a reaction to human provocation: "God's anger lasts but a moment, a lifetime his loving mercy" (Ps 30:6).

In the New Testament, God's wrath is implied in the gospels primarily in eschatological threats of punishment. In Paul the word for anger, *orgē*, occurs only in 1 Thessalonians and Romans. As in the gospels, it refers to eschatological punishment (eight times), but in 1 Thessalonians 2:16 and Romans 1:18; 4:15; 9:22; and 13:4 it bespeaks God's present action. In both uses it is the anthropomorphic explanation of how a good and loving God could carry out due punishment in true justice: "Is God unjust to inflict wrath on us? For how else is God to judge the world?" (Rom 3:6).

Here we have an example of powerful rhetorical language of the Bible that, misinterpreted over many years and placed in the wrong context, can give rise to some serious misunderstandings about God. The contemplation of God as in a constant state of wrath against the sinfulness of humanity has given rise to a reciprocal alienation of humans from such an angry God. Humans know that when they are overcome with rage at another person, they forsake their love of them for a burning hate. It is all too easy for them to transfer such an attitude to God and think that God has stopped loving them. When people sever relations with God by sinning they lapse into such a dire state that it is easier to imagine that it was God who had severed relations with *them*. It is to dispel this alienation that Paul must expend a great deal of energy in presenting Christ's saving act as reconciliation, reconciliation not of God to us, but of us to God.

In my opinion the "wrath of God" for Paul is an image he uses for effect to vividly portray the catastrophe that results when sinful humans fall out of sync with their true destiny. The outcome appears so bad that it provokes suspicion that God really is angry at them and willfully closed to their approach. But Paul is using this metaphor to help people appreciate the fact that God cannot *unilaterally* overcome the gap left by sin. Paul knows that in reality God loves every sinner, and that the biblical "wrath of God" metaphor is supposed to help them understand the severity of this spiritual death of their own making. It is unfortunate that the metaphor is so easily used to shift the blame of human weakness on to a God "who does not love us anymore." When God's continuing overtures of love are then summarily rejected, the end result is society gone completely awry. The tragedy is complete when humans end up supporting each other in their sin, "they not only do (such sins) but even applaud others who practice them" (Rom 1:32).

Some Modern Categories to Help the Discussion

In order to better understand Paul's teaching about sin let us turn to some insights of psychology and employ the language of existentialism to explain it in a modern way of speaking. Gorgulho and Anderson point out that human nature and the structures of human psychology in themselves do not limit freedom, but since sin is socially inherited by all, it is thus anterior to the freedom of every person's behavior. It is a state of being that humans "find themselves in" without any control over its presence in their lives (2006, 71–72).

Sin pervades the human will and determines it in the direction of wrongdoing with its false orientation to self-preservation, what Paul calls "the flesh," as we have explained above. This ubiquitous yet unnamed anxiety masks creative freedom and the desire for authentic living because even before birth a person is subjected to the wrong-headed actions of parents and siblings. As children grow they are aware of how their loved ones act and react, and they hear them giving the advice of traditional wisdom: "Never back down from a fight! What's mine is mine! Those 'ethnics' are to be feared because . . ."

As we grow up the sin of a friend or relative against us may teach us to think that ultimately we can expect only evil from even our most trusted loved ones. Such betrayals inhibit our freedom to respond lovingly to the gracious overtures of our fellow human beings, and even of God. We become afraid of being hurt again to such a degree that we do not give anyone the chance of coming close enough to do us harm. This appears to be self-protection, but is in fact a great diminishment of our human life. Then when someone actually sins against us we are not ready to act with the loving patience and forgiveness that should have been built up by a trusting relationship. Instead, we counter with a sin of our own, thinking that self-protection at any cost is preferable to being hurt, no matter what that makes us do.

Paul considers the tragedy of human sinfulness to be an enslaved condition, but not as some irremediable corruption of human nature itself. This is a very important point for his understanding of what God gave to humanity in the Christ event. Christ was not some alien being who came to earth to magically transform humanity into another kind of being that is worthy of God's love. Humanity was already created in the image and likeness of God and never lost that potential. In his human nature Christ was a fully human, historical person who, with divine assistance, was able to live an authentic life under normal conditions. He was not some superman who lived in a utopian bubble. Thus Paul believes that Christ is a New Adam who is able to show us what is necessary for God to restore full human life in us. As our new patriarch and Lord Christ can guide our return to the original creative and authentic existence that God gave to the first Adam (and Eve) before the Fall.

We can use Murphy-O'Connor's existentialist language to help us understand, in an abstract, theoretical manner what Paul was teaching in his concrete, symbolic way when he spoke of "our inner nature" and "our outer nature" (literally, "our inside person" and "our outside person," *anthrōpos*) in 2 Corinthians 4:16. First, let us illustrate the difference between ontological and ontic possibility by comparing the action of a horse and a human. While the horse is ontologically incapable of rational thought, a human has this ability ontologically; it is one of the defining characteristics of human nature. However, a human may be prevented ontically from thinking rationally as the result, say, of a blow to the head. While the human is still ontologically (essentially as human) capable of reason, the accident may impede that particular man or woman's ability to be rational ontically, that is, in the realm of existentially possible activity, until such time as the injury is healed. There is nothing that can make the horse think rationally.

Human nature was not "ontologically" ruined, that is, it was not vitiated in its very essence, but the sin of our ancestors brought on a massive disorientation to their descendants, the whole human race. This made it nearly impossible to act freely. Here it is again important to recall how fully the ancients appreciated the communality of human being. The failure of Adam as head of the human clan is inherited by his offspring, we might say, as a false value system that humans grow up in, where dishonesty is quite acceptable and seen as necessary for self-protection. By the time they are old enough to choose their actions for themselves, children are already ontically helpless to choose the right action because they have adopted a second nature of selfishness and mistrust. The structure of their own (sinful) familial and societal existence has already determined their actions in the wrong direction.

The Untruth of Paul's Society

Since human existence is essentially social, the results of sin in human life take form in the concrete structures of society's institutions and validate injustice in human comportment. Egocentric behavior and defensive aggressiveness become the norm and the law, blinding people to their right to freedom and integrity as children of God. This has been the *modus operandi* of empire from time immemorial. From the earliest empires in Egypt and in Mesopotamia, selfishness and deceit have been the ruling factors that have allowed a warrior elite to dominate the vast majority of the population by violence, propped up by a state religion, and sustained by a "justified" exploitation. Leaders set themselves up as absolute dictators by the ruthless and unhesitating use of violence against any person or group that would challenge them.

Since sinful humanity worships power and control, it is an easy thing to develop a state religion that guarantees the divine sanction of the emperor and his minions. In it, the clergy are educated and sustained by the ruling class, and the popular theology they devise at the behest of their suzerains reinforces the worship of the gods who have given them victory. A "myth of reciprocity" guarantees the protection of the commoner from imagined outside forces in return for a ruthless burden of taxes and tolls that extracts from the peasant population as much as possible of the produce of the land (See more on this in Maloney 2004, 13–23).

In the time of Jesus and Paul it was the Roman Empire that controlled almost all of Mediterranean civilization and dictated the rules of society. With its all-pervasive propaganda it masqueraded as the perfect society, the epitome of what the very gods wanted for human stability and prosperity. Every coin, every temple, every forum (site of legal and political activity) and every marketplace was filled with images of the emperor and the slogans and monuments of his mastery of the world. This empire was the "world" in which Paul was living, an enormous and all-encompassing system of privilege, graft, and exploitation that affected all of its inhabitants. The self-seeking and violent results of sin in personal interaction in the empire became institutionalized, perpetuating injustice in every aspect of its governance and commerce. The untruth perpetrated in the idolatry of the emperor produced injustice of every kind, legitimating and institutionalizing the interests of the imperial family and their chosen aristocracy over all others.

This propaganda insisted that the divine emperor was "Lord" of all, approved by the gods in every victory of the Roman legions, bringing "peace and security" to all its denizens. Paul mocks this slogan when he points out that at the Parousia of Christ, "Just when they say 'Peace and security,' then sudden destruction will come upon them" (1 Thess 5:3). The only "good news" (*euangelion*, "gospel") in empire is that of the accession to power of a new and even more powerful emperor. The privilege of a state visit (*parousia*) by him promises that all evils will be corrected. In return, the populace had to submit to a patronage system, a completely arbitrary valuation of their dignity as human beings based on their willingness to adhere faithfully and submit unconditionally to their supreme "Lord" and master and his unscrupulous retainers. Society was based squarely on divisions between people, and the result was the covetousness of the "have-nots" to somehow gain status and the covetousness of the "haves" to attain ever more, both groups acting in the egocentric greed of hopelessness, trying to fill up the emptiness of their meaningless lives.

This is the "world" that parodies God's will for humanity and that God will judge (Rom 3:6). Its ideology, "the wisdom of the world" is false since it does not know God (1 Cor 1:20-21), but only the idolatrous image of God that is used to justify and cement the interests of one group over another. In this way "the spirit of the world" misunderstands what is truly divine and what is truly human (1 Cor 2:11-12). But this is also the world to which God is bringing reconciliation in Christ, the real Lord of all. His followers have become a remnant, chosen to live by God's grace, who "have not bowed the knee to Baal" (Rom 11:4-6). They are the ambassadors of Christ who announce the good news (*euangelion*) of a new creation, the message of reconciliation begun by God in Abraham and accomplished by Christ so that humanity "might become the righteousness of God" (2 Cor 5:17-21).

Chapter 2

The Beginning of God's Plan for Salvation

The Bible shows that God was unable to abide the sinful situation of his beloved creatures. God planned to restore humanity to the pristine loving existence lost by Adam's sin by forming a people. God instructed Israel how to live correctly, that is, "in righteousness," to be a witness to all the nations of the excellence of life under a loving God (Mic 4:2). God did this by making a covenant with them, giving them the Law—the biblical Torah—to guide them to live in true freedom and responsibility for all of creation the way that God had originally created all humans to live. They were to be a "holy people," a community set apart, special in their closeness to God and devotion to God's will.

To mark the Israelites as special, the Torah imposed the practice of circumcision whereby the male members of the covenant would be physically marked as set apart to do God's will. Furthermore, the diet of all Jews was to be special. They could only partake of those foods which were "clean" or "pure" according to a large set of regulations (spelled out in Leviticus chap. 11) that looked back to paradise and recalled the order of original creation. Finally, they would imitate God who rested on the seventh day of creation by doing no work on the Sabbath, a weekly feast day and part of a yearly festive calendar that marked and celebrated significant saving deeds of God for Israel. The reason for all this specialness (= holiness) was that Israel was to be God's instrument, a clearly identified priesthood for all the other peoples of the world (Exod 19:6). Their priestly ministry would enable the nations to freely accept a loving relationship with God because they would see in Israel all the benefits of living according their Creator's plan.

Paul's Critique of Israel's Response

When we examine Paul's criticism of Israel's response to covenant and law we must remember two things. First, Paul's struggle to explain the obsolescence of the law was not the center of his evangelization, his "good news" to the Gentiles. A new life for all people, both Jew and Gentile, was his basic message. He addresses the problem of the law at length only in his letters to Galatia and then to Rome. There the resistance of some Jewish Christians to the unencumbered entrance of Gentiles threatened to derail the authentic direction of the kingdom of Jesus Christ.

Not long after Paul moved on from the Galatian Christian communities that he founded, some Christian teachers arrived there to challenge the completeness of his instructions to them. They apparently insisted that only by following the whole Jewish law could the Galatians fully join the ranks of the followers of Jesus who was, after all, the Messiah sent by God to fulfill God's promises to the Jews. Paul saw this as an assault on the validity of the saving work of Christ for all human beings, both Jew and Gentile, for "if justification comes through the law, then Christ died for nothing" (Gal 2:21).

Years later, Paul saw the need to go to Rome in order to carry the Gospel further, even to Spain (Rom 15:23-24). In Rome, however, a deep rift had developed between ethnically Jewish and Gentile Christians, and a controversy raged over the practices of the law. Paul knew that he had to clarify for the Jewish Christians in Rome his earlier teaching so harshly laid out in the controversy in Galatia. At the same time he observed an attitude of some Gentiles Christians in the community at Rome for the Jewish traditional practices that called into question the very legitimacy of God's law. Thus the two concrete situations in two Christian communities (Galatia and Rome) account for the brunt of Paul's developing arguments on the validity and obsolescence of the law.

The second thing to remember is that although Paul could be very harsh in his argumentation against the imposition of circumcision and kosher food laws on his newly baptized, mostly Gentile, flock, he was always proud of his Jewish heritage (Gal 1:14; Phil 3:5-6;

2 Cor 11:22). He had only the greatest respect for his people, and when he criticizes them, he does so with the love and high regard of a Jewish prophet criticizing his own people—never as some outsider, some member of a superior religion. He explicitly uses the language of the Jewish prophets of old when he claims that it was "God who set me apart before I was born and called me through his grace" (Gal 1:15; see Isa 49:1-6; Jer 1:5). As N. T. Wright points out: "The prophet's task is to speak from the heart of the tradition, to criticize and warn those who, claiming to represent the tradition, are in fact abandoning it" (1997, 83).

Paul also upholds the unquestioned authority of the Hebrew Scriptures in all his arguments, whether about the justification of Abraham (Gal 3:6-9 and Rom 4), the sinfulness of all of humanity (Rom 3:9-20), the teaching of Deuteronomy on the law (Gal 3:10-14), and so on. He speaks from the heart "from the point of view of the Jew who believes that the crucified and risen Jesus is the Messiah around whom Israel is now defined" (Wright 1997, 84). Such "speaking from the heart" caused him at times to overstate his case in anger and frustration at the hardheartedness of his opponents whom he always considered his own people. For example, he rails unmercifully against the persecutors of the Jerusalem church and of himself, indicting their motives as purely selfish: "The Jews . . . killed both the Lord Jesus and the prophets, and drove us out; they displease God and oppose everyone by hindering us from speaking to the Gentiles so that they may be saved" (1 Thess 2:15-16). This is an extreme example of Paul's vitriol, and he probably should have either deleted it or at least toned it down when the secretary he used gave the text back to him for final approval. But who among us has not railed against their own family or group, sputtering, "Why, they're all just a bunch of . . .!"

We cannot be too sensitive to today's Jewish population who are only too aware of how Christians for centuries have used New Testament texts like this to persecute them. To understand this early Christian attitude about the sinfulness of the (non-Christian) Jews that Paul shared, we must see it as an attempt to explain how Israel could have rejected its own Messiah and why its leaders persecuted the Church. Paul makes a harsh judgment on his contemporaries among the leadership of his own people. It is not historically valid for all time, as if it could apply to today's Jewish people. Paul is attempting, as a Jewish prophet, to show the errors of those whose assume superiority and complacency and impede others who are seeking God (on this question see Byrne 1986, 61–62).

How Israel Failed

Paul needs to show that becoming a Jew is not necessary for people to embrace Jesus Christ, the universal savior sent by God for all the nations. To do this, he points out that what happened in the history of the Covenant people of Israel was not what God wanted. Their distinctness as God's holy people became for them a separateness from their fellow humans, too often with a disdain for their religious inferiors. Somehow they forgot the main reason for their specialness to God: their duty to bring belief in the one transcendent God to the whole world. Instead of engendering an openness to God's will in others, Paul claims, they began to think of themselves as privileged, superior to the Gentiles, and automatically righteous because they possessed God's law (Rom 2:13).

Paul further indicts his own people for regarding the Gentiles, who could not keep a law they didn't know, as hopeless sinners. They began to think of the Gentiles as the enemy of God, when in fact the real enemy was sin. It was sin that estranged the Gentiles from God by idolatry, but it was sin, too, Paul says, that somehow found "an opportunity in the commandment [the Torah]" (Rom 7:8) and made the law ineffective. It estranged the Chosen people from their duty to fulfill the task for which they were chosen. As a matter of fact, Paul comments, the prevalence of sin in their own daily lives made the commandments of the Torah a new power base for evil deeds for the Jews themselves: "Sin, seizing an opportunity in the commandment, produced in me all kinds of covetousness" (Rom 7:8).

Paul explains this failure of Israel in his letter to the Galatians by stating that the law was to be temporary. It was to be a regimen for the formation of the chosen people as long as they were awaiting the fullness of God's plan in the Messiah. He calls it a kind of tutor or nanny (*paidagōgos*, Gal 3:24) that they would outgrow when the Messiah should come. Instead of welcoming its guidance for a life free from sin, however, the people of God turned this gift of divine supervision into an absolute code of conduct. They exchanged their responsibility toward the world for a response of blind obedience to the law. No longer dealing with reality in all its complexity, many felt they only had to do what the law said.

Paul chides the false teachers at Galatia by loosely quoting the prophets: the righteous life is full of faithful trust in God, whereas living according to the Law just makes one dependent on it for everything (Gal 3:11-12). In this way, Paul says that they turned a great and holy gift from God into a prison of their own making that confined them to only a part of what God wanted. As Murphy-O'Connor says, "Through exaggerated reverence [to the letter of the law] the human obligation to make genuine choices was ceded to the Law" (2009, 117).

The Failure of the Law

Paul soon had to go further than his description in Galatians of the law as temporary. A controversy arose among Roman Christians between those who insisted on the necessity for all Christians to uphold all the traditions of the law and those who repudiated the practice of its regulations by calling into question the original validity of the law. There was no denying the fact that the law had failed, for apart from the relatively few Jews who became disciples of Jesus in the early Church, Israel did not accept Jesus as the Messiah. But to say that the law, the cornerstone of the history of Israel, was a mistake and that it should be completely discarded and forgotten was too much to bear even for Paul and especially for other Christians who had been raised as Jews before becoming followers of Jesus Messiah. Thus Paul had his work cut out for him: he needed to uphold the validity of the law as a gift from God while allowing that because of human weakness, the law had actually failed.

Always speaking in general terms about the majority of the chosen people, Paul maintains that they did not live up to their calling to be witnesses to God's will in their keeping of the commandments. Sin was also prevalent in Israel, and so Paul claims that for the Jew, "In passing judgment on another [the law-less Gentile] you condemn yourself, because you, the judge, are doing the very same things" (Rom 2:1). Instead, Paul accuses, they traded the doing of God's will for the mere possession of God's law (2:17-23, also 2:3).

Paul can speak knowingly to the frustration of Jews who were trying to keep faithful to God in covenant because he himself had been a most fervent keeper of the law. He states, "As to righteousness under the law (I was) blameless" (Phil 3:6). As a Pharisee, Paul knew all of the law and was intimately acquainted with the detailed application of it. He knew from experience that of itself, the law could not bring about the sinless society that God wanted. He knew this because he had *tried* it!

Seeking Righteousness that Comes from the Law

In a notoriously difficult passage (Rom 7:14-25) Paul attempts to explain this paradox of the Jew who wants to keep every part of the law but still misses the mark. He says, "When I want to do what is good, evil lies close at hand" (v. 21). The "I" here refers to a person's inner self, roughly what we might today call the "ego." Here Paul, as someone who has been redeemed by the grace of God in Christ, is addressing the dilemma of fallen humanity that tries to better itself with an *external* code of conduct. He claims that without a fundamental correction of the *inner* problem of the human self (the "I" in this text), a person is "of the flesh, sold into slavery under sin" (v. 14). All who were born into the sinful world were born in a condition of slavery. All have subsequently internalized a life of sinful response to the evil that constantly bombards them. To use Murphy-O'Connor's evocative image, it is like people in a polluted city who have no choice but to breathe in the poisonous air all around them (2009, 95).

No matter how hard "I" try to act correctly, "the law of my mind," the ability to see the right thing to do, is pushed aside by another, more powerful law, the "law of sin" that squelches freedom and pushes me toward further sin. So, no matter how good and holy God's law may be in and of itself, the proper response to it in action becomes impossible, for I am "captive to the law of sin that dwells in my members" (7:23). In fact, omnipresent sin even got into the law itself and made it a veritable base of operations for sin: "For sin, seizing an opportunity in the commandment, deceived me and through it killed me" (7:11). Thus there is no way that humans can live the authentic life of a loving relationship with God expressed through creative and engendering concern for others until that inner defect caused by sin has been rectified.

God gave the chosen people a law that clearly explained how to live rightly in a way especially suited to their manner of life in the Ancient Near East. The problem was that the chosen people as a faith community were never able to live up to their calling to form a sinless environment where all the people would thrive by doing the will of God. They were never able to fully live out that law because of the

effects of sin in their midst. Just when people come to the right conclusion of what they should be doing, the evil actions of others drive
them to react in like manner, sinfully, instead of acting lawfully (Gal
3:21).

The underlying problem in all of this is that evil cannot be overcome by reason or by the human will alone, since we of ourselves
are not equipped to deal with evil. Remember what we said above
about the creation of humans for a loving relationship with God and
with each other and God's prohibition to Adam and Eve about the
knowledge of good and evil. Original Sin, the evil that lies at the
bottom of every other human evil, prompts only further sin in reaction to experienced evil. Our mind wants to identify the evil and
punish the evildoer instead of overcoming the evil itself, as if by
perpetrating a new violence the harm of the first violence might be
erased.

Paul knows this wrongful practice of vindictiveness only too well,
for this is exactly how he felt toward Christians when he was persecuting them, as an evil to be crushed out. In particular his complicity
in the execution of Stephen (recorded for us in Acts 7:58–8:1) must
have haunted him for years, as we see in his anguished admission
of "persecuting the church of God and trying to destroy it" (Gal 1:13).
For although he thought he was acting most lawfully, he knew in his
heart, especially after the heat of the moment, that Stephen was really
a just man. Lucky for us Paul came to know Christ so that he could
show us the right response to evil: "Do not be overcome by evil, but
overcome evil with good" (Rom 12:21).

Romans 7 shows in a very poignant way the dilemma of anyone
who tries to live justly by following the rule of law without complete
reliance on God. These religious people (and this would include
Christians who act in this way) are well aware of their sinfulness.
Fearing the wrath of God and yet untrusting of God's assistance for
a truly free (and thus risky) life, they refuse to leave their nanny, the
law. They refuse, to quote Paul, "to serve in the new life (literally, "in
the newness") of the Spirit," and remain "slaves under the old written code" (v. 6). They revert to a survival mode in order to become
"secure" in their moral behavior by devising a life in which they can
be right all the time. The only way to achieve this is to have a set of
laws that convinces them that compliance with those laws insures
exactly what is necessary to be right. Without total reliance on God,
I know I can't always do the right thing and so I start limiting my

own freedom in order to avoid the "occasion of sin." Thus sin is still the principle of my being, even though my natural human goodness and all my willpower are directed to accomplishing God's commandments.

The sinfulness in me acts to overpower what I really want to do because I am still a slave to sin, not truly open to the transcendent. This schizophrenia paralyzes me, imprisons me, disempowers me and makes me wretched (v. 11). The confusion makes me hate myself as much as I hate sin, and so I try even harder to accomplish my law on my own, by my own will power. Now I am plagued by the law's curse, "Cursed is everyone who does not observe and obey all the things written in the book of the law" (Hab 2:4b). I now believe that it is up to me to "correct the record" and become fully responsible for my own righteousness. The result is a complete lack of spiritual growth, the only activity a constant battle with sin. One's state of mind becomes an anxiety of despair with a growing pessimism that no human being can ever change. This paralysis can never bring human fulfillment and satisfaction, but only a misery that dampens human joy and curtails freedom. Just thinking of someone in this state causes Paul to cry out for him, "Wretched man that I am! Who will save me from this body [= concrete life] of death?" (v. 24).

To sum up: the result of the evil caused by Original Sin in the world is a vicious cycle of further sin that compounds human sinfulness and brings on even more evil. It suppresses the truth about our human freedom that can only be fulfilled by absolute trust in God, and not by anything we do by ourselves. Without that trust our freedom ebbs away and we substitute idolatry for our true orientation to the Transcendent. We make a god out of a set of regulations and our own interpretation of them. We begin to believe that a preset system of laws can answer every situation in life, and so we abrogate our responsibility to meet reality with merciful love and the resultant growth of virtue that is true "life." Lovelessness quickly becomes selfishness, and selfishness is the greenhouse for injustice and cynical despair.

The Threat Posed by Some Jewish Christians

Although the religious leaders of Paul's own beloved Jewish people resented the Roman Empire deeply, they had in fact accepted it as an inevitable political reality. By bowing to its awesome political and military power, they won a certain freedom in their own internal religious affairs as a *religio licita*. This meant that Rome accepted Judaism as a "legitimate and permissible cult"—but the price was high. The Jewish leadership made themselves blind to the claims and demands of empire and instructed their faithful to do the same in order to protect their customs and devotions. For this they received certain exemptions from the explicit worship of the emperor, but in Paul's mind they were quite wrong in considering themselves free. In fact, they were completely dominated by the exploitative imperial social and economic systems. They became closed in on themselves and substituted a rigid legal existence as a clearly definable *religio licita* for a life of true justice inspired by trusting faith in God and tempered by God's mercy. They renounced their lawful duty to be faithful to the covenant by bringing to the Gentiles the true faith and worship of God, the real goal of the law. "Israel, who did strive for the righteousness that is based on the law, did not succeed in fulfilling that law. Why not? Because they did not strive for it on the basis of faith" (Rom 9:31-32). In fact, Paul must indict them further for not accepting their own God-sent Messiah in Jesus: "I can testify that they have a zeal for God, but it is not enlightened" (Rom 10:2).

For Paul, Christianity was an inner Jewish development that clearly rejected the hateful structures of the Roman imperial system that separated Jews from Greeks, slaves from free, and men from women. Submitting to the law's requirements for circumcision meant the acceptance of imperial values of division, since the whole point of circumcision is to give males added religious status as over and against Gentiles (and women!). Paul called out the Jewish-Christian teachers of the Galatians on their true motive for advocating circumcision: it was to preserve their *religio licita* status. "It is those who want to make a good showing in the flesh that try to compel you to be circumcised—only that they may not be persecuted for the cross of Christ" (Gal 6:12).

Indeed, for Paul, the rigid legal existence adopted by Israel only added to the divisions mandated by the empire. It seemed to justify and cement the empire's covenant of slavery and false security. It was only his gospel of freedom that showed God's true will for the concrete experience of fraternity in freedom. Only in this way could God create a new people, "the Israel of God," which would be a "new creation" where those former dichotomies would become meaning-less (Gal 6:15). Paul's communities were to be new carriers of the power of liberty throughout the enslaving Roman Empire. In them (as "the body of Christ") Jesus existed and communicated his life in human history by the formation of "the new person." Only this, and not Greek philosophy or Jewish law, could free them from oppression and the alienation of empire. It is only the saving death of Christ and his ongoing presence in the Christian community that could begin a community where sin is disempowered because it is met with love, not violence. In the next chapters we shall examine Paul's explanation of this saving remedy from God.

Part Two

God's Gift to Humanity "in Christ"

Chapter 3

The Effects of the Christ Event: Part 1

When Christians talk about what God did to resolve the human dilemma, they most frequently use the words "salvation," or "redemption." These are classic Christian ideas based on concrete images Paul uses to express what happens to believers because of Christ. But there is much more to Paul's teaching on God's remedy for humanity than those two words as they are typically understood. In addition to the two aforementioned images, Paul discusses the accomplishment of God's plan for all men and women in three large areas of consideration: 1) other metaphorical images of the consequences of the Christ event, namely, grace, expiation, justification, sanctification, reconciliation, liberation, transformation, new creation, glorification; 2) the gift of the Spirit; and 3) the unity of Christians and their participation "in Christ."

These are the basic and indispensable themes of Paul's soteriological teaching, his doctrine on salvation. Together they unite the past with the ongoing activity of 1) God the Father through Christ's saving deeds, 2) the Spirit as the power behind the new life, and 3) the Son who creates a new sphere of being for believers. All three complement each other as different ways of presenting the reality of the early Christians' conviction that they were being saved by the will of God as dynamically worked out "in Christ" through the Spirit. These three themes, then, will be the subjects of this and the following five chapters of our study.

Pauline Omissions?

Readers of the apostle Paul may be surprised by the rarity in his letters of two key terms central to the teaching of Jesus and to the proclamation of the early Church. "Covenant," the renewal of God's special relationship with human beings, was the decisive effect of the death and resurrection of Jesus Christ. Of the few times that Paul does use the word, he is usually referring to the old or Sinai covenant (thus the "Old Testament"), given through the ministry of Moses (2 Cor 3:14; Gal 3:17; 4:24; Rom 9:4; 11:27). Once it means someone's "last will and testament" (Gal 3:15), but Paul does speak of the "new covenant" in Jesus' words, "This cup is the new covenant in my blood" (1 Cor 11:25). He is perfectly clear about the idea when he says, "[God] has made us competent to be ministers of a new covenant" (2 Cor 3:6).

The problem is with the word itself. While the idea of "covenant" was quite at home in the languages of the Old Testament and of Jesus and the earliest church (Hebrew *berit*; Aramaic *berita*ɔ), the Greek word used to translate it (*diathēkē*) usually had the meaning of "last will and testament." The author of the Letter to the Hebrews plays with this ambiguity, likening the new covenant to a last will and testament of Christ that came into force only at his death (Heb 9:15). The new covenant is also behind the English name that the Church gives its Christian Scriptures, but it is translated literally as "New Testament." The fact that the Greek word *diathēkē* usually refers to one's last will and testament explains its infrequency in Paul—and also why many Christians today do not know that the New Testament is really about the New Covenant.

The second, and perhaps even more surprising near omission of a key term is "kingdom," that new state of being for believers who come together into the presence of God to do God's will. Scholars agree that this was the central teaching of the ministry of Jesus himself. In five of Paul's few uses of it he refers to inheriting the predicted fullness of the *future* kingdom (1 Cor 6:9, 10; 15:50; Gal 5:21; 1 Thess 2:12). Nevertheless, Paul does reassure us that he is well acquainted with the idea of the kingdom as present, when he says, "For the kingdom of God is not food and drink, but righteousness and peace and joy in the holy Spirit" (Rom 14:7; also 1 Cor 4:20; 15:24). As Gordon Fee has pointed out, "its casual appearance here indicates that [kingdom] was part of his own understanding of the gospel"

(1994, 120). The problem again was with the word "kingdom" itself. Paul's communities lived under the rule of an emperor, not a king, and so the very Jewish idea of "kingdom" or the total rule of God as a reigning king might be confusing to them, for whom a "king" was usually a puppet of the emperor.

The Pauline Images

We may now begin our discussion of eleven images that Paul used to elaborate the outcome of God's saving action in the cross and resurrection. In my seminary teaching I like to use the image of Michelangelo's famous statue of David in Florence in order to explain Paul's approach to the mystery of the Christ event. Each of Paul's classic images is like a view of the statue from a different vantage point in the Galleria rotunda where it stands. We cannot have a complete 360 degree view of the statue at any one time, but we may walk completely around it to gain one viewpoint after another and so come up with a more complete appreciation of the work of art than from any single standpoint. It is also important to realize that although Paul's eleven images gave rise to most of our often quite abstract doctrinal expressions of how we are saved, the early church and Paul chose them because they reflected common activities in their culture. Thus, to get the full impact of their meaning for Paul, we need to understand the religious or secular activities referred to, and then examine how Paul uses them to highlight each aspect of God's saving work in Christ.

Paul presents all these images as the product of God's initiative in Christ. We may study this bestowal of God's grace from two points of view, corresponding to the two biblical portrayals of the neediness of humanity that we have studied in chapter 1: first, the sinful state of humanity and then the condition of humanity as "flesh," imperfect and closed in on itself. In a discussion on justification Paul gives us the basis for our distinction: "[A]ll have sinned and fall short of the glory of God; they are now justified by his grace as a gift, through the redemption that is in Christ Jesus, whom God put forward as an expiation by his blood, effective through faith" (Rom 3:23-25). In this long statement we note Paul's twofold affirmation of the deficit of all humanity as 1) owing to sin and 2) as lacking "the glory of God," that is, not attaining the fullness of their creation "in God's image"

(Gen 1:26). This establishes our distinction of human imperfection as 1) caused by *sin* and 2) as the result of being *flesh*, that is, of standing alone bereft of "the glory of God."

Thus we may present all eleven of Paul's images of the results of God's loving action in Christ in two chapters: first, grace itself, and then the images that flow from the Christ event as expiation of sin, including justification, sanctification, and reconciliation. In the next chapter, we shall continue with those images that flow from redemption of the flesh, including liberation for true freedom, transformation to new creation, and glorification, with the final image, salvation, being the end result of the whole process.

Grace

This very important biblical term (Greek *charis*) is not usually listed among the effects of the Christ event because it primarily refers to the favor God (the Father) shows toward God's people. However, since Paul closes every letter with wishes for "the grace of the Lord Jesus Christ," we should examine "grace" here as an effect of Christ's selfless death and his ongoing presence to the Christian community.

Word Background and Meanings

In secular Greek, *charis* means the favor one person shows to another in acts of benevolence, especially a patron's gratuitous donation of goods. But it can also mean the gift or favor itself, and even the gratitude ("thanks") shown by one who receives the gift. From the Old Testament, the Hebrew noun *hēn*, "favor" and its verb form *hānan*, "to show favor" are usually cited as central to Paul's meaning of the Greek *charis* (*hēn* was commonly translated as *charis* in the Septuagint). *Hēn* is most often used of a favorable act to someone in need, done for no apparent reason other than the good pleasure of the one showing favor, like Esau showing favor to his estranged brother Jacob (Gen 33:8) or Boaz's acceptance of Ruth (Ruth 2:2). A second Hebrew idea, however, is needed to complete Paul's understanding of *charis*. The word for it is *hesed*, God's loving kindness as the source of God's favor. This is a love that is above all faithful in a covenant relationship with humans, completely gratuitous on God's part, and deeply committed to the welfare of the other. In the Hellenistic culture *charis*, "favor," is an image common enough, but in Paul we pick up strong overtones of God's gracious love unknown in that patronage system. (On all of this see Dunn 1998, 319–23.)

The Pauline image of *charis* is usually translated into English as "grace" (from Lat. *gratia*, "favor toward another, liking, love") to accent the gratuity of its kindness (Hebr. *hesed*). At other times "favor" (from Lat. *favere*, "to favor, show partiality") is the more appropriate English word (= Hebr. *hēn*), to underline the favorable good will behind such a great gift.

The Pauline Texts

In Paul's letters the term *charis* preeminently signifies the favor of God's saving will towards humans that brings about new life: "We have obtained access to this grace (*charis*) in which we stand" (Rom 5:1-2; also 3:24; 4:16; 5:17, 20, 21; 6:1, 14, 15; 11:5, 6 (*bis*); 1 Cor 1:4; Gal 2:9, 21). With this image Paul can call to mind the totality of the effects of God's gift in Christ both now and in the future. Thus all the images that we shall study in this and the next chapter can be said to be the effects of God's *grace* given through the Christ event.

If it is God's favor (*charis*) that is ultimately responsible for the effects of the Christ event, then it can be said that it is the favor of Christ himself for humankind that was necessary for salvation. Thus Paul speaks of the favor of God and the favor of Christ in parallel: "Much more surely have the *grace of God* and the free gift in the *grace of the one man, Jesus Christ*, abounded for the many" (Rom 5:15). Paul can even ascribe this bestowal of favor to the Lord Jesus Christ alone. Thus for Christians all of God's favor comes through the mediation of Christ that invites imitation of his selfless life: "For you know the generous act (*charis*) of our Lord Jesus Christ, that though he was rich, yet for your sakes he became poor, so that by his poverty you might become rich" (2 Cor 8:9), "the Son of God who loved me and gave himself for me" (Gal 2:20). Grace is the power behind the ministry of Paul, "who called you (in his apostolic ministry) in the grace of Christ" (Gal 1:6), and it is Christ's grace that brings peace in its own transcendent way: "My grace is sufficient for you, for power is made perfect in weakness" (2 Cor 12:9).

Conclusion

God's grace/favor is the prerequisite for entrance into the messianic community and the source of all the saving effects of Christ's life. It nullifies human shame and condemnation and brings a life of peace. Grace is the dynamic principle of faith-filled Christian living in rectitude and missionary outreach, in freedom from sin and the law's restraint. Christ's grace/favor is the basis of our union in peace with Christ and with each other in a cruciform life, life in imitation of the cross of Christ.

Expiation

This image is the first of a group of soteriological images that explain the result of the cancelation of sin in the believer's life: expiation, justification, sanctification, and reconciliation. The idea of the expiatory value of Christ's death occurs infrequently in uncontested Paul, however, and we may be brief in our presentation of it here, but I highly recommend that the reader take the short time necessary to look at Joseph Fitzmyer's exceptionally clear presentation in its entirety (1990, 1399–1400).

Word Meanings

The image in question is from the Old Testament description of the gold-covered lid of the ark of the covenant, called the *kappōret* in Hebrew (translated into Greek as *hilastērion epithēma*, "the expiating cover" in the Septuagint at Exod 25:17, and simply *hilastērion* six times thereafter in 25:18-22). The text describes the expiatory ritual in ancient Israel in which once a year, on the Day of Atonement, the high priest sprinkles the *kappōret* with the blood of an animal sacrificed in order to expiate the people's sins of the past year (Lev 16:14-20).

The Day of Atonement ritual was never thought of "as a vicarious punishment meted out on an animal instead of on the person who immolated it" (Fitzmyer, 1990, 1399). For Paul, *hilastērion* does not refer to some "propitiation" or placation of a blood-thirsty God, as in some pagan religions of the time. Neither does Paul mean that payment was necessary to appease an angry God. This idea came in later in medieval exegesis of these texts, and need not detain us here.

The idea behind the biblical practice of expiation was that blood must be shed in order to purify objects and persons dedicated to the service of God to consecrate them in a special covenant. Such a pact could be ratified only if it was sealed in blood because of the ancient belief that "the life of the flesh is in the blood" (Lev 17:11). This means that life itself was thought to reside in the blood, so that when the blood ran out of an animal, its very life went with it. An animal's lifeblood then could be used symbolically to represent the life of the persons who gave the victim and were offering the sacrifice. Sprinkling the blood on the holy *kappōret* in a ritual gesture was meant to solemnly dedicate people's lives totally to God. Thus were they cleansed of sin, the main obstacle to relationship with God, and fully united to God in a holy union.

Two English words have been employed to translate the Greek word *hilastērion* as Paul used it. "Expiation" (from the Latin preposition *ex*, "out of" and the verb *piare*, "to act with reverence to a deity") brings out the effect, or what comes out of reverence for the divine as "purification by a religious act." "Atonement" (from Middle English *atonen*, literally "to be *at one* with") originally emphasized the resultant unity of the covenant relationship with God, the reconciliation of humans with their creator. While the correct use of the English word "atonement" may mean "expiation," it is also commonly used for a later and non-Pauline theology of the "propitiation," or the appeasement of an angry God (see Tambasco 1991, 12). Since such "propitiation" does not figure in Pauline theology, we have decided not to use the ambiguous and unbiblical word "atonement" for *any* of Paul's images.

Paul's Usage

In several texts Paul shows that he is aware of the earlier Christian belief that Christ's death was an expiatory shedding of blood. He uses this tradition as necessary background to his more developed images of our participation in Christ's saving deeds.

It is in Romans where Paul makes the connection between his special theology of the justified sinner with the blood of Christ shed on the cross: "[All] are now justified by God's grace as a gift, through the redemption that is in Christ Jesus, whom God put forward as an expiation (*hilastērion*) by his blood, through faith. He did this to show his righteousness, because in his divine forbearance he had passed over the sins previously committed" (3:24-25). In this text Paul is emphasizing the grace of God whereby God justifies (puts in a right covenantal relationship) all (both Jew and Gentile) through "Christ's blood." Now this all happened "in Christ Jesus" who, through his faithfulness, was obedient to the prompting of God's will and offered himself ("gave himself out of love for me," Gal 2:20) as a sacrifice of expiation ("by his blood," Rom 3:25).

Only God can forgive sins and God "passes over past sins" by accepting this expiatory sacrifice of Jesus Christ on our behalf. This is what Paul means when he says that "For our sake God made him [Christ] to be sin who knew no sin, so that in him we might become the righteousness of God" (2 Cor 5:21). With this paradoxical language we are given to understand a profound exchange between God and humankind. As the sinless Christ died on the cross for us, he became sin for us, "stood in" for us, as it were, as an expiatory sacrifice for our sin. God now offers to believers this sacrifice as a means of receiving the effect of God's own righteousness given for the obedience of Christ. Paul can say all this simply: "we have been justified by his [Christ's] blood" (Rom 5:9a). The new state of affairs then guarantees what is possible in the future for those united in covenant to God, that "we will be saved through him [Christ] from the wrath of God" on Judgment Day (Rom 5:9b).

In his discussion of food offered to idols in 1 Corinthians 10, Paul calls upon this theology to point out the grave results of participation of believers in pagan temple services. He shows that just as the Eucharist is a sharing in the body and blood of Christ, so any sacrifice to pagan idols by believers would be a sharing exchange with the pagan deities, in which they would become "partners with demons" (v. 20). This is the reason he gives for the prohibition against idol worship: "You cannot partake of the table of the Lord and the table of demons" (v. 21).

Conclusion

Paul is fully conversant with the earlier Christian theology of the expiatory effect of the cross. He takes up the question in Romans when he defends his theology of justification by faith, not works, perhaps to form a stronger theological link with a community founded not by him but others. The reason that he does not dwell at length on expiation in any of his letters may reflect his own upbringing in Diaspora Judaism in which the temple sacrifices did not play a significant part. At any rate, Paul's image of Christ as God's expiatory sacrifice (*hilastērion*) for the forgiveness of sins is one of many rich images of the effects of the Christ event. It brings out strongly the cost to the Son of God, who "loved me and gave himself for me" so that "I might be justified through the faithful deed of Jesus Christ" (Gal 2:20, 16).

Justification

We now come to an image that Paul uses mainly in Galatians and Romans. It has become a subject of enormous contention since the Reformation in the sixteenth century, and there has been so much written about Paul's use of this idea that we cannot begin to address all the religious and theological issues related to it here. In order to present this one of nearly a dozen Pauline images of the effects of the Christ event, we can only look briefly at the uncontested Pauline texts and attempt to make a clear if limited presentation of Paul's under-standing of justice between God and humans.

Word Background and Meanings

First, however, we must consult the Old Testament, that basic en-cyclopedia of theology for Paul, especially in its Greek translation, the Septuagint, which served as Paul's Bible. The Greek root in ques-tion here, *dikaio-*, derives from *dikē*, which originally meant "custom, usage" but then came to represent "law" or a "judgment of law." Thus in secular Greek words with the stem *dikaio-* came to identify what is right or just, especially a righteous person. This root is used in the Greek Old Testament most often to translate the Hebrew root *sdq* in three basic forms: 1) *dikaios* (= Hebrew *saddiq*) "something/one that is just, righteous" in the sense that it meets a standard; 2) The causative verb form *dikaioō* (translating a causative form of the verb *sdq*) meaning "to declare or make righteous," traditionally conveyed in English by the word "justify," but also by some newer attempts at rendering it, "to rectify" or even "to right-wise." From this verb came the abstract nouns *dikaiōma* and *dikaiōsis*, words Paul uses a few times to designate the result of the justifying action. 3) It takes several English words to convey the exact meaning of the abstract derivative noun *dikaiosynē* (from Hebrew *sedeq* or *sedāqāh*) in its various contexts:

it may refer either to the process of making one "righteous," with the translation "justification" or "rectification," or to its result of "righteousness" or "uprightness."

Paul's Early Usage

In Paul's use of these terms the root *dikaio-* (*sdq*) bespeaks a certain kind of right relationship between God and human beings in which one is vindicated of any charge of wrongdoing and is righteous (or upright) in ethical matters, e.g., "O let the evil of the wicked come to an end, but establish the *righteous*" (Ps 7:9). Again and again the Old Testament makes clear that humans are not righteous unless they are acting in accord with the law of God, because God is also righteous. Some texts indicate that such good conduct establishes a claim on God for deliverance from evil, e.g., "Even if Noah, Daniel, and Job, these three, were here, they would save only their own lives by their righteousness" (Ezek 14:14). Many of the later books of the OT, however, add an eschatological emphasis, one which emphasizes the idea that because of the sinfulness of humanity, one must rely on the mercy of God on Judgment Day to be acquitted, e.g., "No one living will be considered righteous in your sight" (Ps 142[143]:2 Septuagint; Isa 51:4-5).

Turning to Paul's uncontested letters, we see that in the earlier letters he uses the *dikaio-* words in a normal Jewish sense of righteous or correct behavior, as in the only occurrence in his first missive, "You are witnesses, and God also, how piously, righteously, and blamelessly we acted toward you believers" (1 Thess 2:10). Here the three adverbs "piously, righteously, and blamelessly" are used almost as synonyms, defining the correct and proper behavior of persons with other persons. Moving on to 1 Corinthians, we see that Paul again uses the word simply to indicate correctness (4:4; 15:34).

Near the beginning of 1 Corinthians, however, we see his first specifically Christian uses of these terms when he considers the Gospel as the wisdom of God. No one should boast because "[God] is the source of your life in Christ Jesus, who became for us wisdom from God, and *righteousness* and sanctification and redemption" (1:30). Secondly, no one should boast about themselves because they were "washed, sanctified, *justified* in the name of the Lord Jesus Christ and in the Spirit of our God" (6:11). Evidently the early Church before

Paul had used all these terms, and linked righteousness to sanctification in their baptism ("washing").

The Faith of Jesus Christ in Galatians

It is in the Letter to the Galatians that Paul first expounds on the ramifications of the Christ event in terms of justification. Some other Christian missioners had come to his community in Galatia and insisted on observance of the Jewish kosher laws and feast days, along with the practice of circumcision. Paul tells the story of his earlier confrontation with Peter at Antioch over Jewish and Gentile Christians sharing table fellowship (and Eucharist!). In Galatians 2:14-21, he probably updates what he had earlier said to Peter in light of the present problem in Galatia. He identifies the controversy over kosher food (and the implied uncleanness of all Gentiles!) as a contradiction to the membership of non-Jews in covenant with God. Paul argues that no "works of the law" can justify a person, and so the law of Moses as such is not necessary for covenant membership because "if justification comes through the law, then Christ died for nothing" (2:21). It is the faithful deed of Jesus Christ, Paul insists, that is responsible for the justification of people now in the new era of salvation history. Faithful submission and commitment to that example of Christ ("believing in Christ") constitute the believer's acceptance of the new covenant with God.

Here we may point out a recent discussion about the words *pistis Iēsou/Christou*, which may be translated either as "the faith *of* Jesus/Christ" according to one view, or "the faith *in* Jesus/Christ" in the more traditional interpretation. Technically, the difference depends on what kind of Greek genitive we have in the phrase. It is easier to see the way the genitive may be used in Greek in another Pauline phrase, "the love of God," a phrase that can indicate the "love of God" as God's love for us (subjective genitive), or as our "love of God," with God as the object of *our* love (objective genitive). Again, without going into all the details of this dispute, we may take a stand on the translation that seems best. The "faith *of* Jesus Christ" is the translation that explicitly recalls the *faithful deed* of the cross, the saving action that Jesus Christ underwent in obedience to the Father, as the primary factor in salvation. We shall thus render the phrase with the subjective (or authorial) genitive, "the faith (meaning his faithfulness or the faithful deed) *of*

Jesus/Christ," knowing full well that Paul also expects believers to commit themselves to Christ. When Paul speaks of "believing in Christ," however, he uses the preposition "in" and not the genitive. Compare the genitive phrases "the faithfulness (*pistis*) of God" (Rom 3:3) and "the faith of Abraham" (Rom 4:12, 16), where faith *in* God or Abraham is clearly not what is being spoken about, but precisely the faithfulness *of* God and the faith *of* Abraham.

Other Texts in Galatians

Paul's opponents must have used the example of Abraham as decisive proof that for anyone who wanted to be in covenant with God, circumcision was necessary, regardless of how disagreeable or even repulsive the custom might seem to most non-Jews. They undoubtedly cited the passage where God demands circumcision of Abraham and all his male offspring (Gen 17:9-14). Paul immediately takes up the challenge with four counterarguments (Gal 3 and 4). 1) The Galatians had unmistakably received the gift of the Spirit *before* they ever heard of the Law and its requirement of circumcision (3:2). 2) Abraham himself shows the precedent set by God since, according to Gen 15:6, it was his *belief* that "was reckoned to him as righteousness" (3:6), and that this act would serve as a type since "all the Gentiles shall be blessed in you" (3:8). 3) The law had become a curse for the Jews, but "Christ redeemed us from the curse of the law by becoming a curse for us," the curse of that very law (3:10, 13). 4) The promises (of blessings to the Gentiles) were made to Abraham and to his offspring (literally "to his seed," a word in the singular). Paul does not take "seed" in the usual collective sense, but insists that its singularity can refer to only one person, Christ (3:16). Thus the inheritance of Abraham comes to Jew or Gentile only through Christ, to whom the promise was made, and not the law of the Jewish people (3:18).

Paul does not want to denigrate the law, however, since it is God given. Thus he imagines it as a kind of "nanny" given to believers to watch over them until the time of the *faithful* life and death of Christ: "Therefore the law was our *disciplinarian* (Gr. *paidagōgos*) until Christ came," but "in Christ Jesus you are all (adult) children of God through faith" (3:24, 26). Finally, in the exhortation in chapter 5, Paul sums up his argument against Gentile Christians taking up the works of the law, especially circumcision: "In Christ Jesus neither circumcision nor uncircumcision counts for anything" (5:6a). Paul finishes the thought with an emphasis on the eschatological element of justification: "the only thing that counts (at the judgment of God at the end of the Christians' life) is faith working through love" (5:6b).

Philippians and 2 Corinthians

In parts of Philippians and 2 Corinthians we see Paul's reaction to a group of teachers who are demanding more conformity to the practice of the Jewish-Christian churches. With great invective Paul calls them "dogs" and "evil workers" because they want to "mutilate the flesh" (= circumcision in Phil 3:2). He laconically names them "superapostles" (2 Cor 11:5) because, from what Paul says of them, they are highly trained in rhetoric (2 Cor 11:6), they willingly accept the financial support of the Corinthians (11:7-9), and they boast about their apostolic pedigree and their exploits in preaching the Gospel (11:12-13). Paul has no use for them. He calls them "his [Satan's] ministers who disguise themselves as ministers of righteousness" (11:15), since he had seen the havoc that similar "teachers" had caused in Galatia.

At any rate, his first salvo against the "superapostles" in 2 Corinthians is to call the practice of the law a "ministry of death" (2:7) and a "ministry of condemnation" (2:9). They place a veil of ignorance over the minds of those who follow them (3:15). This he opposes to his law-free Gospel which he calls "the ministry of the Spirit" (3:8) and "the ministry of (real) justification" that "abound in glory" (3:9). He says this because he is firmly convinced that the old covenant of the law could not give life; indeed he says that "the letter (of the law) kills, but the Spirit gives life" (3:6; see also Gal 3:2). True justification is based on the faithful deed of Jesus Christ and comes from the outpouring of the Spirit at baptism (1 Cor 6:11; Rom 14:17).

Far from denying the truth of the law, however, Paul states firmly that believers are not to descend into lawlessness as a result of their freedom from law. True believers are those who practice a heightened form of virtue because they act in cooperation with God's will (6:1). They are to live as Paul does, accepting adversity, with a whole arsenal of virtuous acts, as "the weapons of righteousness" (6:7). He likes to call the fruit of righteous living "the harvest of righteousness" (9:10; Phil 1:11), yet insists that he "be found in Christ, not having a righteousness of my own that comes from the law, but one that comes through the faith of Christ, the righteousness from God based on faith" (Phil 3:9).

The Letter to the Romans

Finally, spurred on by misunderstanding, and with his thinking much clarified by recurring argumentation over his earlier writing and preaching, Paul comes to write up his most thoroughgoing and connected thoughts on justification in the Letter to the Romans. He starts off boldly, announcing the Gospel as God's power for salvation and the revelation of God's righteousness. He proclaims its newness while insisting that it is seated firmly in the Hebrew tradition, for the Gospel of Jesus Christ was prepared for and came first to the Jews (1:16). At the same time, Paul states right up front that this righteous salvation is a matter of faith, not law, citing Habakkuk 2:4 as he understood it to mean that life comes from *faith* for the truly justified and righteous person (v. 17b).

Next, Paul turns the tables on the "Judaizers," those who demand the full acceptance of Jewish law for Christians. He points out that just because people *have* the law of God, they are not saved if they themselves do evil, even if they *are* Jewish. This proves that *it is not the law* that saves, but one's inner disposition. Paul states, "Real circumcision is a matter of the heart" (2:29). This inner disposition is our faith-filled response to God's free gift of a "new covenant" (2 Cor 3:6).

In chapter 4 Paul sets out a long disquisition on the righteousness of the patriarch Abraham, whom the Old Testament presents at the inception of God's plan. He reiterates the point he made to the Galatians, namely that Abraham's faith was "reckoned to him as righteousness," not his works, and adds that Abraham was a type for all who would enjoy righteousness through faith (vv. 24-25).

Chapter 5 first gives a resume of the results of God's justification of believers: peace in our access to grace and then the hope it brings of sharing God's glory (vv. 1-2). We have seen how verses 12 to 15 show Adam's part in the entrance of sin into the world. The rest of chapter 5 shows how the free gift of salvation in Christ repairs the damage, namely, that God's justification in Christ overturns the judgment that sin brings upon all (v. 16). The results of this free gift are effective now and for the future, "leading to eternal life" (v. 21).

Paul goes on to say that, free from sin, we "have become slaves of righteousness" for God's purpose of "sanctification" (6:19-20). So now, "if Christ is in you, though the body is dead because of sin, the Spirit is life because of righteousness" (8:10). Apart from a right relationship with God our humanity ("the body") would be "dead," that is, incapable of living as we were created to be. But now, our spirit is enlivened by God's Spirit that gives our whole life its newness and authenticity.

At the end of chapter 8 Paul sums up the process of salvation for believers in Christ from its beginning in the mind of God to its culmination in our eternal glory at the last judgment: "Those whom he *foreknew* God also *predestined* to be conformed to the image of his Son, in order that he might be the firstborn within a large family. And those whom God predestined he also *called*; and those whom he called he also *justified*; and those whom he justified he also *glorified*" (8:29-30). The five main verbs here appear in the past tense because all have been accomplished in and for Christ. Because of God's loving foreknowledge of every human being, God has predestined each person for conformity with Christ, and so calls them, justifies them, and begins the process of glorification that will be culminated in eternal life. Believers have nothing to fear on Judgment Day: "Who will bring any charge against God's elect? It is God who justifies" (8:33).

Paul says that Christ is the *end of the law* because the law by itself cannot save, for it is incapable of bringing life because of sin (Rom 10:4). Rather, we share in Christ's righteousness, the only true fulfillment of the law, and so the just requirement of the law may be fulfilled in us because we share in the life and death of Christ. As for the law itself, all it can do is show what true righteousness would be like. Thus for the believer Christ is the "end" of the law in both senses of the word. First, he has *put an end* to the observance of law that, without faith, was never able to attain righteousness. Second, Christ has become the end of the law as its *goal*, since the righteousness of God that the law was meant to manifest has been accomplished by Christ's faithful deed, his saving death in faithful obedience to the Father (Rom 5:19; see Barrett 1957, 197–98).

Summary and Conclusion

Paul acknowledges the Old Testament concept of righteousness as a covenant member's compliance with the law, but he sees a new era in God's plan. He learned from the early church that God had produced something totally new through the mediation of God's Son. Before Christ, according to Paul, both Jew and Gentile had been under the domination of sin. Any Jew could see that the Gentiles were completely off track with God, but Paul knew from his own experience that fulfillment of the whole law was not possible even for the Jews, and it merely compounded their anxiety because the law clearly pointed out their failings (Rom 7:5-25).

On the other hand, when someone thinks that they are literally keeping every part of the law, it is easy to arrogate a kind of self-righteousness that seems to make God beholden. This kind of delusion had inspired an uncharitable zeal in Paul's own life that demanded such "perfect" law observance from others. Paul knew that he had been guilty of some very ungodly behavior towards those who did not measure up to *his* standards of righteousness. One can see this particularly nasty trait in people who have what we call today an authoritarian personality. Once they believe in the unlimited priority of law, they become its slaves in an almost addictive compulsion. It blurs the value of other considerations, and, as Paul knew in his own former life, preempts even the love that Christ enjoins for one's brothers and sisters.

God's solution was that the righteous practice of the law was fulfilled completely in Christ. Participation in Christ's faithful deed inaugurated a new era: attainment of its saving effect was now open to all, both Jew and Gentile. No need, therefore, for Gentiles to become covenant members under the old, ineffective law; their justified membership in the new covenant was guaranteed by their faith in Christ. This faith meant the acceptance of God's will as the center of human life and commitment to imitation of the cruciform ministry of Christ.

Justification has a great effect for the Christian right now in a life sanctified by the Spirit of Christ, but Paul puts strong emphasis on the future judgment as well. The payoff of a justified life, what Paul calls "the hope of righteousness" (Gal 5:5), will be the positive judgment of one's life at the resurrection and one's entrance into eternal glory. In Christ, God is not declaring the guilty to be innocent, but is "providing a way for the unjust to actually become just, to turn from injustice to justice" (Jennings 2009, 220).

Sanctification/Holiness

In English we use two word sets to translate the Greek word group (*hagio-*) that Paul uses for this image: 1) "holy/holiness" (from the Old English *hālig* through Middle English *hool*, "whole; unhurt"), a word that we commonly use in the sense of spiritual wholeness and moral perfection; and 2) "sanctify/sanctification" (from the Latin root *sanct-*, the past participle of the verb *sancio*, "to render sacred; to establish as inviolable," with the verbal suffix *-fy* from *facere* "to make"). This information will be helpful for English speakers who might think of holiness only in the sense of personal piety, but it is to Paul's letters themselves that we must turn to unpack this rich biblical image.

Word Background and Meanings

In secular Greek the word *hagios* refers to things or persons devoted to the gods, like a temple or cult statue, or a pious person intent on pleasing the gods. But as usual, at the heart of Paul's use of a Greek word is his version of the Bible, the Septuagint. There the Hebrew adjective *qadosh* is almost always translated by the Greek *hagios*, "holy." However, unlike the common English meaning of moral superiority or inner piety, the biblical word means "having been set apart; separate," and therefore in a state of readiness for divine use or for an encounter with God. Someone or something that is holy (*qadosh*) is somehow different from the usual object or person, like a special place, the Temple or a shrine, or a person called to a special vocation like a prophet or a priest, and even Israel itself. The Old Testament Levitical Code demands this specialness for all Israelites when God says, "You shall be holy, for I am holy" (Lev 11:44), with the result that God will dwell among them and walk with them as God's own people (see Lev 26:11-12). Thus while Old Testament holiness includes cultic holiness, it involves more than that. Israel as a people has been invited into covenant by God. God's elective call to intimacy demands adherence to a morality that is worthy of the Deity and does not blaspheme that relationship.

Paul uses the simple adjective "holy" (*hagios*), along with the verb form "to sanctify/make holy" (*hagiazō*), and two noun forms, *hagiosunē*, referring to the quality of holiness, and *hagiasmos*, referring to the process and especially the result of being or becoming holy. Both can be translated as either "sanctification" or "holiness." It is above all the church that Paul calls holy, routinely calling its members "the holy ones," often rendered as "the saints" (some twenty-five times) in our modern translations.

The Pauline Texts

This image of "holiness" dominates Paul's first recorded letter, where he speaks of God's election of the community in the power of the *Holy* Spirit (1 Thess 1:4-5). We learn that a life of holiness is what God calls everyone to: "For this is the will of God, your sanctification" (4:3; also 4:7). One does not become holy by one's pure ethical conduct, however. Rather, God gives the holy Spirit, that is to say, it is God's Spirit that makes one holy (4:8). The gift of holiness takes effect immediately in a new way of living that is different from that of nonbelievers. It "reflects a strong outward focus wherein individuals are consistently moving toward others in a selfless and loving way" (Howard 2007, 186). The result of the gift will be readiness for the parousia (3:13), but God's gift for now in holiness is peace (5:23). This makes possible a very countercultural life in the Roman Empire: it is chaste (4:3-7), fair in the treatment of outsiders (4:12), and joyful even in persecution (1:6).

In the greeting of his next letter, 1 Corinthians, Paul gives us a fuller explanation of his idea of sanctity when he addresses the members as "those made holy/sanctified in Christ Jesus, called holy people (*hagioi*), together with all those who in every place call on the name of our Lord Jesus Christ" (1:2). First, we see that church members have been sanctified "in Christ Jesus," that is, because of their union with the person of Christ. Then we note how Paul links the Corinthian *ekklēsia* with the members of all the other churches where Christ is acknowledged as Lord.

Paul continues his teaching on the holiness demanded of those who live "in the name of Christ," that is, under his lordship. They are to be called "holy people" because they have taken on the characteristics of Christ's own holiness. That is, they are committed to live as Christ did. Holiness, then, is a characteristic of Christian life now, begun with baptism (6:11). God is "the source of your life in Christ Jesus" (1:30), that is, all of Christian life comes from God's love, and Christ has become for us "sanctification," our human imitation of the life of God.

This holiness, however, is not so much an inner, ethical quality as a personal dedication to the will of God, to being like God as much as is humanly possible as God's obedient servant (Rom 6:19). Murphy-O'Connor explains how living a sanctified life is not the same thing as making the faith decision that begins it (2009, 161–66;

253–56). For one thing, Paul never denies the sanctity of the Hebrew people (even those who do not believe in Christ; Rom 11:16) or the sanctity of the law (even though it has been vitiated by sin; Rom 7:8-12).

Surprisingly, Paul points out that children (those not old enough to have a developed moral life) as well as unbelieving spouses of Christians may be considered holy because of their attachment to members of the church (1 Cor 7:14). Here we see the communal dimension of Christian holiness. Paul sees that union with a believing spouse puts even a nonbeliever in the holy community, presumably in mutual love and support of the spouse in all matters, including his or her union with the other believers in Christ. The children are holy because of the sanctified ambience in which they now live. We have a great insight here: the Christian community itself provides a sphere of holiness where goodness and mutual aid are the order of the day.

Throughout 1 Corinthians, Paul maps out various practical insights into the behavior of holy Christians as "God's temple" (3:16), dealing with a whole array of negative practices (chaps. 5–6), and then speaking positively on marriage, virginity, and celibacy (chap. 7), advising about food offered to idols (chaps. 8 and 10), proper liturgical behavior, and the use of spiritual gifts (chaps. 11, 12 and 14).

From all this, we see that the gift of holiness, the *fact* of being sanctified, does not mean that individuals necessarily become completely virtuous all of a sudden. Even though they had been freed from the slavery to godlessness and had submitted to a new Lord, Paul had to teach his newly sanctified converts some ways of behaving that were very new to them, often quite contrary to what they were brought up to believe. At the base of holiness, then, is a dynamic option of being separated from the world of nonbelievers, much as the chosen people of old. But now non-Jews too may be sanctified as children of God, brothers and sisters of Christ, God's own Son.

The ritual practice of the "holy kiss" practiced in Paul's communities underscores the sanctity of the Christian union as they greet one another (1 Thess 5:26; 1 Cor 16:20; 2 Cor 13:12; Rom 16:16). The reality of holiness in the community does not depend on legalistic practices like circumcision or purity laws concerning food. The temptation among the Galatians to adopt a rigid adherence to the Jewish law will bear no fruit. Because of their failure in this regard there is no hint of holiness language in any part of Paul's letter to that community.

In order to more fully explain his notion of the sanctity of the Christian community, Paul describes it with the image of a temple (1 Cor 3:16-17; 6:19; 2 Cor 6:14-18) and frequently explains Christian life with cultic metaphors, imaging believers as cultic sacrifices (Rom 9:3), the community as holy dough (1 Cor 5:6-8; Rom 11:16), as liturgy (Phil 2:17; 2 Cor 2:14-16; Rom 12:1; 15:16), as anointed (2 Cor 1:21), as unblemished sacrifice (Phil 2:17; 2 Cor 7:1), as altar ministry (1 Cor 9:13; Rom 12:1), as excluding the worship of idols (1 Cor 10:14-22), and more—even the collection for Jerusalem is presented as an act of worship (2 Cor 8:4; 9:1, 12; Vahrenhorst 226).

Conclusion

We may conclude that in his earliest letters Paul explained the effect of the death and resurrection of Jesus Christ on believers in a developed theology of sanctification. With this cultic image, he shows that believers receive holiness—are made special—by the free gift of God's grace in Christ Jesus, transmitted through the Holy Spirit, to live a life of love in action. This requires a life apart in an engendering community, much like the separateness of a temple in the midst of its profane surroundings. The existence of such holy believers is to be like that of a willing servant of a benevolent lord.

In my own teaching, I find that modern Christians so abhor every aspect of slavery that they react negatively to the very mention of it when Paul explains holiness as a beneficent slavery. On the other hand, the image of a child growing in a loving and supportive family does well to communicate Paul's message of holiness for today. Such children are completely subject to parental authority (not so very unlike a favored slave), yet they know that they are special. They act as special, with growing ability to trust others, to love, and to be honest. They willingly imitate an older brother who has devoted himself completely for the honor of the family, a model for the way to live greatly. Anyone who has dealt with a deeply dysfunctional family knows what the unloved child is like: furtive, dishonest, untrusting, and cantankerous—deprived of and incapable of authentic love. They are slaves of their sin and that of others; Paul would say they are under the dominion of death.

The beloved child is very different. He or she genuinely tries to please the loving parents, to get along with brothers and sisters, to have caring and trusting relationships with friends, and to represent the family well when dealing with outsiders. Although they are far from perfect, their behavior grows in excellence even as they are corrected in their mistakes, even punished for the occasional wrongdoing. Similarly, Christian believers live in the separate and protective ambiance of an extended family, with older and loving siblings to mentor them. As they increase in love they become more and more like Christ, who is the perfect image and revelation of God, "and represents what the community is to become in eternity" (Howard 2007, 184).

Reconciliation

Another image that Paul uses to explain what has happened to humankind in the Christ event is "reconciliation." This idea is based on the all-too-frequent breakdown of human relationships and the necessity of resolving a state of estrangement that results from one party offending another. Because sinful humans know that their unvirtuous conduct offends God, they are given to think that "God's wrath" is God's permanent attitude toward them. Their imagined rejection by God festers into a state of despair over the worthlessness of their lives. This only confirms them in their desperate sinfulness, so that they end up "hating God" (Rom 1:30).

Word Meanings

The Greek word for reconcile has the root *katall-* (made up of the prefix *kata* "over against; in answer to," and *allos*, "other") that yields the idea of a "response to another; an exchange." In personal relationships it is used to designate the change from enmity to friendship or cordial relations. There is no Old Testament word for such an action with respect to God. In Hellenistic usage, it is always humans who must initiate reconciliation with the gods. Paul's understanding is different: it is God who has taken pains to bring about reconciliation, even though it is God who has been offended and rejected by the sin of humans. Paul speaks of this divine offer of "reconciliation" at length in two key texts.

Paul's Usage

In Romans 5:6-11 Paul lays out his theology of reconciliation: the death of God's own Son is offered as an indisputable example of God's selfless love and desire for the end of any human alienation. Imagine the enmity that would exist between one party who has always been good to the other, loving and engendering growth, but who is constantly rebuffed by the disdain and hurtful behavior of the other. This is *not* the focus of Paul's image! Rather, Paul knows that human beings misunderstand God and are blinded by their guilt. They think that a good and creating God *must* reject them because of their imperfection, their sin, their apathy. They surmise that because of their bad behavior a just God must be at odds with them: distant, angry, and waiting for reparation. Doesn't the human ego all too frequently take the goodness and nobility of another as a reproach to its own misbehavior? Such imagined enmity often turns into hatred of an innocent party by the other who cannot abide comparison to a paragon of the good. Think of the intense resentment that a younger sibling might have toward an older, successful brother or sister.

Paul carefully explains how God, in reality, does not disdain human beings, but loves them without limit. We have seen that God's "wrath" is the biblical image sometimes used to explain the result of human sin. For when sin breaks one's relationship with God, the resultant self-imposed distance from God seems like an angry rejection of their person. The reality of the case is the complete opposite: God loves humans very much and wants to end any alienation between the divine and the human. The death of God's Son offers a sacrifice of reparation to the very ones who are at fault for the broken relationship, "while we were still weak . . . still sinners . . . while we were enemies" (Rom 5:6, 8, 10). Instead of casting humanity aside as unworthy of love, God offers them a chance to regain their intimacy, for "God proves his love for us in that while we still were sinners Christ died for us" (Rom 5:8). More than that, Christ's decision to do God's will did not come from some forced obedience, but from "the Son of God who loved me and gave himself for me" (Gal 2:20). In sum, God so wants the reconciliation of humanity that "in Christ, God has absorbed the cost of sin, freeing human beings to engage in restored relationships" (Colijn 2010, 182). Whereas "justification" in Christ describes the repair of the covenant relationship of humans with God in legal terms, "reconciliation" describes the end of their alienation with the image of a restored human relationship.

Paul anguishes over the difficulty experienced by his law-observant brothers and sisters who have only the law, "for the letter kills, but the Spirit gives life" (2 Cor 3:6). Their rejection of the seeming weakness and foolishness of Christ has made it easier for the rest of the world to be reconciled, but Paul is optimistic about their final conversion: "For if their rejection (of Christ) is the reconciliation of the world, what will their acceptance be but life from the dead!" (Rom 11:15).

In an earlier letter Paul points out the ramifications of this marvelous reality: "God has given us the ministry of reconciliation. . . . So we are ambassadors for Christ, since God is making his appeal through us" (2 Cor 5:18b, 20). In this letter Paul is pleading with the Corinthians to be reconciled to his leadership in spite of the recent harshness he needed to use on behalf of the Gospel. For Paul the reconciliation that Christ has brought about with God should spill over into a relationship of trust among all Christians as brothers and sisters. Moreover, the mutual love in a community of believers is the primary means by which God's true self is revealed to other members of the world community.

Conclusion

Paul uses a powerful image from human interaction to explain how the rift that exists between a sinful people and their all-merciful God has been mended. Reconciliation is at the heart of Paul's theology, because it speaks to the depth of human hurt and the alienation that so permeates the lives of ordinary people both then and now. When we realize that it is not God who needs to be reconciled to our imperfect selves, but *we* who need to be reassured of God's unswerving love, we can realize that in Christ "everything old has passed away; see, everything has become new!" (2 Cor 5:17). This new life brings with it a new depth of prayer in which all anxieties are brought to God. They are dispelled because of Christ's obedient love, they are released to God with a trust in the future that rests on God's unwavering love for us (Phil 4:6-7). This is the center of the Gospel of which we are God's ambassadors for the whole world to see, even for God's chosen people themselves to observe and grow "jealous" (Rom 11:11), if only we live like Christ in joy and peace with one another.

Chapter 4

The Effects of the Christ Event: Part 2

We continue with our list of images that Paul uses to define the effects of the Christ event. Four images follow upon the image of Christ as ransom for our slavery: 1) his death as redeeming price of our freedom, or "liberation" (which we study together with "redemption"); 2) transformation into a "new creation"; 3) "glorification"; and finally, 4) we shall detail the image for the end point of the whole process, called "salvation." The chapter will close with a brief summary and conclusion on all eleven of Paul's soteriological images.

Redemptive Liberation

Paul is aware of an early Christian understanding of the new possibility for humanity in Christ that reverses the image of the cruelest oppression of ancient society. The institution of slavery was well known in the cities of Paul's mission, where an estimated one fourth to one third of the population was enslaved. Paul uses three terms to elaborate a rich theology of the antithetical social status of believers as compared to that of those completely in the control of worldly power. They describe the "redemption" (or manumission) of a slave, the actual "purchase" of their release, and the "freedom" that they thus attain.

Word Meanings

In an early letter Paul quotes what is probably a fragment of the preaching (*kerygma*) of the early church that summarizes God's saving action in Christ, "[God] is the source of your life in Christ Jesus, who became for us wisdom from God, and righteousness and sanctification and redemption" (1 Cor 1:30). The order of these three images is probably meant to be progressive, showing the movement of believers as first put into a right relationship with God, then being formed into a special (holy) community, and thereby receiving a new status as "redeemed," freed from the evils of this world, variously understood as "elemental powers," ignorance, the flesh, human masters, the false religiosity of the law, and sin itself as a constraining power. Note that our English translation, "redemption," derives from the Latin "buying back" (from *re* + euphonic *d* + *emptio*, "purchase, a buying"), a very apt word as we shall see. Since Hellenistic Greek prefers to speak of the release from slavery as *apeleutheria*, "release," literally "a freeing from," we must look for the Christian terminology of "redemption" (*apolytrōsis*) in the Septuagint. Here this Greek word refers to the practice of "ransoming" (translating the Hebrew root *g'l*, literally, "releasing from") a person out of slavery, e.g., "If [a slave] does not please her master . . . he shall let her be *redeemed*" (Exod 21:8).

The theological idea behind the Christian usage is the touching Old Testament image of God as "redeemer" (Hebr. *gô'ēl*), the kinsman whose duty it was to buy back an enslaved or captive relative, e.g., "They remembered that God was their rock, the Most High their *redeemer*" (Ps 78:34). Basic to Paul's understanding of the image is the Old Testament narrative of God's redemption of Israel from their enslavement in Egypt. God "redeemed" them and "acquired" them as God's own possession (Exod 15:16; 19:5; Ps 74:2; here we follow the excellent summary of the background and meaning of these three Pauline terms in Fitzmyer, *NJBC*, 1400).

The terminology of "buying" ([*ex*] *agorazō*) someone out of slavery comes from Hellenistic practice rather than from the Old Testament itself, and we note that Paul must have thought long about this redemptive process. We shall see this in Paul's careful application of the idea of freedom (Greek root *eleuthero-*), both the negative idea of freedom *from*, and the more positive notion of freedom *for*.

Paul's Usage

Paul's use of the terminology of redemption and buying back is very limited, for he is more interested in the resultant freedoms for the believer. In addition to the (probably) kerygmatic fragment in 1 Corinthians 1:30 (cited above), he uses the abstract word for "redemption" (*apolytrōsis*) only two more times and does not employ any of its related noun or verb forms that occur so frequently in the Old Testament. In Romans 3:21-31 he explains justification, pointing out that believers are "justified by God's grace as a gift, through the redemption that is in Christ Jesus, whom God put forward as a sacrifice of expiation" (v. 24). As we noted above in chapter 3, Paul is saying here that what is happening is the restoration to a covenant relationship. This occurs because of Christ acting as our *gô'ēl*, our redeemer in his sacrifice for us. In Romans 8:23, the third use of *apolytrōsis* signals the present incompleteness—the eschatological aspect—of the process of salvation: "We wait for adoption, the redemption of our bodies." By this he means that the unfreedom of our mortal lives is only fully dispensed with at our resurrection from the dead.

Paul underlines the Galatians' freedom from the law by using the word "purchase; ransom" (*exagorazō*) a couple of times: "Christ *ransomed* us from the curse of the law by becoming a curse for us" (Gal 3:13), and repeats the idea of freedom from the law in his discussion of God's adoption of believers: "God sent God's Son . . . in order to *ransom* those who were under the law, so that we might receive adoption as children (of God)" (4:4-5). Here Paul points out that Christ's ransoming us from the law was necessary, freeing us for the Spirit to enact our adoption into God's family. Finally, in his discussion of sexual morality, Paul uses the simple marketplace verb *agorazō* when he reminds the Corinthians that "you are not your own. For you were *bought* with a price; therefore glorify God in your body" (1 Cor 6:20; again in 7:23). Paul does not specify the entity to whom the "price" was paid; he uses the metaphor only to indicate concretely that believers belong to God now.

With regard to the freedom (with the root *eleuthero-*) that redemption brings about, we may note that Paul can use the term in its usual, non-theological sense of "free" (person), as the opposite of "slave" (1 Cor 7:21, 22; 12:13; Gal 3:28; 4:22, 23, 30, 31). Nevertheless, "freedom" (*eleutheria*) is the basic *image* he uses to speak of the result of Christ's redeeming death: a Christian is free from the flesh (Gal 5:13), from sin (Rom 6:18, 20, 22; 8:2), and from the law (1 Cor 7:39; Rom 7:3). Believers "belong" to the Lord Jesus (1 Cor 7:22) in a positive sense, and enjoy the rights of citizens of a free city or state: "Our citizenship is in heaven" (Phil 3:20).

This newfound freedom is the product of the indwelling of the Spirit, for "where the Spirit of the Lord is, there is freedom" (2 Cor 3:17). Paul recognizes this state of being as predicted in the Book of Isaiah, where God's deliverance would make all the people "righteous" (60:21) and "called 'The Holy People, The Redeemed of the Lord'" (62:12). Christian believers will act differently in their true freedom of conscience (1 Cor 10:29) and will be the envy of the pseudo-religious (Gal 2:4). Such freedom is to be in a realm of God's power where believers stand as delivered from the evil powers of the world (Gal 4:8-9), from the "yoke of slavery" of the law (Gal 5:1), and from the impulsive desires of the self-indulgence ("the flesh"; Gal 5:13).

Like Paul, believers are free to choose God's will or deny it. They can forego certain rights and imitate the freedom of the Apostle in service of the Gospel: "For though I am free with respect to all, I have made myself a slave to all, so that I might win more of them" (1 Cor 9:19). This glorious status of freedom will finally extend to the whole of creation after time's struggle with the "cosmic elements," when "creation itself will be set free from its bondage to decay and will obtain the freedom of glory of the children of God" (Rom 8:21).

Conclusion

Although "redemption" is not one of Paul's major images for the effects of the Christ event, its outcome, "freedom" is. At base is the Old Testament idea of the "redeemer" (*gô'ēl*), where God is the author of redemption, but now the ransoming of believers that takes place through Christ's saving deeds. The resultant freedom is a work in progress in which the lingering power of the flesh is offset by the power of the Spirit in the Christian community. There the members, as slaves of God, "through love become slaves to one another" (Gal 5:13b). In this way the members provide a loving space for each other to grow in freedom, for "We do not live for ourselves, and we do not die for ourselves" (Rom 14:7). Such is the glorious existence that we are called to, a destiny to be shared by all of creation which "will obtain the glory of the freedom of the children of God (8:21).

Transformation into a New Creation

Transformation

Paul observes that he and the people of his communities are becoming the very "image" of Christ through the power of God's Spirit (2 Cor 3:18). Humanity in the image of God hearkens back to the creation scene of Genesis where "God created humankind in his image; in the image of God he created them" (Gen 1:27). Indeed, the first Adam was enjoying a perfect life of grace, but, Paul says, when Adam sinned, "the judgment following one trespass brought condemnation," and all his descendants "by the one man's disobedience were made sinners" with the result that "sin exercised dominion in death" (Rom 5:19-20).

What Paul is pointing out in his image of transformation, then, is the restoration of human beings to their original state of godliness, their pristine loving and free relationship with the Creator. We have seen how in the Christ event "the free gift following (humanity's) many trespasses brings justification/righteousness" (5:16), that is, a rectified covenant relationship with God. With his image of transformation, Paul considers the positive change of humankind to new life that can only happen through Christ as the New Adam, when "the last Adam became a life-giving spirit" (1 Cor 15:45). Christ did this according to God's plan for us whom "God predestined to be *conformed* to the image of his Son, so that the Son might be the firstborn within a large family" (Rom 8:29).

When this transformation occurs within a large "family" (the whole community of Christ believers), we see the formation of a counter-culture, a small society in which the worldly standards of conduct of daily life in the Roman Empire (or any other empire, for that matter) no longer have precedence. The old order, in which value and privilege were determined by one's status, has passed away. Here we have Paul's second use of the word transformation. Every act, every decision should derive from a new point of view. As Paul says, "Do not be conformed to this world, but be *transformed* by the renewal (*anakainōsis*, literally "a newing up") of your minds, so that you may discern what is the will of God—what is good and acceptable and perfect" (Rom 12:2).

The new life in Christ is above all reasonable, springing from "the renewal of your minds." Paul declares that the manner of knowing people and things in Christ is different: "From now on we regard no one from a *merely human point of view*" (*kata sarka*, literally "according to the flesh"; 2 Cor 5:16). One must be aware of traditional guidelines of law and custom, of course, and we see this in Paul's own frequent use of the Old Testament and even of Stoic moral principles. But the process of discernment is different now. Believers are to regard the norms and criteria for good with a new freedom, "liberated to be able to assess and evaluate the[ir] efficacy and validity," no longer as they are in themselves, but only as they help our orientation to others in love (Munzinger 2007, 183–84).

Decisions made by the body of Christ are directed communally by the renewed minds of those have been transformed by their obedient faith and cruciform life in Christ. Their authentic understanding is shaped by the sacrifice of the cross whereby they have the same self-less attitude that was Christ's: "Let the same mind be in you that was in Christ Jesus" (Phil 2:5), an outlook that cannot happen "until Christ is formed in you" (Gal 4:19). Good-hearted people will practice the right behavior when it is taught to them by someone who has already been conformed to Christ's death. They will see the power of the resurrection acting in those who boast only in "the cross of our Lord Jesus Christ, by which the world has been crucified to me, and I to the world" (Gal 6:14; see also 1 Cor 1:17).

New Creation

Such a tremendous change can only be called a "new creation." As Paul exclaims, "Everything old has passed away; see, everything has become new!" (2 Cor 5:17). This new creation reconciles Jew and Gentile in a new covenantal relationship with God that both Jeremiah (31:31-34) and Ezekiel (chaps. 36–37) predicted, "a new covenant, not of letter but of spirit" (2 Cor 3:6). Thus "neither circumcision nor uncircumcision counts for anything; but there is a new creation!" (Gal 6:15). In fact, none of the dichotomies or antinomies of the Old Age have significance any longer, "for all of you are one in Christ Jesus" (Gal 3:28). The new creation is a world where the status of an individual is not what counts, but rather their participation in the new community.

The new creation is the beginning of the final coming into being of what God promised to Israel centuries before: "new heavens and a new earth; the former things shall not be remembered or come to mind" (Isa 65:17). The background here is the biblical image of God's creating power in God's Spirit: "When you send forth your Spirit, people are created; and you renew the face of the earth" (Ps 104:30).

Paul has witnessed the development of many faith-filled individuals into communities dedicated to love and service in the name of Christ. Transformation is a change that happens individually, but also to the group. The group provides the initiation of baptism, as they all together experience the power of the Spirit in their lives for the "upbuilding" of the church (1 Cor 14:3-5). Their awareness of the importance and dignity of one another brings about their unity as the body of Christ. He does not mean here that we are all becoming the same. Paul's disquisitions on the diversity of the members of the Body of Christ and their gifts in 1 Corinthians 12 make that abundantly clear. But Paul understands that as we all participate in the life of Christ, we are all being transformed—each in our own way according to God's plan—into the same glory of humanity's original creation, a veritable new creation.

Resurrection

Yet there is more. Since the transformation of each person is a gradual emulation of the glory of their risen Lord Jesus Christ, the final goal in God's plan is that "[the Lord] will change (*metaschēmatisei*) our humble body so that it may be conformed to his glorious body" (Phil 3:21). For this change Paul uses a verb (*metaschēmatizō*) very similar in meaning to his word "to transform" (*metamorphoō*), the former perhaps emphasizing a bit more the final mode of its appearance, since in the end the faithful will be changed into the final, glorious state of the risen Christ. This general resurrection will take place so that "all will be made alive in Christ . . . at his parousia" (1 Cor 15:22, 23). The end of the present age will come after the power of Christ destroys all ungodly powers (15:24), when all the world will be subjected to God, with believers then in the full glory of their own resurrection. Only then will believers fully understand the mystery of God's plan, "For now we see in a mirror, dimly, but then we will see face to face. Now I know only in part; then I will know fully, even as I am fully known" (1 Cor 13:12). This will be the culmination of God's eternal plan for the world, "so that God may be all in all" (15:28).

The Present Transformation

Paul, however, has already observed the initial effects of this ongoing process. It is a remarkable phenomenon, not the least so in him. By his own admission, Paul had been very self-righteous (Phil 3:4-9), and his zeal for Jewish tradition outstripped his contemporaries (Gal 1:14). After his conversion, however, and because of the overwhelming experience of the Spirit in the conversion of his communities, he says of his former accomplishments: "I regard everything as loss because of the surpassing value of knowing Christ Jesus my Lord. For his sake I have suffered the loss of all things, and I regard them as rubbish . . . not having a righteousness of my own . . . becoming like him in his death, if somehow I may attain the resurrection from the dead (Phil 3:8-11).

Here Paul lists the entire process of transformation, from the necessary shedding of any self-congratulation to the recognition of complete dependency on Christ, from the sharing with Christ of the burden of evil, to a "death" like his, to the hope of total union in resurrection.

The Transformation of Creation Itself

Finally, in Paul's thinking, this creative process of human development will culminate in the transformation of all of nature. Far from the violence and destruction of the usual apocalyptic scenario of the end of this Age, for Paul the *parousia*, the coming of the Lord Jesus will bring about God's promise of a new creation, as in Isa 65:17 (cited above). This cosmic event will mark the full revelation of a reality already nascent in creation's present form. Thus the liberation of nature will allow its full potential to come about by regeneration rather than destruction (Polaski 90).

Paul says that, in the present, "creation waits with eager longing for the revealing of the children of God; for creation was subjected to futility" (Rom 8:19-20). Here Paul is again using the ancient Hebrew understanding of causality that we mentioned earlier in chapter 1. We might paraphrase Paul's words to say, "Because of what humans did in sinning against God, God *allowed* their natural rapport with nature to disintegrate." This Paul learned from the story of the Fall, where, according to the same ancient Hebrew mentality, God is said to curse the ground and make difficult the tasks of human life (Gen 3:17-19).

Nature now appears to be purposeless and thus futile with regard to its original function of revealing "God's eternal power and divinity" to human beings (Rom 1:20). Yet, as Paul says, God "subjected creation in hope" (Rom 8:20), that is, God always left the hope that creation would be set free. Paul further points out that "the whole creation has been groaning in labor pains until now" (8:22), suffering indeed—but with the hopeful anticipation of new birth. Creation "awaits with eager longing for the revealing of the children of God," for it must be set free by the same agents, humanity, that caused God to permit "its bondage to decay" (8:19). Only thus can creation's total destruction be avoided, destruction at the hands of humans who no longer see any reason to care for it because they no longer see the reflection of God in it.

Paul maintains that the only solution to this dilemma of both humans and creation is the Spirit of God. This is how it will come about: first humanity will be transformed and regain their knowledge through the image of God that they share in Christ. Their unity with Christ will break their conformity to a godless world and their minds will be renewed (Rom 12:2). With humanity finally free from sin and its last enemy, death (1 Cor 15:26), nature itself will complete its process of becoming a new creation, transformed in glorious freedom to once again demonstrate the being and power of God. The labor pains of creation have not been hopeless anguish but are the sign of something coming: a new birth or rebirth of all of creation, the only possible location for the assured happiness of humans in eternity, finally raised fully from the dead with Christ.

Conclusion

To sum up Paul's reflection on how individuals and communities in union with Jesus Christ are transformed, we note first that Paul needs a rich variety of images to fill out this very rich idea: "transformation," becoming the "image" of the Lord, the gift of "new life," "conformity" to the glory of Christ, "new creation," a new way of knowing ("having the mind of Christ"). His overall picture is of a new creation, a thorough renewal of the whole world, in which believers will share God's glory by their participation in the death and resurrection of Christ, God's image. Christ, as the new Adam and head of humanity, is the firstborn of the many who are predestined to be conformed to his image (Rom 8:29). Their newness of life is a share in Christ's risen life even in the present time, a life completely dedicated to doing God's will. With it they are able to endure the suffering needed to put sin completely to death as they live out their lives in hope of their resurrection and that of all the living and the dead. All of this takes place in a world that is itself groaning to be changed, to be renewed back to its original purpose of demonstrating the glory of God and thus serving as the backdrop for the happiness of all (Ijezie 129).

Glorification

Word Background and Meanings

The Greek noun Paul uses for glory, *doxa*, refers to the high opinion of something honorable, and so can indicate that "honor" or "glory" itself. Paul's use of it reflects the Hebrew word *kābôd*, the root meaning of which is "weight" or "heaviness." It connotes importance in a relationship and thus the "honor and glory" that such weightiness demands. *Kābôd* evokes the idea of God's greatness in creation, especially that of God's creation of human beings, "whom I created for my glory" (Isa 43:7), as well as God's glorious presence resplendent in creation's appearance (Exod 24:17). The acknowledgement of glory is connoted by the verb form *doxazō*, "to give honor and glory; to glorify."

The Pauline Texts

Like the Old Testament writers, Paul can use the word "glory" to describe the high worth and honorability of a person (1 Thess 2:6, 20; 1 Cor 12:26; 2 Cor 6:8; Phil 3:19). He applies the words *doxa* and *doxazō* most frequently to God and to those who share the glory of God. Paul's original insight into God's glory is that God graces believers to share in it (Rom 5:2). He first writes of glory as something that God calls believers to receive, along with "kingdom," if they should "lead a life worthy of God" (1 Thess 2:12). The paralleling of glory with kingdom is a basic clue for understanding Paul's frequent reminders of the goal of Christian life as "the glory of God." Kingdom is not a place, but a way of being for believers. It means the state of affairs where people are joined together with God as their king, that is, where they perfectly do what God the supreme ruler wants them to do.

Similarly, "the glory of God" has to do with something that humans actively participate in. Murphy-O'Connor explains this sense of the phrase "the glory of God" as using an objective genitive in which "God" is the object of "glory" (= our giving glory to God), just as the phrase "love of God" can mean "our love toward God." Thus when Paul says that because humanity was without God's righteousness, "all have sinned and fall short of the glory of God" (Rom 3:23), he means that they were not giving glory to God as they should (Murphy-O'Connor 82). Paul chides pagan humanity precisely for this defect, "So [the pagans] are without excuse; for though they knew God, they did not glorify him as God" (Rom 1:20-21).

Moreover, even though the law "came in glory so that the people of Israel could not gaze at Moses' face because of the glory of his face," this glory has now "been set aside" by them. Paul knew that his former righteousness, his life as "perfect" according to the law, did not result in the life that God wants for every human being. He saw hints of this true life again and again in his Scriptures, in the stories of the greatness of the patriarchs and matriarchs, of the prophets and individuals like Job and, at times, King David. But he recognized that his life was not like theirs. Something was lacking in his life of strict law observance, because "the letter kills, but the Spirit gives life" (2 Cor 3:6). In Paul's works, "life" can have several meanings. In a simple sense, of course, life means our mortal existence before we die. It can also refer to eternal life after the last judgment. In a few texts, however, Paul has a special use of the term "life" to indicate a higher level of human existence, one empowered by God's own Spirit to embody the perfect fulfillment of human nature as God created it in Adam, perfect human life as it was before Adam lost it in the Fall (1 Cor 15:45). Murphy-O'Connor writes that when we live authentically, free from the impact of sin, we give glory to God, just as obedient children honor and glorify their father (see Mal 1:6). For this reason, Paul quite frequently invites the members of his communities to do everything "for the glory of God." Moreover, believers are "being transformed into the same image (of Christ) from one degree of glory to another" (2 Cor 3:18).

The authenticity of human life and consequent glory for God, however, does not come about fully at the moment of conversion to faith.

The transformation of the lives of believers is incremental because they still live in a world dominated by sin. The believing communities must increase in number as the members ever more fully embody in every facet of their lives the creative love that was characteristic of Jesus, "so that grace, as it extends to more and more people, may increase thanksgiving, to the glory of God" (2 Cor 4:15). This growth is essential for the community, for the members themselves are God-given opportunities for the deepening of the authentic life. Real growth comes about in loving and caring for others, for "to those who by patiently doing good seek for glory and honor and immortality, [God] will give eternal life" (Rom 2:7; see also 2 Cor 9:13). Paul knows that the Christian life is a process, and so he prays "that your love may overflow *more and more* with knowledge and full insight, . . . to produce the harvest of righteousness that comes through Jesus Christ for the glory and praise of God" (Phil 1:9-11).

In all these texts that emphasize the glory in store for believers we wouldn't expect to hear about life's more negative aspects. Yet for Paul the necessity and value of suffering for the children of God who follow the example of Jesus Christ is quite clear: we are "joint heirs with Christ if, in fact, we suffer with him so that we may also be glorified with him" (Rom 8:17). Such is the hard truth about following Jesus to glory. But Paul is quick to add, "I consider that the sufferings of this present time are not worth comparing with the glory about to be revealed to us" (8:18; see also 2 Cor 4:17). Full glory comes only at the end of a good life of authentic and creative love, the final state of God's process of refashioning human beings in conformity with his Son, "For those whom God predestines he also calls; and those whom he calls he also justifies; and those whom he justifies he also glorifies" (Rom 8:30—my translation has all these verbs expressing a timeless truth).

Conclusion

We have seen how Paul speaks of the glory that believers give to God, but there are some texts that seem to dwell on the believers' own glory, that is, glory that is bestowed upon them as a reward for their authentic lives, "glory and honor and peace for everyone who does good" (Rom 2:10; see 5:2; 9:23; 1 Cor 2:7). This glory is a share in God's own glory, and it comes to the believer through Christ. Finally, and by way of the marvelous conclusion to God's eternal plan, "the creation itself will be set free from its bondage to decay and will obtain the freedom of the glory of the children of God" (Rom 8:21).

So, what is the glory of God, the ineffable majesty of the loving Creator of all? I think that Paul gives us a strong hint at God's own revelation of that glory: "For it is the God who said, 'Let light shine out of darkness,' who has shone in our hearts to give the light of the knowledge of the glory of God in the face of Jesus Christ" (2 Cor 4:6). We behold this knowledge "seeing the light of the gospel of the glory of Christ, who is the image of God" (2 Cor 4:4). Now the message of the Gospel is that, according to the divine plan, "For our sake God made Christ to be sin who knew no sin, so that in him we might become the righteousness of God" (2 Cor 5:21), and that it was Christ, "the Son of God, who loved me and gave himself for me" (Gal 2:20). If Paul considers that the children of God are "heirs of God and joint heirs with Christ—if, in fact, we suffer with him so that we may also be glorified with him" (Rom 8:17), then the glory of God is the unique power of the Creator to deal with the most difficult human problem of all, the problem of evil. God's own glory shows us in God's loving Son just how humans are to deal with evil. God's own glory becomes ours when we, like Christ, allow God's power to *absorb* evil, to destroy it, to overcome it—even in death: "Where, O death, is your victory? Where, O death, is your sting?" (1 Cor 15:55).

Salvation

The final image that we shall look at in this catalogue of the effects of the Christ event is "salvation." Our English term has a broadness of meaning where salvation is used for the general goal of religion, the possibility of being brought through the evils of life to a happy eternity with God. On the other hand, many Christians ask the question "Have you been saved?" in the narrow meaning of "Have you been converted to Christ?"

Word Background and Meanings

In Paul, the full comprehension of the term depends on its Old Testament usage of "safety and well-being." The Hebrew stem *yšʿ* has a root meaning of "broadening" that in most cases connotes the idea of obtaining space necessary for freedom and security as opposed to being hemmed in, in some confined status, "in straits" (McKenzie 1965, 761). It is used mostly of God's help, the deliverance of Israel with God, or someone God sends, as savior. In secular Greek the noun *sōtēria* denotes a "saving" or deliverance from some danger, a "safe return" home, or the idea of keeping safe.

The Pauline Texts

Paul uses the noun *sōtēria* fourteen times and the verb form *sōzō* nineteen times, almost always in the religious sense of the deliverance from the threat of evil and the promise of eternal life in Christ. Remarkably, however, he only once calls Christ *sōtēr*, "savior," the agent who saves (Phil 3:20). The reason for this may be the commonality of that title in a very popular mystery religion dedicated to the healing god Asklepios. But Jesus Christ is so much more than that! Paul often speaks of salvation in general or as coming from God (seventeen times), but he also connects it explicitly with Christ, the cross, or the Gospel of Christ (twelve times), or the mediation of a Christian (six times). As in all the effects of the Christ event, Paul sees God as the initiator of the saving process that is carried out through Christ, "For God has destined us not for wrath but for obtaining salvation through our Lord Jesus Christ" (1 Thess 5:9).

I think that too much has been made of an understanding of salvation "in three tenses," that is, in past, present, and future time (e.g., Colijn 2010, 124). Certainly the cause of salvation for believers is the past events of Christ's death and resurrection, but Paul doesn't ever speak of Christians having been already "saved." Rather, the verb *sōzō* is regularly used in the future tense or in the aorist subjunctive to denote the (possible) future in fourteen of the nineteen times it occurs. It never appears in a truly past tense. Paul only uses the aorist indicative once and that is most likely what is called a "gnomic aorist" (from Greek *gnomē*, "maxim") that is used to indicate a timeless, general fact: "In hope we are saved" (Rom 8:24). As for the noun form *sōtēria*, Paul refers explicitly to its futurity (Rom 13:11; Phil 1:19; 2:12; 1 Thess 5:9) or points out some aspect of God's plan as *for* our salvation (nine times).

How then are we to understand salvation in Paul? Let us begin with what he says we are being saved *from*. He doesn't mention it very often, but when he does, it is very clear: "We will be saved through Christ from the wrath of God" (Rom 5:9; see 1 Thess 5:9). Paul's imagery of the "Day of the Lord" (1 Cor 5:5) is very powerful. To the sinner Paul warns, "you are storing up wrath for yourself on the day of wrath, when God's righteous judgment will be revealed" (Rom 2:5-8; also 2 Cor 5:10).

We have seen above (in chap. 1) that the wrath of God is part of the biblical anthropomorphic picture of God: the One who is all holy forcefully rejects everything that is not. This metaphor identifies the seriousness of not being saved. When people pass out of this life without having cooperated with God's goodness to "do good," when they do not live up to their destiny to be truly human, the loveless-ness of their lives will have its consequences: to the good "God will give eternal life," while "there will be anguish and distress for every-one who does evil" (Rom 2:9). What could be more terrible than that?

To move on now, what does Paul say we are being saved *for*? The eschatological component of salvation is very clear: at the last judg-ment Jesus Christ will be our savior (Phil 3:20). There will be no condemnation because it is Christ "who indeed intercedes for us" (Rom 8:34). On the other hand, salvation promises the end of the affliction and suffering of this life, with the bonus of "glory and honor and peace for everyone who does good" (Rom 2:9-10).

While it is true that the final effect of the salvation made possible by the Christ event remains in the future, Paul speaks of it in our present lives as an ongoing process. Moreover, he refers to those "who are being saved" as important in the lives of other believers since they are like the fragrance of incense to God in an already triumphal procession (2 Cor 2:15). They make present the urgency of the proc-lamation of the "message of the cross" (1 Cor 1:18), for "now is the day of salvation" (2 Cor 6:2). Their "striving side by side with one mind for the faith of the gospel . . . is evidence of their [opponents'] destruction, but of your salvation" (Phil 1:28).

Since, however, we have not yet received resurrection, "we groan inwardly while we wait for adoption, the redemption of our bodies. For it is in hope that we are saved" (Rom 8:23-24). It is the great hope that Christians have of their final salvation that enlightens daily life, with the "Spirit [who] helps us in our weakness" (Rom 8:26). Brenda Colijn sums up her excellent exposition of the idea thus: "The comple-tion of salvation awaits the age to come, when God's people, fully restored and in resurrection bodies, experience with the rest of creation the blessings of God's saving reign" (143; see all of 121–43).

Conclusion

Paul admonishes that salvation is an inchoative process that demands growth for its future consummation. Because the stakes are so high, Paul admonishes "Work out your salvation in fear and trembling" (Phil 2:12). This understanding of the eschatological reality, bolstered by hope in the Gospel of Jesus Christ, breaks in at baptism and confirms the faith commitment of Christians until the last day. Christ's saving deeds have guaranteed final salvation for all on Judgment Day, the end of all earthly suffering with glory and peace beyond comprehension. Thus believers do not fear condemnation but, strengthened in their hope by the Spirit, live an enlightened daily life in their common struggle to keep faith with the Gospel. Their witness to one another of authentic life guarantees that they will not have lived a meaningless existence. They will have "worked out their salvation," in order, when their days are fulfilled, to present their honorable existence to God as "the aroma of Christ . . ., a fragrance from life to life" (2 Cor 2:15-16).

General Conclusion to Chapters 3 and 4

Paul was convinced that God had begun the final act of salvation of the world and all its creatures in the death and resurrection of Jesus Christ. The Christ Event inaugurated a new age that believers could now participate in even before the end of the old one. Basing his theology squarely on the presence of God in the history of the Hebrew people and the kerygma of the nascent church, he used a dozen or so soteriological images to give us a 360-degree perspective on this axial event. He described in his theology what was given for the present life and what was to be expected of the life to come. In the "faith of Christ," believers had the model of a cruciform life that alone would engender an authentic manner of living and growing together "until he comes in glory."

With the grace of Christ, believers receive a sense of their own giftedness. In gratitude, they may grow in a selfless life that shows its own favor by engendering love in others and, with God's help, by absorbing evil in the world. Such favor underlines holiness, the specialness of being God's elect people. In a graced community, the intimacy of God's love brings about a naturalness of living—a joyful, moral, and peaceful existence that imitates God's own being as revealed in the life of Jesus. The hope of future salvation sustains the Christians in affliction and in the seeming meaninglessness of so much of life, as they "stand firm in one spirit, striving side by side with one mind for the faith of the gospel." In this way, even affliction becomes "evidence of your salvation" (Phil 1:27-28). Such a life is the beginning of glorification, promised to all and to creation itself as believers grow into that love for God and for each other that denies sin's power and puts the lie to mere law observance as the life God wants for us.

Paul uses the earlier Christian doctrine of expiation (not propitiation!) to point out Christ's love in his obedient death that reveals God's selfless love. Here we understand how God's own Son has become the ritual victim with whom believers can identify and, through him, offer their own lives wholly to God. God's selfless gift in allowing the death of the beloved Son proves God's true attitude of love toward all sinners. Believers can now be reconciled to God and live in peace, healed from their alienation from the God they mistakenly thought of as condemning and vindictive.

Paul's teaching on justification, the right relationship of humans with God, rests on two great insights: 1) God alone is the source of all human righteousness, 2) only Christ has accomplished all that the law requires. Since only Christlike love can "fulfill the whole law" (Rom 13:8), humans may be justified by their faith commitment to Christ. This faith commitment is lived out by imitating his cruciform life. Law observance as a way of doing God's will has serious drawbacks: 1) it is divisive in that it deliberately sidelines Gentiles; 2) it places roadblocks in front of the spontaneity of Christlike behavior, 3) it enslaves humans with a new addiction to being right instead of being godly, that is, acting as God does in love, 4) it creates the anxiety of perfect compliance instead of the freedom to choose right action as "second nature" in conformity to Christ, and 5) its harsh demands of uniformity actually impede the process of sanctification of both individual and community.

Paul acknowledges the progression of justified Christians as they become more holy in Christlike attitude and behavior. In this way they may benefit ever more fully from the redemptive act of Christ so that, bought out of slavery and adopted into God's family, they may be freed *from* the bonds of sin and death. Their freedom is *for* their dedication to God's will as citizens of the divine ("heavenly") sphere on earth in which they fulfill their human glory and contribute to the process whereby all the "cosmic elements" that restrain creation itself are overcome. The power of the Spirit is thus set free in the Christian community, marking the beginning of a glorious existence yet to come.

Transformation defines the restoration of humans to the state of being that God intended for them at creation, namely, a loving and fully authentic humanness in a community of like-minded believers that becomes a new creation. In this new habitat all personal accomplishments are left behind, all distinctions of status made invisible in complete dependence on God. The result is a counterculture where the renewal of the mind fosters a different response to reality: an other-centered way of acting for the growth of the human spirit in contact with the life-affirming Spirit of Christ.

Now that we have studied the images that Paul uses to explain God's eschatological activity in Jesus Christ, it remains for us to examine his explanation of the working of the indwelling Spirit and the new connectedness that believers have "in Christ."

Chapter 5

The Identity and
Experience of "Spirit" in Paul

Paul describes the process of salvation in Christ in yet another way—one that we might describe as experiential—when he speaks with the imagery of "spirit" in the many contexts of his theology of Christian living. In this chapter we shall explore the various meanings of "s/Spirit" in Paul; we shall describe the experience of "spirit" and its consequences for living in the presence of God made available to believers by the death and resurrection of Jesus Christ.

Paul uses the one word "spirit" (Greek *pneuma*) with a great deal of variety and nuance. Some uses are drawn from the Old Testament, but with a radical newness in light of the Christ event. Using the word, he can refer to: 1) the spirit as something that characterizes a human being, 2) a level of human living that is opposed to the realm of flesh, 3) the Spirit of Christ, and most frequently, 4) the Spirit that belongs to and emanates from God. We shall use the capital letter "S" with "Spirit" when it clearly refers to God's Spirit or Christ's Spirit, and the lower case for all other uses.

The powerful arrival of *pneuma* seems to have been experienced in every one of Paul's Christian communities, and it is Paul's writings in the New Testament that devote the most attention to its effect on the lives of believers. The Evangelist Luke, writing two decades after the death of Paul, has given some narrative descriptions of people actually receiving the Spirit in the Acts of the Apostles. Luke is also responsible for the *consistent* use of the phrase "the holy Spirit," originating its use in later theology where the phrase "the Holy Spirit" becomes a technical phrase, a proper name. This is somewhat different from the Pauline use of the phrase "holy Spirit" (thus without capital "H") which denotes only one aspect of the Spirit, namely holiness. However, it is Paul who delves into the mystery of the presence of *pneuma* in believers, its importance and its great effect on their lives. He speaks of diverse experiences of the Spirit in a less uniform way than Luke, yet it is from Paul that the Church derives the main tenets of its pneumatology (theology of the Holy Spirit).

In the Greco-Roman world of Paul's time, the Greek term *pneuma* referred to an elementary power of nature that encompassed and guaranteed the cohesion of the whole universe. Sometimes it is described as a mantic force that can possess a person in an irrational way. Among the Stoics, it was considered the rational soul of the whole universe that was shared by the divine and the human. Despite this, it was not nearly as central an idea for first-century Stoic thought and speech as it was, for Paul. For example, Paul's contemporary, the Stoic philosopher Epictetus, uses the word *pneuma* only half a dozen times in the four books of his *Discourses*, an oeuvre more than twice the size of Paul's uncontested letters. By comparison, Paul uses *pneuma* more than a hundred twenty times.

It is widely recognized that Paul based his understanding of *pneuma* on the Old Testament usage of the Hebrew word *ruah*, but greatly developed its meaning because of the widespread reception of the Spirit in his communities. Paul believed that something new had happened to the world through the Christ event, and every aspect of *pneuma* in Paul reflects the centrality of Christ to the Christian.

"Spirit" in the Old Testament

Ruah in the Old Testament, in its most basic meaning, denotes the moving of air in the throat, the breath of life. From there it is used figuratively to indicate an active force that is beyond the regulation of human beings, whether it is the motion of the wind that passes by, or the life energy of livings beings both human and suprahuman, including even God. As we see in the creation story, God's Spirit is likened to "the breath of life," the principle of human life that God breathes into Adam's nostrils (Gen 2:7), and will take away again in death, when God says, "My Spirit shall not abide in mortals forever, for they are flesh; their days shall be numbered" (Gen 6:3). Here we see also that God's "Spirit" is contrasted with "flesh," the mortal weakness of the human state. Psalm 78 uses an apt metaphor to emphasize just how ephemeral the lives of humans are when compared to the eternity of God: "[God] remembered that they were flesh, a wind (*ruah*!) that passes and does not come again" (v. 39). The weakness of flesh is also brought out when it is spoken of in conjunction with the sinfulness of humanity, e.g., "And God saw that the earth was corrupt; for all flesh had corrupted its ways upon the earth" (Gen 6:12; see Ps 65:2-3).

In the Old Testament, "spirit" can refer to the seat of vital activity of men and women, of their intelligence and will, and God is said to stir up the spirit of men and women to accomplish some action, e.g., "And the LORD stirred up the spirit of Zerubbabel . . . and the spirit of all the remnant of the people; and they came and worked on the house of the LORD of hosts" (Hag 1:14). The word spirit frequently indicates a person's state of mind, e.g., "Happy are those . . . in whose spirit there is no deceit" (Ps 32:2); "God had hardened [Sihon's] spirit and made his heart defiant" (Deut 2:30). We notice that in many texts God is said to act upon the spirit of men and women.

The Spirit of God in the Old Testament (with a capital "S") is the effective force that God bestows upon humans to empower them for some superhuman service in God's saving plan, as for example, in the case of Samson's great strength (Judg 14:6), or the extraordinary leadership of Othniel (Judg 3:10). It is especially employed in the oracles of the prophets, who are the instruments of God's revelation to the people in word and deed. The prophets claim to speak in God's own voice when they say "*na'um YHWH*," (literally the "utterance of the Lord"), e.g., "And now the Lord God has sent me and his Spirit. *Na'um YHWH*, I am the LORD your God" (Isa 48:16-17). God's "Spirit," too, can be personified as an actor for God's ends, e.g., "For the mouth of the LORD has commanded, and his Spirit has gathered them" (Isa 34:16). Finally, God's "Spirit" is seen as the inner nature of God whose presence carries unfathomable power to renew and create: "My Spirit abides among you; do not fear" (Hag 2:5).

After the Exile Israel is seen as deficient in the prophetic activity of God's Spirit (Ps 74:9), but it is expected that the Spirit will be poured out fully on the Day of the Lord (Joel 2:28-29). The Spirit is expected to empower the expected Davidic king (Isa 11:2; 42:1; 61:1; texts applied effortlessly to Jesus as Messiah in the Gospels, e.g., Luke 4:18), and the Spirit of God was to be poured out over the whole people of God at some future date (Isa 44:3; Ezek 39:29; Joel 2:28-29). It is easy to see how Paul understood the arrival of the Spirit in his new communities as proof of the New Age that was inaugurated in the coming to faith in Christ. In the great vision of Ezekiel, God's Spirit is predicted to bring Israel back to life by clothing their dead bones with flesh and putting God's Spirit/breath (*ruah*) within them (37:14). Paul saw in the resurrection of Jesus the beginning of this prophecy's fulfillment with its promise for the resurrection of all those who do God's will as the new people of God.

The Meaning of "Spirit" in Paul

In Paul we see nearly all the meanings of this very Jewish concept, except its most basic meaning of "wind/breath." But Paul never has occasion to speak about the "wind" or "breath" in his letters. Paul's use of the term *pneuma* takes the Old Testament idea of spirit to a new level of importance, both in the way he speaks of the human spirit's interaction with the divine, and in the personification God's "Spirit" as the agent of the newness in Christian life. Clearly Paul's earlier understanding of "spirit" as a Pharisaical Jew has been radicalized by his very personal involvement with God's Spirit in his conversion experience and in his work with the community of believers in Christ.

We should keep in mind that the idea of spirit was always dynamic in the Old Testament. It was an invisible, animating power that is "the force of life from God" (Dunn 1998, 428). This is all the more so for the recipients of Paul's letters who spoke Greek. They always heard something active in the word, stemming from the etymology of *pneuma*, whose verbal root *pnew-* means "to blow or rush like the wind," and its suffix *–ma*, which indicates the result of an action. We might use the obsolete English word "spiration" to get the idea across today. True, "the Holy Spiration" might not work very well in modern theology, but it would be just fine for Paul. In any case, it is well to keep the energy of spirit in mind, for there is an opposite tendency for us today to think of the human and even the divine spirit as a fixed entity, a static substance, rather than as the dynamic living energy that Paul always describes in experiential terms.

The Spirit of God

Paul uses *pneuma* to indicate the divine Spirit about eighty out of one hundred twenty five times. Sometimes he employs the typical Old Testament identification of "the Spirit of God" (fifteen times). Sometimes he uses the non-technical phrase "the holy Spirit" (eleven times) to highlight the sanctifying power of God's Spirit, especially as it effects right action in the community. Most frequently, however, Paul simply uses the word *pneuma*, with or without the definite article, to indicate God's Spirit, in the general sense of God's powerful agent of salvation, much as it is used in the OT. Thus Paul often links *pneuma* with "power" (nine times), with "life" (eleven times) and with the act of revelation (fourteen times).

So pervasive in Paul's theology is God's Spirit that he employs a wide variety of metaphors to help unpack this reality. Thus *pneuma* does not lend itself to a uniform description, even though it is an experience known in all his communities. As Gordon Fee points out, Paul cannot describe spirit only as a miraculous power responsible for signs and wonders—which it was!—but he must show how the Spirit also empowers one in the midst of weakness and adversity, "For whenever I am weak, then I am strong" (2 Cor 12:10). Moreover, all the drama of Christian life takes place as we await the final glory of our own resurrection, which the Spirit guarantees (Fee 1994, 8).

The Spirit is spoken of as the cause or vehicle of the effects of God's saving activity, like "joy" (1 Thess 1:6), the various charisms (1 Cor 12:3-11), and prayer and song (1 Cor 14:2, 13-15). Since it is God's Spirit, Paul can attribute the same precise activity to God (the Father) and to the Spirit. Compare: "It is the same God who *activates all of these* [charisms] in everyone" and *"All of these* [charisms] are *activated* by one and the same Spirit" (1 Cor 12:6 and 11; see Rom 8:11 and 2 Cor 3:6). Thus the Spirit's activity is often presented as personal, as sharing in the very personal saving activity of God, for example, "the Spirit itself witnesses with our spirit" (Rom 8:16), "the Spirit searches all things" (1 Cor 2:10), "if you are led by the Spirit" (Gal 5:18), "the Spirit intercedes" (Rom 8:26), and often. In its variety and richness, however, Paul's Spirit language can also employ the images of some well-known items of daily life: "God . . . has given us the Spirit as guarantee" (2 Cor 5:5); "Do not quench the Spirit" (1 Thess 5:19); "We who have the first fruits of the Spirit" (Rom 8:23).

The Human Spirit

Paul can speak in a very Jewish way of the human spirit as the seat of vital human existence, calling it to *pneuma tou anthrōpou*, literally, "the spirit of the human being that is within" (1 Cor 2:11). Thus when he says, "The grace of our Lord Jesus Christ be with your spirit" (Gal 6:18; Phil 4:23; Phlm 25), he is wishing that the Lord's grace penetrate to their innermost self, permeating the whole of their being (also "my spirit" in 1 Cor 5:4; 14:14; 16:18; 2 Cor 2:13; Rom 1:9; "our spirit" in Rom 8:16; "his [Titus'] spirit" in 2 Cor 7:13). He sometimes employs "spirit" as the center of human willing and feeling with a certain disposition as, for example, when he asks the Roman Christians to be "ardent in spirit" (Rom 12:11), or whether he should visit the Corinthians "with love in a spirit of gentleness" (1 Cor 4:21).

This usage does not mean, however, as some exegetes maintain, that for Paul the word "spirit" is coterminous with the Greek idea of "soul" (*psychē*), the immortal, immaterial essence of the human being. As a matter of fact, Paul does not use the Greek word *psychē* in that sense. For him *psychē* always has the sense of the Old Testament Hebrew word *nepesh*, "the living being, the life of a person," as when he says that Epaphroditus "came close to death for the work of Christ, risking his life (*psychē*)" (Phil 2:30). As a matter of fact, Paul never indicates with any language that he believes in an immortal soul in the classical Greek sense, namely, that some aspect of the human being lives on "automatically" after death. Rather, he says that at the resurrection we will be clothed with a spiritual body (*sōma pneumatikon*) and that we will leave behind the present body, which he identifies as the *sōma psychikon*, literally, "the psychical body," or the body that pertains only to this life (*psychē*)—evidently a mortal aspect of being human (1 Cor 15:44, 46).

This distinction helps to explain Paul's originality in opposing the living person who is *pneumatikos* ("spiritual" or "Spirit-endowed"—certainly not "immaterial"!) to the one who is *psychikos* ("of this life only"), a human being who is not yet spiritual, not truly led by God's Spirit. Thus he can say, "Those who are *psychikoi* (in the sense here of unspiritual) do not receive the gifts of God's Spirit (1 Cor 2:14a). "Those who are spiritual (*pneumatikoi*) discern all things" (1 Cor 2:15; see 2:13; 3:1; 14:37; Gal 6:1a).

To round out our discussion, we note that the opposite of what is *pneumatikos*, and therefore that which is quite closed off from the effects of the Spirit, Paul calls *sarkikos* or *sarkinos*, "fleshly/carnal" (as in 1 Cor 3:1, 3; 2 Cor 1:12; 10:4; Rom 7:14). This adjective describes people who are left in their sin and apartness, and cannot attain to the heights of greatness God promises all who believe and surrender to God's Spirit.

Paul also distinguishes the human spirit from the mind (*nous*). He says, "If I pray in a tongue, my spirit prays but my mind is unproductive. What should I do then? I will pray with the spirit, but I will pray with the mind also" (1 Cor 14:14-15). Evidently for Paul, spirit is different from mind (*nous*), the human intellect, the faculty responsible for judging and for rational thought that produces clear ideas that can be communicated by intelligible words. "What human being knows what is truly human except the human spirit (*pneuma tou anthrōpou*, literally, "the spirit of the human") that is within?" (1 Cor 2:11; also 14:32). When he asks this question, then, he is not simply inquiring about factual data or intellectual content. He rhetorically probes the inner identity of the self *qua* human, to recognize what it means existentially to be a man or a woman, a reality better apprehended by one's spirit than by one's intellect alone.

From these texts we can see that Paul clearly distinguishes the human spirit from life (*psychē*) and mind (*nous*), but a text like Rom 7:6 raises another difficulty. Here Paul claims (literally), "We are slaves not under the old written code but in the newness of *pneuma*." Here the phrase "newness of spirit" is ambiguous: it is not clear if Paul is referring to the human spirit, or the Spirit of God. He could be thinking about freedom from slavery to the old ways "in the newness brought about by the Spirit," for Paul does say that the Spirit is responsible for freedom, for "where the Spirit of the Lord is, there is freedom" (2 Cor 3:17). However, "newness of spirit" here may also refer to a newness of the *human* spirit, since the construction may be what is called a "Hebraic genitive." This is a fairly common construction in which a noun used as a genitive with another noun may be the equivalent of an adjective. "Newness of spirit" thus may mean "spiritual newness" or even "a new spirit," just as when Paul says "so too we might walk in newness of life," we might translate it as "so too we might live with a new life" (Rom 6:4). Thus Paul may be saying in Romans 7:6 that in Christ, "we are discharged from the law, dead to that which held us captive, so that we are slaves not under the old written code, but *with a new spirit.*"

Divine or Human "Spirit"?

It is a commonplace among interpreters of Paul that his understanding of "spirit" is quite fluid. In fact, there are a good number of texts in which scholars cannot be sure whether to interpret pneuma as God's Spirit or the human spirit. The letters of the alphabet in ancient Greek writing did not have a lower case as distinct from the upper case, and so there is no visible distinction between "spirit" and "Spirit" in the most ancient copies of Paul's letters. Most of the time Paul does refer to the Spirit of God when he uses the word *pneuma*, but as we have just seen, he also speaks of the human spirit in the same fashion as do writers in the Old Testament. However, in several Pauline texts there is no clear demarcation between the Spirit of God and the human spirit. This fact is very instructive for our understanding of Paul's ideas of how the Spirit of God interacts with the human spirit.

We must keep two things in mind as we examine this question. First, Paul's conception of spirit is more about the *activity* of God and humans than about the substantial reality of spirit in either. In their excellent commentary on the Letter to the Romans, John Cobb and David Lull make a very important comment for understanding Paul's thought. They point out: "Those shaped by the dominant, substantialist, conceptuality are compelled to translate all this [Paul's] rhetoric into a language that reflects the mutual externality of all things. . . . According to this view, relations are external to substances. Substances are what they are in themselves and are related to other substances only spatio-temporally" (2005, 92). Substances, in this thinking, are always separate. Paul's thinking, on the other hand, is more existential than essentialist (substantialist), that is, he describes *pneuma* in experiential terms rather than with abstract concepts, since he is thinking primarily of what *pneuma* does rather than just exactly what it is. It will help us here to remember our mention of the action implied in the old English word "spiration" as a translation for *pneuma*. A few authors even speak of believers being "in-Spirited."

The second point to reflect on is that, for Paul, as a Christian, the Spirit of God that was *only hoped for* in the Old Testament has been given to all believers already. Paul says that the death of Jesus under the law occurred "so that we might receive the promise of the Spirit" (Gal 3:14). Thus while Paul's communities know some of the extraordinary effects of God's Spirit on certain individuals in the Old Testament, they have a much broader experience of in-spiriting, for it is the inheritance of *all* as adopted children of God, who "has sent the Spirit of his Son into our hearts" (Gal 4:5). Paul would not ask a person if they were Christian. He would *observe* whether or not they had received the Spirit.

In several texts, as we have seen in Romans 7:6 above, there does not seem to be a clear demarcation between the divine Spirit and the human spirit, especially when the activity of the human is pictured as enlivened by the divine. Thus commentators dispute whether Paul means the divine or the human spirit in the frequently occurring phrase *en pneumati*, literally, "in spirit." In like fashion, the connotation of the phrase *kata pneuma*, literally, "according to spirit" is somewhat ambivalent (Rom 1:4; 8:4, 5; 1 Cor 12:8; Gal 4:29). True, *kata pneuma* refers to the status or activity of one in whom the Spirit of God dwells—probably even the resurrection status of Christ in Rom 1:4—marking them off from those who have not received the Spirit. However, it is the human side of spirit that is affected in these verses, in contrast to the stated opposite, "according to the flesh," which clearly refers to the humanity of those in question.

If Paul himself does not take pains to always distinguish grammatically or stylistically between the action of the divine and the human spirit, we may take it that he does not segregate the activity of the two in his mind. Rather, *pneuma* in Paul always refers to a level of being that is transcendent to those who live merely "in the flesh."

We conclude that Paul *always* considers the activity of the Spirit of God upon the human spirit as an interaction in which both the divine and human partners participate at the deepest level. This is the case whether he is emphasizing one or the other, or both. We should remember that for Paul, the human spirit itself is a gift from God (as in Old Testament usage), and so not a completely independent natural faculty. It is not the philosophical "soul," or some aspect of human psychology. The human spirit is "evidently that dimension of the human person by means of which the person relates most directly to God" (Dunn 1998, 77). Or, as another scholar puts it, "The believer's spirit is the place where, by means of God's own Spirit, the human and the divine interface in the believer's life" (Fee 1994, 25). Thus we may say that for Paul, *pneuma*, Spirit, is the divine force that interacts with the inner person who may then be said to "have" *pneuma* or to live or act by it. But if the divine Spirit is not present, that dimension acts as if it had been turned off, something like what happens when a radio receiver is receiving no signal. It is interesting that the medieval mystic Meister Eckhart uses the image of *fünklein* (diminutive of Middle High German *funk*, meaning a little "spark" or "sparkling point"; Latin *scintilla*) to speak of the abiding presence of God in the human soul. In later German the word *funken* has become the word used for transmitting by radio.

The Roles of the Resurrected Christ and of the Spirit of God

Another difficulty for many readers of Paul is the fact that he does not always distinguish clearly between the role of the risen Christ and that of the Spirit, e.g., "*giving life*" is attributed to the Spirit in 2 Corinthians 3:6, but in 1 Corinthians 15:45 the risen Christ is said to be "*life-giving*," in fact, he is "a life-giving spirit" in that text. Christ is "the *first fruits* of those who have died" (1 Cor 15:20), just as "we ourselves have the *first fruits* of the Spirit" as we await "the redemption of our bodies" (Rom 8:23). Paul even equates the Spirit's activity with the powerful presence of the Lord Jesus Christ in the appropriation of his saving deeds: "You were washed, you were sanctified, you were justified in the name of the Lord Jesus *and in the Spirit*" (1 Cor 6:11; also in Rom 8:4 and 14:17). Finally, Paul speaks of the Spirit of God dwelling "in" and Christ being "in" believers in the same text: "You are in the Spirit, since the Spirit of God dwells in you. . . . But if Christ is in you, though the body is dead because of sin, the spirit is life because of righteousness" (Rom 8:9-10).

Actually, throughout his letters Paul redefines God's Spirit again and again by the work of Christ. In his recognition of the fullness of God's Spirit in the life, death, and resurrection of Jesus, Paul actually gives greater definition to God's Spirit as the power by which God works salvation in Christ. As Fee points out, just as "the glory of God has been imaged for us in the one true human who bears the divine image," so "Christ has put a human face on the Spirit as well" (1994, 6). Thus Paul explains the operation of the Spirit of God as existing in the risen Jesus Christ in a very complete way, and therefore gifted to the members of the Church which is his body (McKenzie 1965, 843).

"Spirit of God" and "Spirit of Christ"

Paul develops the idea of spirit with even more complexity when he speaks of the "Spirit of Christ" in several texts (1 Cor 6:17; 15:45; Gal 4:6; Phil 1:19; Rom 8:9 and possibly Rom 1:4 and 2 Cor 3:17-18). Paul knows that in the Old Testament, the presence of God's Spirit can be attributed to an extraordinary human being. For example, we read in the hymn to Israel's illustrious ancestors in the Book of Sirach about "the prophet Isaiah, who was great and trustworthy in his visions. . . . By his dauntless spirit he saw the future and comforted the mourners in Zion" (48:22-24). Isaiah's "dauntless spirit" is undoubtedly the result of Isaiah's being "in-Spirited" by the dynamic power of God's Spirit, but the writer feels free to speak of it as "his spirit."

Paul can say much more than this about the Spirit of Christ. As Son of God and because of the resurrection, Christ lives now at a heavenly and divine level of being, uniquely possessing God's Spirit in his human spirit and able to share in spiritual union with the church more intimately than imaginable for us who are still in the flesh (McKenzie 1965, 483).

Thus Spirit remains preeminently the Spirit of God but it is communicated to believers now by the "spiritual" Christ whose life, death, and resurrection opened the way and made the fullness of this communication possible. Paul knows that God's Spirit has been fully expressed in the life, death, and resurrection of Jesus Christ, and can even speak of the "Spirit of Christ" as the location of the Spirit's action, especially when that action conforms to the selfless life of Christ.

Paul never says, however, that the Spirit is Christ or that Christ is the Spirit, because he differentiates the identity of the two. In fact, Paul can set out a triadic lineup of Father, Son, and Spirit in at least eight texts that point up different functions for each (1 Cor 2:12-16; 6:10-11; 12:4-6; 2 Cor 1:21-22; 13:13; Gal 4:4-6; Rom 5:1-5; 8:14-17). This manner of speaking is very important as a biblical base for the later full-blown theology of the Trinity that developed over the following centuries. However, we need not read such later metaphysical clarity back into the more experiential—and practical—teachings of Paul.

Paul doesn't distinguish between the Spirit and the risen Christ as clearly as we might like, but this itself is important testimony to the way Paul thinks. The problem for theologians is that, once again, Paul is speaking existentially of the action of the Spirit and does not try to give it an abstract dogmatic definition. Suffice it to say that a dividing line cannot be neatly drawn between the experience of the Spirit in the believing community and the context of their living unity "in Christ." Paul was a great saint and theologian who claims to have experienced the risen Christ as well as the ongoing and even the ecstatic reception of the Spirit. His testimony is most important for believers who are trying to identify the work of the Spirit in their lives in community and the way they are to live "in Christ." His manner of speaking should be very helpful for the *ressourcement* (or rediscovery of ancient sources) demanded for theological expression today.

The Experience of the Spirit

When we consider the great diversity of Paul's communities, we wonder just what happened to cause such a striking turnaround for them to become followers of Christ. The answer is that the initial experience in each one of them was a mighty outpouring of the Spirit, an event that Paul compares to God's act of creation in Genesis: "For it is the God who said, 'Let light shine out of darkness,' who has shone in our hearts to give the light of the knowledge of the glory of God in the face of Jesus Christ" (2 Cor 4:6). He recalls this moment of transformation several times. The most vivid recollection of it is in his letter to the Galatians, his first Christian foundation after his blowup with Peter and subsequent departure from Antioch.

Paul tells us that on the way across Asia Minor he became ill, probably with a flare-up of some kind of skin ailment. This malaise affected his vision, disabled him, and probably made him rather unpleasant in appearance. So there he was, having failed in Antioch, without friends and in a strange country, very sick, and quite unable to continue his mission to preach the Gospel. But the Spirit changed all that! He recalls with delight to the Galatians how "though my condition put you to the test, you did not scorn or despise me, but welcomed me as an angel of God, as Christ Jesus" (4:14).

Several years later, when Paul heard that other Christian missioners were trying to require his Gentile converts in Galatia to embrace the full observance of Jewish law, he was surprised that many were becoming convinced of such a step backward. Evidently the memory of those wonderful early days had been swept aside by their nagging sense of inferiority and the overpowering presence of the new "teachers." He upbraids them harshly: "Foolish Galatians! Who has bewitched you?" (3:1), and then reminds them about the awe-inspiring beginnings of their faith in Christ when they received the Spirit. Of their generous response to his illness he says, "You would have torn out your eyes and given them to me" (4:15). How could they forget about that wonderful and extraordinary experience that happened long before they had even heard about Jewish legal observance? Paul asks, "Did you receive the Spirit by doing works of the law or by believing what you heard? Did you experience so much for nothing?" (3:2, 4). The law, he points out, could only enslave them again to the flesh, "But if you are led by the Spirit, you are not subject to the law" (5:18), and the fruit of the Spirit produces in them a Christlike existence in freedom (5:22-25). For "God has sent the Spirit of his Son into our hearts, crying, 'Abba! Father!' So you are no longer a slave but a child, and if a child then also an heir, through God" (4:6-7). All old religious obligations are void now, "For neither circumcision nor uncircumcision is anything; on the contrary, there is a new creation!" (6:15).

Paul doesn't have to recall the initial experience of the Spirit in so many words when he writes to the Philippian community, his first foundation in Greece. They had perhaps the most favorable response to the Spirit, for they immediately became Paul's helpers in the mission to preach the Gospel of Christ. He is supremely confident of the tight unity of this, perhaps his most beloved, community. Their unity was the result of their "sharing in the Spirit" (2:1) that made them "stand firm in one Spirit" (1:27). Their prayers flow from their compassionate lives. Paul can count on them in his prison predicament at the time he is writing to them. He needs only to gently encourage them to continue to live together in full accord, relying on the Spirit to guide them in their total covenant response to God: "For it is we who are the circumcision, who worship in the Spirit of God and boast in Christ Jesus and have no confidence in the flesh" (3:3).

Paul gives encouragement to his Thessalonian community as well, reminding them of the power and conviction and resultant upright-ness of their conversion: "Our message of the gospel came to you not in word only, but also in power and in the holy Spirit and with full conviction" (1 Thess 1:5). Remembering how they combated persecu-tion with joy, Paul is quick to mention that their Spirit-filled reception of the Gospel set an example for all other communities that he founded in Greece, "For in spite of persecution you received the word with joy from the holy Spirit, so that you became an example to all the believers in Macedonia and in Achaia" (1 Thess 1:6-7, my translation).

This is Paul's earliest extant letter, and is our best artifact of his early preaching. Here we see that he does not have the problem of the Jewish law on his mind as when he wrote to the Galatians and Philippians. Neither is the false sophistication of popular philosophy the center of his concern as it is in the Corinthian correspondence. What we see in this letter to the Thessalonians is an overwhelming sense of the holiness that the Spirit brings. He calls the Spirit the "holy" Spirit three out of the four times he mentions it, and his prayer for them is for the love that flows from holiness. He teaches them to obey and imitate him as their teacher in the Spirit, saying, "whoever rejects this [the call to holiness] rejects not human authority but God, who also gives his holy Spirit to you" (4:8). Finally, he exhorts them to continue their holy lives in openness to the ongoing direction of the Spirit through those who exercise prophecy in the Spirit in their community: "Do not quench the Spirit. Do not despise the words of prophets, but test everything" (5:19-21).

Turning now to Paul's Corinthian correspondence we see that the Spirit's effect on that community must have been truly profound! At the top of his first letter to them, Paul expresses his admiration for their more than enthusiastic reception of the Spirit and the spiritual enhancement of their lives, "for in every way you have been enriched in Christ Jesus, in speech and knowledge of every kind—just as the testimony of Christ has been strengthened among you—so that you are not lacking in any spiritual gift (*charisma*)" (1:4-7).

We can tell that Paul was impressed by the spiritual response to his first preaching in Corinth. Early on in his mission in Corinth, Paul writes to the Thessalonians and makes it a point to exhort that church, "Do not quench the Spirit" (1 Thess 5:19). But the joyous reception of the Spirit at Corinth soon turned into a difficulty for Paul owing to several factors, not the least of which was their spiritual immaturity. Their overenthusiasm led them to see the gift of the Spirit as a kind of personal enhancement that made them prize their individuality in an un-Christian manner. This led to many problems that Paul had to address in a series of letters to Corinth.

Paul emphasizes the unifying power of the Spirit at the very outset of 1 Corinthians when he notes that they enjoy the gifts of the Spirit in a new mode of living, an eschatological existence different from the striving for individual excellence of their contemporaries. He underlines the lordship of Christ, that is, the new orientation into a new kind of community under a new kind of leadership when he says that "by [God] you were called into the fellowship of his Son, Jesus Christ our Lord" (1:9; cf. "the fellowship of the Spirit" in Phil 2:1). He addresses their divisive factionalism by reminding them, "Do you not know that you are God's temple and that God's Spirit dwells in you (*hymin*, the plural form of "you")?" (3:16). When he addresses the special gifts of the Spirit that they are using to form further divisions, Paul chides them by recalling their initial unity, "For in the one Spirit we were all baptized into one body, . . . and we were all made to drink of one Spirit" (12:13).

Though he did not found the Christian community in Rome, Paul feels that he must write them "to share with you some spiritual gift to strengthen you" (Rom 1:11), namely, by explaining the theology and consequent tolerance necessary for Jew and Gentile to live and worship together "in Christ." After a long disquisition on the sinfulness of both Gentile and Jew, he reminds all the Romans of the new life their faith brings them since "God's love has been poured into our hearts through the holy Spirit that has been given to us" (5:5). This sense of God's love brings about a new attitude of living in freedom, for "we are not slaves under the old written code but in the newness of the Spirit" (7:6).

We see that when Paul speaks of his evangelization of each community, he neatly catalogues for us the initial effects of the Spirit on rather disparate groups. First, we note the overwhelming power of the experiences of the Spirit that call forth openness and generosity and joy. Next, we hear of their coming to faith and the profound changes that reoriented their once pagan lives: the holiness of a new life, enrichment in knowledge, and boldness in speech. Then we hear Paul recount how a new unity was born among them, a oneness of mind and selfless action brought about by the pouring out of divine love upon them. The result was nothing less than a new creation!

Even though Paul does not discuss the Spirit in his very short, personal letter to Philemon and his community, he shows their awareness of the connecting point between the believer and Christ when he wishes that "the grace of our Lord Jesus Christ be with your spirit" (Phlm 25). N. T. Wright sums it up well: when Paul preached the Gospel of Jesus Christ, people "found this announcement making itself at home in their hearts and minds, generating the belief that it was true, and transforming their lives with a strange new presence and power" (Wright 2005, 100). That power Paul called "the Spirit."

The Presence of God

N. T. Wright has formulated a rich vision of Paul's "rethinking God." He says that Paul's theology is actually a fuller understanding of monotheism than was possible before Christ. For the God of the Exodus (in the Old Testament) has now sent God's Son to redeem the world. God also sent the Spirit as God's new presence, renewing and completing the former dwelling of God with the people of God in the sanctuary. The Spirit leads those who believe in Christ, those whom the Spirit has formed into the renewed people of God, not to the Promised Land (nor to "heaven"!), but to "the new, or rather renewed, creation, the cosmos which is liberated from its own slavery, to experience its own 'exodus'" (Wright 2005, 98). Thus the Spirit is *"the absolutely essential constituent of the whole of Christian life"* (Fee 1994, 898) This "real presence of God" is the eschatological outpouring of the Spirit that the prophets promised to the people of God: "I will put my spirit within you, and make you follow my statutes and be careful to observe my ordinances" (Ezek 36:27; see Gorman 2004, 124). The longing for God's presence was often expressed with great poignancy in the Old Testament, but now the Spirit has been gifted to all believers as "the way God is now present" among and within God's people (Fee 1994, 7). As we have seen, the initial outpouring of the Spirit in Paul's communities was a powerful event that changed their lives forever. It was an intense personal and communal experience, touching each person deeply, awakening deeper faith in God, building community, and giving rise to an *ongoing* affective component in their religious experience.

This presence of God first of all fills them with "God's love [that] has been poured into our hearts through the Holy Spirit that has been given to us" (Rom 5:5). Believers know they are loved by the author of creation. They have been adopted into the intimacy shared by God's own Son, so much have they become God's own children, the beneficiaries of God's promise to Abraham. They know that they are on the right track to accomplish their full destiny as human beings as well as what their loving Father asks of them in behalf of others. Their whole attitude is as secure as that of a cherished child that is thriving in a good family, in contrast with one who knows no love and flounders in dysfunction. They act in the full freedom of the Spirit and their ability and openness to communicate with God is surprising. They are conscious of their shared identity with Jesus Christ and with each other and can use the very language that the Son of God used in prayer, "Abba! Father" (Gal 4:6; Rom 8:15).

Consequently, God's Spirit gives them a more integrated and confident way of reciprocating their love of God, replacing their "hearts of stone" with "hearts of flesh" (2 Cor 3:3, alluding to Jer 31:33). They long for God now, not out of a sense of emptiness, but with assurance: "Such is the confidence that we have through Christ toward God . . ., who has made us competent to be ministers of a new covenant, not of letter but of spirit; for the letter kills, but the Spirit gives life" (2 Cor 3:4-6). Christians, in fact, make God present since "in Christ we speak as persons of sincerity, as persons sent from God and standing in his presence" (2 Cor 2:17). Paul tells the Corinthian faithful that their actions "show that you are a letter of Christ, prepared by us, written not with ink but with the Spirit of the living God, not on tablets of stone but on tablets of human hearts" (2 Cor 3:3; see also 3:7-8). Unbelievers, for their part, should see in them "the light of the gospel of the glory of Christ, who is the image of God" (2 Cor 4:4). God's presence in the Spirit will convict unbelievers of their sin and lead them to acknowledge the one true God: "But if all prophesy, an unbeliever or outsider who enters is reproved by all and called to account by all. After the secrets of the unbeliever's heart are disclosed, that person will bow down before God and worship him, declaring, 'God is really among you'" (1 Cor 14:24-25).

Believers worship God not out of fear or constraint, not by blind obedience, but in freedom and equality with their peers. They know a deep security in their election: "For we know, brothers and sisters, beloved by God, that God has *chosen* you" (1 Thess 1:4). Because of their intimate access to God they know the deep and abiding peace that Paul greets them with at the beginning of every letter he writes. They celebrate the purity of their faith and their self-esteem, "for we are the temple of the living God; as God said, 'I will live in them and walk among them, and I will be their God, and they shall be my people'" (2 Cor 6:16).

Summary and Conclusion

"Spirit" is an image used by the early Church to describe a very complex reality in the Christian life. Paul sees continuity with the Old Testament identification of the Spirit as God's creative, prophetic, and renewing presence in the world, but he now knows the Spirit with a radical newness. The seeming absence of God's Spirit in the life of the chosen people was reversed with the death and resurrection of Jesus Christ. The Spirit broke into the world with a powerful, life-changing effect in that event and with astounding effects upon those who received the Spirit in faith. Thus Paul preaches three new and important realities: 1) God's Spirit has been fully revealed by the life, death, and resurrection of Jesus Christ who possessed it fully; 2) God's Spirit is united to the believer's spirit in a new and permanent way "in Christ"; 3) the Spirit builds a fellowship of believers who are the adopted children of God and members of the body of Christ. Since God's "Spirit" is the vehicle for God's revelation, Paul sometimes predicates the exact same activity of both God and the Spirit in the church, and often describes the Spirit's activity in very personal terms.

The human spirit is the seat of vital human existence, but is never spoken of as something immortal and separable from the human being, as the "soul" is in Greek philosophy. It is the whole person that is called "spiritual," but the whole person might be "unspiritual" in another case. Moreover, the human spirit is not presented as separable from God's Spirit, and so we should think more of God's activity in the human person rather than the precise nature of one separate agent working on another. The overall effect of God's action might best be called God's "spiration" in the believer.

Paul presents the image of "spirit" as a very fluid and dynamic reality that he describes in experiential language rather than in the static, essentialist categories of later theology. He bases his understanding on his own experience of the Spirit and on his observation of the working of the Spirit in his faith communities. The human spirit refers to the deepest level of human thought, emotion, and activity, while God's "Spirit" expresses God's outgoing activity and enlivening presence. "Spirit" is also the vivifying power of the risen Christ himself (1 Cor 15:45), and so Paul speaks of God's Spirit as Christ's Spirit.

The Spirit is God's gift to all believers in Christ, making them the temple of God's presence now and co-heirs with Christ of the promise of the Old Testament, with the hope of their own resurrection. Paul himself felt the full force of the Spirit of Christ in his mission when he was welcomed with joy and generosity, in spite of his physical problems and his sometimes contentious behavior. Even though he lacked some of the human qualities that people of the time expected in a leader, his communities recognized in him the working of God's Spirit as they had never experienced it before.

Paul saw that in the conversion of so many men and women, God was breaking open a new revelation of God's own self, making possible a new kind of presence to form a new people of God. God was now with people in an intimate union in order to build up a new, liberated world over the course of time. All of history is moving toward an inevitable conclusion that God has ordained, when, after the last enemy to be overcome, death, will have been defeated, "God will be all in all" (1 Cor 15:28).

Paul is not as clear as we might like on the difference between the Spirit and the presence of Christ, but he does show that the power of the Spirit is experienced as more dynamic at some times than at others. Believers may even slip back into "fleshly" behavior, but, as we shall see, their presence in the unity constituted by Christ in his body the church abides even in dark times. Christians are always "in Christ," yet as Ernst Käsemann says, "The Spirit of God is defined by pointing to Christ, keeping him in mind and heart, and laying down a witness with one's life" (2010, 99).

Taking our cue from Ugo Schnelle, we might conclude that for Paul, the Spirit is primarily the life-giving power of God the Creator, "but is at the same time the new mode of being and working of the risen one himself, his dynamic and effective presence" (Schnelle 2003, 487). We might go even further and say that love, the ultimate truth about the Father, is poured out in the Spirit in the life and person of Jesus Christ. God's Son in turn shares that love with the faith community in the Spirit that is now perfectly his, returning the gift to the Father as filled out and ever more completed by the faithful lives of the believing community. Far from being a separate facet of human existence, spirituality—the spiritual life of believers—is, for Paul, their whole life as guided and empowered by the Spirit.

Chapter 6

The Effects of the Spirit

The outpouring of the Spirit, as we have seen, is not confined to the last times, but is conferred with the faith-filled acceptance of the Gospel by believers and their formal acceptance into the new community at baptism (1 Cor 12:13). More than a "guarantee" of what is to come, then, the Spirit is in fact the "first fruits" of an ongoing process of salvation, the eschatological struggle for the completion of God's plan for the salvation of the world (Rom 8:23). The conferral of the Spirit constitutes the gifted new life of the Christian as a "new creation" (2 Cor 5:17; Gal 6:15), a radically new style and purpose of "living to God" (Gal 2:19), that is, of "placing oneself humbly in the ocean of [God's] mystery" (Penna 1996, 2:234). We remember that the Spirit for Paul is now identified with Christ, the human face of God, the dynamic presence and effective mode of being "in Christ," and that "anyone united to the Lord becomes one spirit with him" (1 Cor 6:17).

This power of the Spirit is by no means the final perfection of the renewed people of God, but the sure path to "maturity in Christ" needed for the Eschaton (Fee 1994, 826). Paul lists the results of the working of the Spirit in the life of the believer in Galatians 5:18-26: "If you are led by the Spirit, you are not under the law. [You will] inherit the kingdom of God . . . [and enjoy] the fruit of the Spirit [which] is love, joy, peace, patience, kindness, generosity, faithfulness, gentleness, and self-control. [You] have crucified the flesh with its passions and desires. [You are] guided by the Spirit . . . not conceited, competing against one another, or envying one another." In this text we have a resume of the effects of the gift of the Spirit for the eschatological struggle that is Christian living: 1) a new covenant with God, not in law but in true freedom, 2) the hope of future salvation in the fullness of the kingdom of God, 3) the power of the Spirit to live as Christ did, 4) the guidance of the Spirit in ethical matters, and 5) the basic understanding of a charismatic and unselfish common life in Christ.

The New Covenant of the Kingdom

We have seen the reasons why the words "covenant" and "kingdom" occur relatively infrequently in Paul's letters, and that when he does use them he connects them rather closely to the Spirit. This is because, when considering the creation of the new covenant of the kingdom of God, Paul points out the Spirit's work in empowering the soteriological effects of the death and resurrection of Christ for this new kind of life (1 Cor 4:20; Rom 14:17).

Whereas in chapters 3 and 4 we identified some eleven metaphors or images of the effects of the death and resurrection of Jesus Christ, we must now point out an "overlap" of the work of Christ and of the Spirit because most of these same soteriological metaphors, God's saving work "in Christ," are carried out in the ongoing activity of the Spirit in the church. We may take justification as an example. Paul's use of the image of "justification/righteousness," as we have seen, is crucial to his whole argument for the entrance of non-Jews into the covenant in Christ. The saving action and fulfillment of the law are preeminently the result of the death and resurrection of Jesus Christ. However, since the power behind the believer's faith-filled acceptance of the gift is the Spirit, "justification" can be attributed to the Spirit "in terms of the believer's appropriation" of it (Fee 1994, 856, n. 10). Thus Paul can invoke both the "name of Jesus Christ" and "the Spirit" when he speaks of the believer's justification in 1 Corinthians 6:11. In Romans 14:17 the effect of justification is said to govern personal and ongoing "righteousness of behavior." So also the following images are seen as gifts effected by Christ and appropriated in the Spirit: redemptive liberation (2 Cor 3:17; Gal 4:5-6, 29-31; Rom 8:2, 23), sanctification (1 Cor 6:11), expiation/cleansing (1 Cor 6:11), transformation/new creation (2 Cor 3:18;), glory (2 Cor 3:8, 18; Rom 8:21-23), and the idea of salvation itself (Phil 1:19; Rom 8:23-24).

The Hope of Future Salvation

In Paul's time all Israel (and many in the Gentile world) was await-ing a new development in God's plan for the salvation of the world. They expected a great upheaval of empires and nations, God's de-struction of evil, a reorienting of the whole world to God's will, and a resurrection of the dead. Theologians call this aspect of theology "apocalyptic eschatology," the description (Gr. *logia*) of the final or last (Gr. *eschatos*) events of God's plan that God would reveal (Gr. *apokalyptō*) for the salvation of the world. Christians claimed that all of this commenced at the death and resurrection of Jesus Christ, the first to be resurrected from the dead. This Christ event, however, did not bring about the Day of the Lord, the final judgment of the nations by God, the reconstitution of Israel, *or* the resurrection of all the dead. It was this discrepancy with received Jewish thinking on the end time (*Eschaton*) that was such a stumbling block for Israel, and undoubt-edly for Paul himself when he was still persecuting Christians.

The problem was remedied for Christians, and eventually for Paul himself, by their experience of the Spirit. The Spirit was God's "guar-antee" (or "first installment," Gr. *arrabōn*) for the completion of the world's salvation in the following scenario: "God establishes us with you in Christ and has anointed us, by putting his seal on us and giv-ing us his Spirit in our hearts as a first installment" (*arrabōn*; 2 Cor 1:21-22). All of this was, of course, according to God's plan since "we have the same spirit of faith that is in accordance with scripture . . . because we know that the one who raised the Lord Jesus Christ will raise us also with Jesus" (2 Cor 4:13-14).

Paul, who was always proud of and beholden to his Jewish heri-tage, was fully aware of the eschatological dimension of God's promise to Israel and to the Gentiles. Although he never uses the world "eschatology," he shows that he understands the problem in three texts where he uses the adjective *eschatos*. He explains the present time as a period of struggle between the accomplishment of God's salvation in Christ and the forces of evil that still await destruc-tion. The resurrection of all was to be at Christ's glorious return, the *parousia*, after he overcomes the powers of oppression and his king-dom will have grown in power to completion (1 Cor 15:22-24).

In the second passage, Paul images Christ as the last (*eschatos*) Adam, the representative of a restored humanity, reversing the effect of the first Adam and his sin (1 Cor 15:45, citing Gen 2:7). Paul shows that he is very aware of the great Jewish apocalyptic tradition in which God's eschatological act would be a sudden revelation (*apo-kalypsis*) of power to reverse the fortunes of humanity. This scenario was replete with a set of traditional visual effects and other literary accouterments, symbolic images of the Day of the Lord. Paul uses some of these when he speaks of the parousia of Christ: "For the Lord himself, with a cry of command, with the archangel's call and with the sound of God's trumpet, will descend from heaven, and the dead in Christ will rise first" (1 Thess 4:16).

In the third text Paul uses Jewish eschatological tradition combining the word *eschatos* with the "apocalyptic stage prop" of the sounding trumpet when he describes the parousia as happening "in a moment, in the twinkling of an eye, at the last (*eschatē*) trumpet. For the trumpet will sound, and the dead will be raised imperishable" (1 Cor 15:52). For Paul it is the indwelling of the Spirit that guarantees that God will raise all believers to eternal life: "If the Spirit of him who raised Jesus from the dead dwells in you, he who raised Christ from the dead will give life to your mortal bodies also through his Spirit that dwells in you" (Rom 8:11).

Thus Paul's letters proclaim that the eschatological promises to Israel have begun to be fulfilled decisively in the Christ event. In hope believers await their fulfillment in the reorientation of the whole world to God's will. In hope they look forward to the resurrection of all those who will have died before the parousia. This hope is the sure belief about the future that completely changes the way believers live in the present. As Gorman says, "Hope is the future tense of faith" (2004, 122).

For Paul, eschatological hope is one of the main results of a believer's reception of the Spirit. Paul prays for it as he concludes his instructions to the Roman community: "May the God of hope fill you . . . so that you may abound in hope by the power of the Holy Spirit" (15:13). Just as Abraham "hoped against hope" (4:18) for the future through his promised heir and offspring—even though the prospect seemed hopeless by human standards—so Christians hope for their own future resurrection as heirs of the glory of God, in spite of the difficulty of their present lives (8:18). Their adoption as heirs is the result of the redemptive suffering and death of Jesus Christ because

"God has sent the Spirit of his Son into our hearts . . . so you are no longer a slave but a child" (literally "a son," the male heir; Gal 4:6-7). This connection of adoption to redemption is in effect even now, "but we ourselves, who have the first fruits of the Spirit, groan inwardly while we wait for adoption, the redemption of our bodies" (Rom 8:23). Only the eschatological future will bring the perfection of being and becoming fully the children/heirs of God (Bird 2008, 109).

True wisdom understands that with "the power of God" Christ crucified becomes Christ resurrected, "the first fruits of those (believers) who have died" (1 Cor 15:20; 2 Cor 5:5; Gal 5:5). This knowledge gives rise, then, to a hope of future glory that believers can base on the following factors of their own experience: 1) the joy they know in Christ, 2) the groaning of their spirit, 3) their success in overcoming the flesh, living a Christlike life of virtue and generosity, and 4) the resultant peace they experience in their lives.

1) Joy is a Christian experience that Paul calls forth in every one of his letters, where the noun "joy" and the verb "to rejoice" occur over forty times. If possession of the Spirit is a sure sign of a Christian believer, joy is a sure sign of the Spirit. Joy should be the constant companion of all the justified, along with peace in the Holy Spirit (Rom 14:17). It is the inward and outward manifestation of hope of believers (Rom 15:13; 1 Thess 1:6). It is contagious (2 Cor 2:3) and abounds even in affliction (2 Cor 7:3; 8:2), especially in prayer (Phil 1:4). Our loving relationship with other Christians is the proleptic experience of full union with the Lord. They are "our hope and joy and crown of boasting before the Lord Jesus at his coming. Yes, you are our glory and our joy" (1 Thess 2:19).

2) Paul does not often speak about what we might call today the psychology of the believer when considering the effect of the Spirit. However, one intimate detail he does bring up several times is the "groaning" of believers as they progress in this life of the Spirit. We all know what this existential outpouring of our longing is like, and Paul puts it very well along with his metaphor of our present life as mere tent-dwelling, awaiting the fuller and better dwelling of eternal life: "For in this tent we groan, longing to be clothed with our heavenly dwelling" (2 Cor 5:2-4; see Rom 8:23). The existential groaning of the believer is not despair, but a deep longing as "we hope for what we do not see" (Rom 8:25). This so touches God that the Spirit cannot help but join in, turning our moaning into prayer: "Likewise

the Spirit helps us in our weakness; for we do not know how to pray as we ought, but that very Spirit intercedes with groans too deep for words" (Rom 8:26).

So also, though Paul never says to rejoice at the passing of a loved one, he reminds those mourning of his teaching on the resurrection, "so that you may not grieve as others do who have no hope" (1 Thess 4:13). Since "at the parousia of the Lord . . . the dead in Christ will rise first" to be united with "[us] who are alive, who are left," it is clear that all the faithful "will be with the Lord forever" (4:15-17). Thus our eschatological hope consoles even at the death of our dearly departed.

3) Believers are also strengthened in hope because of the experience of their success at overcoming the flesh and living a Christlike, cruciform life. The New Age of Jesus Messiah brings a new regime of the Spirit to replace that of Sin, fulfilling the dream of the prophets Jeremiah (31:33) and Ezekiel (36:27-28): the new plan for humanity as truly free, without external norm, and animated in their depths by the Spirit, the very action of God in them (Casalegno 2001, 256). Their sufferings and afflictions produce endurance and proven character. This fact that they know about themselves actually builds hope (Rom 5:3-5), a primary element of the Christian character in the Spirit's transformation of the believing community on the road to resurrection (Byrnes 2003, 276). Hope both brings them peace of mind (Rom 15:13) and prepares them for bold action and any further necessary suffering on behalf of the kingdom of God (2 Cor 3:12), full of strength for a life free from domination and open to greatness (Rom 8:9).

4) Notable in the Christian life is the quality of peace. Paul opens every letter and closes most with warm wishes for peace, a word much abused in the Roman Empire's propaganda slogan "Peace and security!" Paul mocks this false claim (1 Thess 5:3), because real tranquility comes from a right relationship with the Creator. The rich Hebrew idea of peace, *shalom*, stems from a Semitic root that connotes completeness, so that *shalom* means a "filling up" so that nothing is lacking. For Paul, "since we are justified by faith we have peace with God . . . because the love of God has been poured out into our hearts through the holy Spirit" (Rom 5:1, 5). Peace is fostered by worthy living (Phil 4:9; Rom 2:10; 3:17) and it should characterize the Christian assembly (1 Thess 5:13; 1 Cor 7:15; 14:33; Phil 4:9; 2 Cor 13:11;

Rom 12:18; 14:19). Finally, he sums up the connection between the Spirit and the peace that hope brings in his beautiful wish to the Romans: "May the God of hope fill you with all joy and peace in believing, so that you may abound in hope by the power of the Holy Spirit" (15:13; see 8:6; 14:17; Gal 5:22).

The Power of the Spirit for a Christlike Life

The identifying mark for Paul of what it means to be a Christian is not some external behavior or ritual, but the Holy Spirit. As Paul categorically states, "Anyone who does not have the Spirit of Christ does not belong to him" (Rom 8:9). The traditional identity marker of God's people now becomes "circumcision of the heart, in the Spirit and not in the letter" (Rom 2:29), a sign not limited by gender, race, or social position. It is the Spirit that plays the decisive role in con- verting and shaping the entirety of the Christian life as it unfolds in community (Dunn 1998, 424). Paul's understanding of the Spirit, moreover, is completely centered on Christ, enabling believers to transcend themselves in three ways: 1) to reproduce in them Christ's attitude toward God, 2) to actualize the cruciform life of Christ in them, and 3) to engender the faith and hope necessary to endure suffering as they and their world are transformed into a new creation.

1) "To have the mind of Christ" (1 Cor 2:16): In their justification by the faith of Jesus Christ the Spirit allows believers to have the same mind as Christ, the same faithful attitude that empowered the human Jesus to live his just life, doing God's will even to the point of his untimely death. But what is "the mind of Christ," this key to a Christ- like life, full of faith and hope, with charity for all?

Paul's conversion experience was the moment when he began to understand the wisdom of God's plan for salvation and to assume "the mind of Christ" as his own. For it was then that he experienced the gratuitous love of God "who was pleased to reveal his Son to me," when he was still an enemy, "violently persecuting the church of God and trying to destroy it" (Gal 1:16, 13). It was here that he understood the central mystery of the "mind of God": the power of God's forbearance to absorb hatred and violence and render it im- potent. Paul's own misdirected zeal was dispelled in an instant when he realized that all his wrongdoing made no difference to God's loving outreach toward him. That was the new way of the followers of Christ: love for all, even for those who were persecuting them. Such fair-mindedness and love prohibits the believer from ever using the name of Jesus as a curse: "No one speaking by the Spirit of God ever says '(Let) Jesus (be) a curse!'" (1 Cor 12:3; my translation after Thistleton 2009, 61). Paul states categorically that love can never rejoice in wrongdoing (1 Cor 13:6).

Paul remembers when he was unspiritual, just like "the rulers of this age" who could not understand God's wisdom. If they had understood how the embodiment of God's love in Christ would show all the world the way to end falsehood and oppression, "they would not have crucified the Lord of glory" (1 Cor 2:8). Regardless of their motives, they were wrong: if they were honestly trying to do God's will, they would have recognized the glory of the unconditional love of God in Jesus Christ, the One whom God would make the real Lord of the world. Conversely, and more darkly, if they were dishonestly trying to preserve their own privileged position, they ended up by actually providing the stage for the event that shows the world how evil that kind of self-interest is.

"The mind of Christ" is based on his Sonship, his position of filial obedience to God's will that allows him to carry out his role in the salvation of the world because of his intimate relationship with his Father. We have seen that the Spirit makes us aware that we are also the children of God, adopted children, but able to share the same openness and prayerful intimacy with our heavenly Father as the earthly Christ did, "Abba, Father." The effect of this intimacy with God on our lives brings out the newness of life for Paul's communities. When confronted by the Corinthians with their "super apostles" who boasted letters of recommendation, Paul retorts, "You yourselves are our letter, written on our hearts, to be known and read by all . . . prepared by us, written not with ink but with the Spirit of the living God" (2 Cor 3:2-3).

2) "It is no longer I who live, but Christ lives in me" (Gal 2:20): the initial experience of the Spirit changes one completely, because the Spirit conforms the believer to the mind of Christ. Paul exhorts the Philippians:

> Let the same mind be in you that was in Christ Jesus,
> who, though he was in the form of God,

> did not regard equality with God
> as something to be exploited,
> but emptied himself,
> taking the form of a slave,
> being born in human likeness.
> And being found in human form,
> he humbled himself
> and became obedient to the point of death—
> even death on a cross. (2:5-8)

Although this hymnic text is often thought to concern Christ's pre-existence and incarnation, many scholars see it as also describing Christ as the New Adam who corrects the response of the original Adam. Thus the clause "who was in the form of God," is a way of calling to mind the Book of Genesis where the first Adam was created "in the image and likeness of God" (Gen 1:26). Continuing the allusion, the hymn implies that the first Adam "regarded his equality with God as something to be exploited." This means that the consequent possibility of having a relationship with God, of standing in some way on equal ground with God, was distorted by Adam, resulting in the disobedience of the first sin. In the human Jesus, on the other hand, we see the generous response of heroic obedience to the Father, the self-emptying act of subjecting himself to the ravages of human sinfulness and death, even though he was without sin. This humble and obedient life of Jesus culminated in his death in carrying out God's will.

This, then, is the model for all Christians, and the Spirit actualizes that life in the believer (Gal 5:25). The Spirit is not some external norm or force, but "a new structure of our being that moves us and directs us from our deepest interior" (Masi 1995, 74). Now since the Spirit is the Spirit of Christ, the entire life of a community of believers should be an imitation of Jesus Christ. First, they enjoy profound faith and hope as sons and daughters in the presence of their heavenly Father from the "Spirit of adoption" (Rom 8:15). Second, as Nicolau Masi says so eloquently, their transformation in the Spirit creates in them something like a "second nature" that brings about "a profound desire for what is genuine, for a transparent will and the incapacity to lie." Just as happened to Paul, at the moment that one experiences the freedom of the Spirit, one is enmeshed "in a most exigent love that consecrates one to solidarity, justice and service" (Masi 1995, 74).

Such a life, however, is by no means automatic. Believers must dedicate their lives in prayer and communal support as Paul did. Because of this Paul can rejoice to his Philippian community even about his imprisonment, "For I know that through your prayers and the help of the Spirit of Jesus Christ this will result in my deliverance" (1:19). Although the life of the Spirit receives enormous support from God and from one's fellow Christians, it strictly requires its adherents to set their minds on the things of the Spirit, for, "To set the mind on the flesh is death, but to set the mind on the Spirit is life and peace" (Rom 8:6). Salvation is conditional for all in this life (Gorman 2004, 375), "For if you live according to the flesh, you will die; but if by the Spirit you put to death the deeds of the body, you will live" (Rom 8:13).

Paul never hesitates to identify the characteristics of those who live by the flesh. "Do you not know that wrongdoers will not inherit the kingdom of God? Do not be deceived! Fornicators, idolaters, adulterers, male prostitutes, sodomites, thieves, the greedy, drunkards, revilers, robbers—none of these will inherit the kingdom of God (1 Cor 6:9-10; see other lists of vices in 1 Cor 5:10-11; Gal 5:19). When he, on the other hand, expounds on the "fruit of the Spirit . . . love, joy, peace, patience, kindness, generosity, faithfulness, gentleness, and self-control" (Gal 5:22-23) and the requirements of love (1 Cor 13:4-7), he as much as gives us his "character sketch" of Christ (Dunn 1998, 433), the true model for those "who walk not according to the flesh, but according to the Spirit" (Rom 8:4).

3) "We are always being given up to death for Jesus' sake, so that the life of Jesus may be made visible in our mortal flesh" (2 Cor 4:11). Paul was profoundly moved to spread the gospel by his longing to see God's purposes fulfilled. He wanted to show also that the only way to end strife among humans is God's way of love in Christ. Along with great faith and hope, this witness requires the acceptance of the suffering that comes from other people who might misinterpret the outspokenness of the Christian's authentic love. Paul had no lack of opportunities to demonstrate his profound faith in being conformed to the image of God's Son in this way. To his catalogue of mistreatment at the hands of religious and civil authorities in 2 Corinthians 11:23-29 he adds, "I am under daily pressure because of my anxiety for all the churches" (v. 28). For example, Paul suffered anxiety when his community in Thessalonica soon fell under persecution and

"suffered the same things" from their compatriots as did the churches in Judea (1 Thess 2:14-15).

The suffering of believers, their afflictions, and even their weaknesses, are not the same as they are for others who have no hope. For one thing, the Spirit sustains them in their suffering (Rom 8:26). Moreover, they know that their distress will be replaced by eternal coglorification with Christ: "The sufferings of this present time are not worth comparing with the glory about to be revealed in us" (Rom 8:18).

Here is how Paul explains the present peacefulness of Christians in spite of all difficulties: "We boast in our hope of sharing the glory of God. And not only that, but we also boast in our sufferings, knowing that suffering produces endurance, and endurance produces character, and character produces hope, and hope does not disappoint us, because God's love has been poured out into our hearts through the holy Spirit that has been given to us" (Rom 5:2-5). Paul can boast in suffering because he knows that suffering can be an occasion for real growth. As we might say today, "No pain, no gain!" When we have endured suffering, we know existentially that we were able to deal with it and can probably endure it again. That makes us persons of "proven character," the kind of person that can be relied on even in difficulty. Now such character produces hope, for if by faith we were able to endure past difficulties, we have every reason to believe that we will be able to endure in the future—and that is hope: the future tense of faith. All of this is impossible from human effort alone, but because of the Spirit, God's own love is being "poured out into our hearts."

Guidance of the Spirit in Ethical Matters

The Christian moral life is a reproduction of the life of Christ and a participation in the age to come, when "God will be all in all" (1 Cor 15:28). Yet even now, after the Christ event, the world is still dominated by the perspective of the flesh, that is, of human self-protection and individualism. For the execution of right action, one needs to "be transformed by the renewal of the mind so that you may discern what is the will of God—what is good and acceptable and perfect" (Rom 12:2). While the mind or intellect (*nous*) is necessary for discernment, it alone cannot choose the good and cause one to act on it. In fact, a baptized believer may still lapse into behavior that is "of the flesh." As Paul recalls, "I could not speak to you as spiritual people, but rather as people of the flesh, as infants in Christ" (1 Cor 3:1).

Without the Spirit of God a person is merely *sarx* ("flesh"), that human weakness that is "opposed to the Spirit . . . that prevents you from doing what you want" (Gal 5:17). Without the Spirit of God, humans are incapable of knowing the truth about God's plan of salvation: "No one comprehends what is truly God's (literally "the things of God") except the Spirit" (1 Cor 2:11). Without the Spirit, people are able to rely only on "the works of the flesh" to bring about what they think are their best interests. This is how fornication, idolatry, jealousy, anger, factions, etc., appear as good responses to the difficulties and challenges of life. Even the law of God, without the Spirit, is of no help here. Such a human life is doomed to progressive disintegration, for, as we have seen, even the law was used by human sinfulness to bring destruction to well-meaning people (Rom 7:13).

What the Christ event brings about, Paul says, is freedom from sin (and the law that sin used to enslave him) in the new life of the Spirit (Rom 8:6). The new life of the Spirit gives not only freedom, but also empowerment to live as Christ. In fact, right living can be seen as that, and only that, which is empowered by the Spirit (Gal 5:17). When believers share the Spirit of God in Christ, they have "crucified the flesh with its passions and desires" to live on the battleground of life by "the fruit of the Spirit" (Gal 5:24, 22). If Paul can speak of his own spirit (as united to the Spirit of Christ!) being present in church affairs when he is physically absent (1 Cor 5:3-4), it is because he believes that "anyone united to the Lord becomes one spirit with him" (1 Cor 6:17). Here "the (human) spirit is life" (= "comes alive") because of Christ's righteousness shared with the believer (Rom 8:10b).

Many years ago Rudolf Bultmann put forth the famous dictum that Paul understood whatever actions he advocated for his communities to be based on the eschatological reality of the believers' new life in Christ. What Bultmann called the Christian "imperative" (what to do) is based on the "indicative" that describes God's gift already received by them (Bultmann, 1924, 124). As Romano Penna puts it, "Become what you already are in Christ!" (1996, 268).

The gift of life believers have received from the Spirit can be rejected by them at any time, however, for the Spirit gives everything in freedom. Insofar as believers still live "*in* the flesh" (in this world), they must be led by the Spirit in order not to live "*according* to the flesh" (by the standards of this world). In fact, human beings have no autonomous principle that compels us to do the good, for all goodness comes from God. What we have now, however, is the freedom to choose to be empowered in all our actions by the Spirit—if we want to: "If you sow for the Spirit, you will reap eternal life from the Spirit" (Gal 6:8).

Now if the Spirit's great gifts are freedom and love, the Christian must be free from the motivation of the law, for law quickly squelches the struggle for goodness with a quick and *apparently* doable answer. As we have seen above in chapter 2, a person is easily enslaved by a sense of duty to fulfill the law, and this compulsion can outstrip the accomplishment of the good that that law intends to bring about. True, Paul can proffer guidelines that may be helpful for general attitudes—especially in times of great emotion or stress—but the basic reason for the believer's decision to act should be love, the premier fruit of the Spirit. Only love, which is the real identity of God, can produce the full knowledge needed for right action. For Paul prays "that your love may overflow more and more with knowledge and full insight to help you to determine what is best, . . . having produced the harvest of righteousness" (Phil 1:9-11). Only as agents of the Spirit's power can Christians participate in the God-given, creative task to transform the world and bring about the humanity that God intended at creation.

In Romans chapter 12, Paul explains that Christlike love begins with the dedication of this life "as a loving sacrifice, which is your spiritual worship" (v. 1). We act now as God's children, wanting to accomplish the will of our loving Father in every aspect of our being. The next step is the evaluation of traditional guidelines, whether from biblical tradition or from secular culture, but in the new spiritual way, "by the renewing of your minds, so that you may discern what is the will of God—what is good and acceptable and perfect" (v. 2). Quite the opposite of the non-believer who is "conformed to this world," Christians must be transformed by a new way of thinking humbly about themselves (v. 3). This means always considering oneself as part of the community and acting for the sake of the others, because "we, who are many, are one body in Christ" (12:5; see Matera, 2010, 288).

Notice the use of the plural in Paul's instructions. True discernment can occur only in the communal context, for the Spirit dwells in the Body of Christ, made up of many members. Individualism is a product of the flesh with its tendency to self-reliance and self-protection, as if the ego were the only guardian of one's life. The Spirit provides the righteous orientation to make God and one's fellows the center of meaningful action. As the action of the Spirit in believers conforms them more and more in the image of Christ, their own spirits are "transformed into the same image (of Christ) from one degree of glory to another" (2 Cor 3:18). Again, Paul says, "Those who are spiritual discern all things" (1 Cor 2:15). As a result, then, "The Spirit, as the earnest of the age to come, enables the believer to live, in this age, the life of the age to come" (Barrett 1957, 136). In this way they are empowered to bring about the presence of God in a divine manner of living as God's temple in the world.

The Special Gifts of the Spirit to the Community

We have seen how all of Paul's communities received the Spirit at their foundation and how he recounted the importance of this gift to each of them. As we now turn to Paul's teaching on the special gifts of the Spirit, often called "charisms," we must begin with a clarification of several terms. As a matter of fact, "charism" (*charisma*) is not the only word that Paul uses to describe certain extraordinary gifts of the Spirit.

Let us begin with the adjective *pneumatikos*, "spiritual." This descriptor is used only rarely in Hellenistic Greek, and usually refers to something having to do with the wind (compare our word "pneumatic" today). In Paul's special usage, *pneumatikos* always refers to the human connection to the Spirit, often explicitly opposed to what is "of the flesh" (*sarkinos*), or "the merely human" (*psychikos*). In a majority of instances, Paul speaks about people who are spiritual, or about those things that pertain to spiritual people, that is, believers who are indwelt by the Spirit and the actions these *pneumatikoi* (spiritual people) perform.

The noun *charisma* (plural *charismata*), often translated "spiritual gift," actually has a broader range of usage in Paul. This, too, is a rare word, and it occurs more in the Pauline corpus (sixteen times) than in all of the rest of known Hellenistic literature combined, including the one other New Testament instance of it (1 Peter 4:10; "Serve one another with whatever *gift* each of you has received"). We can expect that Paul chose this word for special reasons. It is made up of the root word *charis*, "graciousness" or "favor," with the suffix –*ma*, indicating the result of an action, and so *charisma* has the basic meaning of "a gifting; something graciously given." Since *charis* in Paul means "grace," the good will of God for the salvation of humankind, *charisma* refers primarily to some favor from God, an outpouring of grace for divine intervention in the salvation of the believing community.

In several texts Paul uses *charisma* without reference to the Spirit, emphasizing the effectiveness of God's grace in the life of believers as a descriptor for the giftedness of one's state of life, married or celibate (1 Cor 7:7), or as a saving intervention by God in Paul's mission (2 Cor 1:11), or for the overall gift of life from God to believers in Christ (Rom 5:15, 16; 6:23) or to the chosen people in the Sinai covenant (Rom 11:29). In Paul, *charisma* has the general meaning of "divine grace come to effect or expression in word or deed" and can be used as such in a variety of contexts (Dunn 1998, 554).

When Paul wants to speak about the *charismata* that pertain specifically to the Spirit, he uses the adjective "spiritual" (*pneumatikos*). He does this in his disquisition on extraordinary gifts in 1 Corinthians 12:1 and in Romans 1:11, where he describes the encouragement of faith, a particularly spiritual effect, that he wishes to exchange with them: "I am longing to see you so that I may share with you some spiritual gift (*charisma pneumatikon*) to strengthen you." Only in 1 Corinthians 1:7 and Romans 12:6 does he use *charismata* by itself to mean "spiritual gifts," but in both texts he names certain gifts that he specifically considered as *pneumatika* in 1 Corinthians 12:1-11.

Now Paul has another perfectly good (and rather common) word for gift, namely *dōrea*, which he uses in various contexts to point out the gratuitous nature of the whole of salvation, e.g., "Thanks be to God for his indescribable gift" (*dōrea;* 2 Cor 9:15). Thus he could have spoken of a *dōrea tou pneumatos*, "gift of the Spirit," if he didn't have a special emphasis in mind when he refers to spiritual *charismata*. We conclude that the *charismata pneumatika* are special gifts of the Spirit. They are not necessarily permanent enhancements of virtue or of the ability of the one who receives them. Rather, they are gracious empowerments by the Spirit for certain members to assist the believing community in its goal of becoming a new creation.

Paul's first written use of the word *charisma* refers to the extraordinary results of the initial outpouring of the Spirit in Corinth (1 Cor 1:4-7). It is in chapter 12, however, that he elaborates on this theme and begins a long discussion on the identification and regulation of the "spiritual gifts" (*ta pneumatika*, literally "the spiritual [things],"– v. 1) of the members. Paul begins his teaching on the *pneumatika* with a double triad: "Now there are varieties of gifts (*charismata*), but the same Spirit; and there are varieties of services (*diakoniai*), but the same Lord; and there are varieties of activities (*energēmata*), but it is the same God who activates all of them in everyone" (vv. 4-6).

Here we have the divine triad (Spirit, Lord [Jesus] and God [the Father]) named as the source of these spiritual activities (*pneumatika*) in parallel with a triad of identifications for them. We interpret this to mean that each of the activities can be called *charisma* ("outpouring of grace"), *diakonia* ("service"), and *energēma* ("activity," another word with the *-ma* suffix, meaning "the result of something working *in* someone"). This means that each one of the members' inspired actions are 1) something that is the result of grace, 2) something meant for service to the community in the Lord, *and* 3) something that the Spirit effects concretely in the community through a special person. These *pneumatika* are all to be directed to the building up (*oikodomē*; emphasized six times later in chap. 14) of the community, and Paul concludes, "To each is given the manifestation of the Spirit for the common good" (12:7). Thus the full identification of each of the extraordinary outpourings of the Spirit (*pneumatika*) listed in 12:8-10 is a "manifestation of the Spirit," that is, something gifted as a grace by the Spirit that works within a certain person but is for service to all the community. The catalogue of special activities in 1 Corinthians 12:8-10 is not meant to be complete. Paul gives briefer lists in 12:28-30; 13:1-3; 14:26-32 and Romans 12:6-8. He knows that *everyone* in the church is specially gifted by the Spirit (1 Cor 12:13), and that each is a necessary part of Christ's Body (1 Cor 12:14-26).

We may now explain the charisms in the longer list:

- *utterance of wisdom*: The phrase indicates that this is not just some gift of wisdom given to a believer, but the actual and effective communication of God's "secret and hidden wisdom" (2:7) that Paul speaks about in 1 Corinthians 1:18–2:13. At times it requires extraordinary grace for a believer to enable someone else to come

to a life-changing understanding of the "foolishness" of the cross
(1:18) and its profound effect on one's life, "what God has prepared for those who love him" (2:9). Paul says, "And we speak
of these things in words not taught by human wisdom but taught
by the Spirit, interpreting spiritual things to those who are spiritual" (2:13).

- *utterance of knowledge*: This is also the declamation of the kind of
  truthful knowledge about the faith, an explanation that moves
  a person to action, perhaps like the deep understanding needed
  to forego one's superior knowledge (like "no idol in the world
  really exists" 8:4), for the sake of edifying action based on knowledge of the real situation of one's fellow believers (like abstaining
  from meat offered to idols).

- *faith*: This *pneumatikon* is a special kind of faith over and above
  that given to every believer who responds to the Gospel. Paul
  sees an extreme example of it in the person whose faith is all-
  powerful, "so as to remove mountains" (13:2), the kind of faith
  that is a model and an effective witness for others.

- *gifts of healings*: The identification by the plural of both words
  here means that the gift is not the actual cure itself but the graced
  moment and effusion of power in the person who effects the
  cure.

- *workings of miracles*: "Miracles " (literally "powers; powerful
  deeds") is a frequent New Testament word for the mighty deeds
  of Jesus and his followers. Paul recalls this effect of the Spirit also
  in Galatians 3:5. The first word, the plural *energēmata*, "workings," refers not to the miracle itself, but to the working of the
  Spirit in a person who performs the miracle.

- *prophecy*: Although practically every religion in the first century
  boasted of their prophets, for Paul the understanding of this
  working of the Spirit was thoroughly based on the Bible. The
  etymology of the Greek word *prophēteia* actually demonstrates
  its Old Testament meaning: the prefix *pro* ("in front of; in place
  of") is added to the word for "speaking" to indicate that the
  inspired prophet is speaking for God, in the place of God, from
  a divine revelation. Hence Fitzmyer defines Christian prophecy
  as "a Spirit-inspired dynamic and effective preaching of the

Scriptures and the gospel, as Paul makes clear below, in [1 Cor] 14:1, 3-6, 24, 29, 31" (2008, 467).

- *discernments of spirits*: The plural spirits here refers to the working of the Spirit of God in the spirit of a believer. "Discernments of spirits" thus means inspired acts of evaluation by one member of the community upon the origin and veracity of the "spirations," the supposedly inspired acts, of another. Recall when Paul admonishes, "Let two or three prophets speak, and let the others weigh what is said" (1 Cor 14:29).

- *various kinds of tongues*: Much has been written on this phenomenon, but our purpose here is merely to identify it among the extraordinary outpourings of grace we commonly call charisms. We may define tongues as a pre-reflective utterance at the common prayer of the community. As we see from 1 Corinthians 14, the sounds emitted in this action are not readily understandable to others because they are not made up of commonly understood language. Rather, they are an emotional outpouring of sounds not unlike those we make before we have time to think upon experiencing something. "Ooh! Mmm! Gee! Ha-ha!" The practice of glossolalia ("tongue-speaking") at common prayer in the church today is very expressive when witnessed and often very satisfying to the one who is thus venting feelings. However, as in Paul's day, the meaning of the extended "nonsense syllables" is far from clear to the bystander.

- *interpretation of tongues*: This gift requires that someone else feel the mood of the tongues-speaker and (probably because of their acquaintance with that person) attempt to put into words that which the other is experiencing so strongly.

Paul concludes this catalogue of special gifts, reaffirming that they are all "activated by one and the same Spirit, who allots to each one individually just as the Spirit chooses" (12:11), and not by individual merit or ability. He develops the idea of their purpose as the "upbuilding of the community" with the beautiful analogy of the body of Christ (vv. 12-26), and gives a kind of ranking system to its gifted members: "And God has appointed in the church first apostles, second prophets, third teachers; then deeds of power, then gifts of healing, forms of assistance, forms of leadership, various kinds of tongues"

(v. 28). Herein we see a sampling of other gifts in verse 28, including "miracles" and "gifts of healing" (both already mentioned in 12:9-10) along with "(acts of) assistance" and "(acts of) leadership" (the plural of these words is used). "Assistance" (literally "supports") indicates various inspired acts related to the "service" mentioned before in verse 5. Similarly, "leadership" (literally "governings") shows that for Paul, even the various acts of administration within the community are to be Spirit-guided. Here we note the last place position of the charism of speaking in tongues as in the longer list above. Even in his rapid-fire final set of rhetorical questions in verses 29-30, he ends with "tongues." This gift was apparently being misused by members of the community as setting them on a higher plane than the others. Paul deals with them by ranking their "special" charism dead last not once but three times!

In Romans 12, Paul begins to address the disparities of communal life that he heard were occurring in Rome. He gives a mini-review of his longer discourse of 1 Corinthians 12, rehearsing what he had taught there on the unity of community as the "one body in Christ." He proceeds to mention "gifts (*charismata*) that differ according to the grace (*charis*) given to us" (Rom 12:6), naming prophecy, ministry (*diakonia*), teaching, exhortation, generous giving, leadership, and compassion. Paul speaks often enough of the first three of these ecclesial offices, but the last four items seem to refer to individual acts of members that Paul includes as among the *charismata*, emphasizing the graced nature of all acts of service for the community.

Although many of the spiritual gifts that Paul discusses take place in communal worship, it is remarkable how infrequently he speaks of the working of the Spirit in the act of praying. While Paul often speaks of prayer, praying, or giving thanks to God (some seventy-five times), he directly mentions the Spirit in connection with prayer only rarely. In two texts Paul prays for the *effects* of the Spirit ("fellowship of the Spirit" in 2 Cor 13:13 and "to excel in hope by the power of the Holy Spirit" in Rom 15:13). In another, he claims that "we who worship in the Spirit of God are the circumcision" (Phil 3:3). In another, he rejoices "for I know that through your prayers and the help of the Spirit of Jesus Christ this will turn out for my deliverance" (Phil 1:9), paralleling the effects of prayer and of the Spirit.

From this we might think that for Paul, the experience of the Spirit does not enter into personal prayer. Yet Paul does mention an intimate connection of the Spirit with prayer in three texts. Twice he refers to the Spirit as responsible for our crying out "Abba! Father!" (Gal 4:6 and Rom 8:15) in the joy of knowing our ultimate acceptance by God as beloved children. Finally, he describes the Spirit's activity in the interior of the human person who is trying to pray: "The Spirit helps us in our weakness for we do not know how to pray as we ought, but that very Spirit intercedes with sighs too deep for words. And God, who searches the heart, knows what is the mind of the Spirit, because the Spirit intercedes for the holy ones according to the will of God" (Rom 8:26-27). Here we catch a glimpse of the reality of the Spirit's action in the very depths of the human person, a subject so personal that Paul simply had few words that could describe it.

Summary and Conclusion

Paul affirms all that is said about the Spirit of God in the Old Testament as the expression of God's presence in the world and of God's creative, life-giving activity, but acknowledges God's greater revelation of the Spirit in Jesus Christ. The Spirit is the first fruits of the believer's life in a community that is engaged in God's ongoing process of the salvation of the world. By the Spirit Christians become a new creation by their radical new way of "living to God" in intimate union with Jesus Christ. We have identified five areas of the Spirit working on believers:

1) The Spirit enables believers to live out their lives as God intended in the new covenantal life that Jesus referred to as the kingdom of God. Immoral conduct is never condoned in the kingdom, but only God's way of understanding other human beings and how they should be treated, as discerned by prayer and spiritual insight in constant conformity to Christ's life.

2) The Spirit is the hope of future salvation in God's plan and the basis of a fellowship of believers joining in the eschatological struggle for what is to come, the fullness of God's kingdom at Christ's Second Coming in the parousia. This hope of future glory is based on the joy that Christians already know in their experience of the Spirit in the loving fellowship of believers. The presence of the Spirit sustains them in their prayerful waiting for salvation, complicated as it is by their own struggles and the death of so many loved ones. Their lives witness to the fulfillment of salvation as they observe growth in their

own conformity to Christ and that of their fellows as they progress through endurance of suffering to live to God.

3) The Spirit gives power for a Christlike life so that believers have in them Christ's attitude toward God's will, the mind of God. This is the power of God's forbearance to absorb hatred and violence and render it impotent. Through this power, the children of God will show the world the way to end falsehood and oppression in newness of life. They dedicate their lives in prayer and communal support as Paul did, in order that the fruit of the Spirit becomes known for the complete transformation of the world as a new creation.

Paul shows how Christ was a model of what the world would deem as weakness but that in fact demonstrates the true power of God. The Spirit sustains Christians in their suffering from the everyday and their human weakness in this present condition, making them persons of proven character—the kind of people that can be relied on even in difficulties impossible to overcome by human effort alone. They are able to do this only because of the Spirit poured out in their hearts.

4) The Spirit guides believers in ethical matters, for the Christian moral life is at the same time a reproduction of the life of Christ and a participation in the age to come. Believers embark on this journey with great hope and a complete change of lifestyle. However, since they still live "*in* the flesh" (in this world), the Christian community must be led by the Spirit in order not to live "*according* to the flesh" (by the standards of this world). With regard to moral decision making, they are to be transformed by the renewal of the mind so that they may discern together what is the will of God. As Matera concludes, "the Spirit is the moral compass that enables the justified to know what is pleasing to God. More importantly, the Spirit enables them to live in a way pleasing to God" (Matera 2012, 167). The basis of the believer's decision to act should be love, the real identity of God and the premier fruit of the Spirit (Gal 5:22).

5) The Spirit is responsible for all the special gifts that are given for the building up of the community. Each of them is defined by Paul as a manifestation of the Spirit, that is, the gracious activity of the Spirit working in a person for service to the community. In addition to these special gifts, Paul meditates on the powerful connection of the Spirit and prayer, noting the reality of the Spirit's action in the very depths of the human person.

The Spirit is the source of faith, hope, and love, of grace, peace, and joy for a ministry that answers the powers of sin and death with the mind of God, in weakness like Christ's, sharing in an effective and responsible communal life with the deep comfort of eschatological hope. The Spirit thus is the dynamic presence of God's love and the principle of a new way of acting (Barbaglio 2004, 203). In a flight of fancy we may liken such a communal life to a cadre of God's agents "in the field" for the development of humanity, all linked by an advanced communication system to the Transcendent that empowers them. They come together in prayerful assembly to share information, receive fuller knowledge, plot strategy, and celebrate their union, each sharing an irreplaceable function in the whole to show the world how to live to God, to live in God's future by God's gift from the future, as a people in whom the new age has come to birth "in advance of the final putting-to-rights of the whole creation" (Wright 2005, 147).

Chapter 7

Paul's Language of the Unity of Christians "in Christ"

We may now focus on the center point of Paul's theology, namely, the existence and praxis of Christians in union with Christ and each other. Paul explains this reality as being "in Christ." The phrase "in Christ" refers to a vital sphere of existence in which believers become a close community, living out and passing on to others the new life made possible by God's saving act in Jesus Christ. As we shall see, being "in Christ" means entering into the process of salvation with God's gift of faith and the reception of baptism. New Christians live in a kind of protected area, a "habitat" for a special life in which they find their true identity and carry on the work of Christ. It is a new eschatological present, already participating in the saving future of the lordship of Christ when he will be present in full glory and power at the parousia.

This new state of being is most frequently expressed in Paul by various relational phrases. First, there are the prepositional phrases "in Christ," "through Christ," "into Christ," "with Christ," and the expression "belonging to Christ" (literally "of Christ"). The variety and frequency of these phrases (some two hundred times in the fifteen hundred verses of the undisputed letters) show how central the union of Christ and believer "in Christ" is to Paul's understanding of Christian living.

It is not necessary to present here the exhaustive exegetical treatment of every example of every expression on which our study is based, but within the necessary limits of space in a work like this, we hope to give an adequate, if schematic, summary of the areas of Christian being and action that these images portray.

116

The Prepositional Phrases with "Christ"

The exact origin of the phrase "in Christ" is disputed. Since it is used so frequently by Paul (some one hundred times!) and hardly anywhere else outside the Pauline corpus (with the exceptions of 1 Peter 3:16 and 5:14—written by a later writer familiar with Paul's language), we may surmise that it is the creation of Paul himself. He undoubtedly came to this bold new way of speaking about the believer's religious experience because of the power of his own personal union with Christ. Clearly, he felt its effect throughout his entire ministry, beginning at his life-changing experience of the Lord on the way to Damascus, and certainly, we should hope, at the moment of his martyrdom. He devised the image of being *in* the sphere of the effects of God's work in the person of Christ, basing it on the language of a similar Old Testament situation. Paul understood that the newness of being "in Christ" was in continuity with God's full plan of salvation history. Paul shows his familiarity with the exact Old Testament idiom when he cites God's words to Abraham, "*in you* all the families of the earth shall be blessed" (Gen 12:3 cited in Gal 3:8; see Gen 18:18).

Scholars derive the core meaning of the phrase from the value of the preposition "in" as either locative (showing an almost spatial relation of "being in Christ") or instrumental (showing "Christ" as the origin and sustenance of the unity), or they distinguish different meanings of the phrase when the object of the preposition is "Lord" and when it is "Christ (Jesus)." These distinctions and nuances, however, seem to be overdrawn, as the wide discrepancy in scholarly opinion demonstrates. In fact, the phrase "in Christ" is used almost interchangeably with the phases "in Christ Jesus" and "in the Lord" that appear in various contexts with no more difference than the common inflections of a single ancient Greek word. The longer phrase, "in Christ Jesus," may carry a bit more solemnity, and "in the Lord" may at times emphasize Christ's present authority in the church, but every instance reminds us of all the other contexts in which the image is used.

At times, "in Christ" calls to mind obedience in this world to a Lord who is not of this world. It articulates the identity of those who do God's will in a special unity. They pattern their lives after the self-giving example of the one who leads them by his special presence in the group. The phrase "in Christ" shows the connection of all believers together to the saving acts of the life of Jesus, as they enjoy the effects of that life in theirs. It enables them to truly be a part of God's on-going reformation of the world by their Christlike actions. Implicit in the phrase is the claim that believers themselves die with Christ, first when their faith led them to be baptized "into Christ," and again and again as they suffer together in fulfilling their mission. They participate in the newness of his resurrected life, looking forward to a resurrected life of their own.

These ideas are picked up and articulated by other turns of phrase. "Through Christ" brings out the belief that all benefits—whether past, present, or future—are mediated by the One who both gave the example of how to live and who guides them now in their ongoing experience of recognizing and doing God's will. "Into Christ" em-phasizes the incorporation of believers into this new realm of exis-tence by their faith and baptism. "With Christ"—as well as several action words compounded with *syn* ("with")—shows how they par-ticipate in and continue the suffering and death of Christ in lives in a way that makes a difference for the good of all men and women: "[we are children of God] . . . *joint heirs with* Christ—if, in fact, we *suffer with* him so that we may be *glorified with* him," literally "co-inheritors . . . co-suffer . . . co-glorified" (Rom 8:17; see also Rom 6:4, 5, 6, 8; Gal 2:19; Phil 3:10, 21).

In four texts (Gal 2:20, 4:19; 2 Cor 13:5; Rom 8:10) Paul uses the expression "Christ in me/you" when he comments on the formation of Christ as the spiritual growth of the Christian community as a whole. As we have seen earlier in chapter 5 of this volume, Paul sees no sharp dividing line between the experience of the Spirit of God and the experience of Christ's spiritual presence ("the Spirit of Christ") in the Christian community. Thus "Christ in me/you" is a kind of shorthand for "(the Spirit of) Christ dwelling in you," refer-ring to the spiritual presence of the risen Christ that empowers and directs the community from within.

Other Terms and Phrases

Closely related to these phrases are certain Pauline expressions that employ specific images to further describe union with Christ. Thus the intimate relationship of believers "in Christ" is also expressed by the notion of "fellowship" with God's Son as the sharing of the whole life of Christ, past and present (Rom 15:26; 1 Cor 1:9; 10:16; 2 Cor 8:4; 9:13; 13:13; Gal 2:9; Phil 1:5; 2:1; 3:10; Phlm 6). As such, it is a participation in God's own Spirit that includes the fellowship of communal life that the Spirit creates and sustains (Fee 1994, 872).

Christians "put on" Christ at baptism to wrap themselves in a new way of living until their union with Christ is completed in their own resurrection (Rom 13:12, 14; 1 Cor 15:53-54; 2 Cor 5:2-3; Gal 3:27; 1 Thess 5:8). The image here is of clothing oneself, an action one does to cover one's nakedness for protection against the elements, but also to adorn oneself for enhanced interaction with others. Since Paul can exhort believers to "put on Christ," even though in baptism they have already done so, we can agree with Gorman "that dressing oneself with Christ—a vivid metaphor—is not a one-time experience. It is a way of life" (2004, 120).

The idea of "belonging to Christ" (Rom 8:9; 14:8; 1 Cor 1:12; 3:23; 15:23; 2 Cor 10:7; Gal 3:29; 5:24) is more than a metaphor. It is a real identification with the Savior that results in an affective union like that of an impassioned follower of a great lord who is both hero and mentor (Dunn 1998, 407). One becomes at the same time a devoted servant to Christ, a partner in friendship and even in brotherhood. Christ has shared all the goodness of his being to effect a complete transformation of believers, one that transcends both life and death. Paul says, "If we live, we live to the Lord, and if we die, we die to the Lord; so then whether we live or whether we die, we are the Lord's" (Rom 14:8).

Ekklēsia is another word Paul uses to refer to the community of believers, usually in a local setting. This Greek term literally means "an assembly of those summoned," usually for political matters in the Hellenistic world. Its use in the New Testament has given rise to our later and broader concept of "church" (itself an English word derived from a different Greek word, *kyriakos*, "pertaining to the Lord"). *Ekklēsia* was already in common use among Christians before Paul, as his free use of it (forty-four times) in the uncontested letters makes clear. Jewish writers like Philo and Josephus used this word, derived from the Septuagint's translation of the Hebrew *qāhāl*, the assembly of Israel, especially when they referred to the assembly of Israelites called together for religious purposes. That the early Jerusalem church adopted this word as its own shows the strong identification by Christians with the Old Testament people of God. Paul makes explicit this relationship when he speaks of all believers as being "Abraham's offspring, heirs according to the promise" (Gal 3:29) and of Gentile Christians as "you, a wild olive shoot, were grafted in their (Israel's) place to share the rich root of the olive tree" (Rom 11:17). The difference is, of course, that while non-Christian Judaism remains with the old covenant of the law, the Christian "*ekklēsia* is the eschatological community of a new covenant empowered by the Spirit" (Matera 2012, 148).

Paul uses *ekklēsia* to identify local faith communities and does not develop its meaning by any further description. Nevertheless, we can see something new in Paul's usage when he calls any and every Gentile congregation of believers an *ekklēsia*, right along with "the churches (*ekklēsiai*) of God that are in Judea" (1 Thess 2:14; see Gal 1:22). He understands *ekklēsia* as a unity that transcends the identity of Jew or Gentile and incorporates them both as followers of Jesus Christ (Fitzmyer 1990, 1412).

In secular Greek, *ekklēsia* usually refers to a political gathering to promote the interests of a given group. Thus Paul comes to see *ekklēsia* as an international movement made up of many communities, local *ekklēsiai*, who share the same faith in Jesus Christ. Such a communion contrasted with the Roman Empire in that its "Lord and Savior" was Jesus Christ and not Caesar. Its egalitarian social structure differed greatly from the social stratification upon which the privileges of Empire relied, and Paul's repeated call for "the upbuilding" of the church flew in the face of the factionalism required by the patron-client system of Rome. Paul reminds his readers that "our citizenship (*politeuma*) is in heaven [not Rome!] and it is from there that we are expecting a Savior, the Lord Jesus Christ [and not Caesar!]" (Phil 3:20).

The Body of Christ

Paul demonstrates great versatility in his use of metaphor when he describes the unity of believers and Christ with the image of the body or "members" (of the body) of Christ. This symbolic language of Paul's has been artfully developed in the Deutero-Pauline letters, where we find their vivid picture of the (universal) Church as the body with Christ as its head. As in all of our analyses, however, we leave aside these contested letters in order to be sure that we have the meaning of the idea in Paul's own theology. In the non-contested letters, we note that Paul develops the idea of the body of Christ in only two of them, 1 Corinthians and Romans, whose communities were rife with inner dissention. The ever-resourceful Apostle elaborated the image in order to respond to this deficiency in those communities.

Paul had encountered the language about Christ's body in the eucharistic liturgy that he had inherited from the churches he first served. Their common (and therefore liturgical) language was Greek and the concept of "body" was rather broad. It was with this tradition, Paul reminds the Corinthian community, that he had instructed them about the events of the Last Supper: "I also handed on to you that the Lord Jesus on the night that he was betrayed took bread . . . and said, 'This is my body that is for you'" (1 Cor 11:23-24). Paul's Greek language tradition had translated the original word of Jesus over the bread, probably the Aramaic *basra*ʾ, "flesh," with the Greek word for body, *sōma*. Jesus had most probably used the sacrificial language of "flesh and blood" in Aramaic to interpret the sharing of bread and wine at that last Paschal meal as referring to his upcoming death "in behalf of" his followers. The traditions of the Last Supper in the gospels of Matthew, Mark, and Luke, like Paul's formula, all use the Greek word *sōma*, but we have possible evidence of the original Aramaic in the text of the "Bread of Life" discourse in John's Gospel: "Unless you eat the *flesh* of the Son of Man and drink his blood, you have no life in you" (John 6:53; thrice more in vv. 54-56). Since the meaning of "flesh" in Semitic languages is different from its counterpart in Greek (*sarx*), the early church did well to render Jesus' word over the bread as *soma* (body), a better translation of the original Aramaic.

Paul takes up this vivid image of the body of Christ in Romans to point to the historical body of Christ in his saving death on the cross in another context. When discussing Christian freedom from the law, he says, "You have died to the law through the body of Christ, so that you may belong to another" (7:4). This argument is based on an idea that we shall look at below, the believers' death with Christ in baptism. Paul uses the idea of the body of Christ here because for him, "body" is a way of talking about the concrete life of a person, and it is the concrete life (the death and resurrection) of Christ that has transformed believers' concrete life in relationship to the law. It was an easy step in Paul's thinking, then, to apply the phrase "the body of Christ" to refer to the living, glorious existence of the resurrected Christ. It is this glorious existence he speaks of as the future eternal life he has promised to bestow upon all believers: "He will transform the body of our humiliation that it may be conformed to the body of his glory" (Phil 3:21).

In 1 Corinthians, Paul takes up the eucharistic symbol of the body of Christ, based as it was on Jesus' use of it at the Last Supper to communicate the saving events about to unfold in his cross and resurrection. He combines it with a rather popular Stoic description of the human community as a body (politic), made up of many members, and fleshes out the comparison to make powerful arguments against four errant practices of some community members:

1) *Participation in Pagan Religious Banquets (1 Corinthians 10)*

In chapter 10, Paul mandates that Christians may never participate in a pagan ritual. First he reflects on the profound sharing that occurred in offering a Jewish sacrifice, and then compares it to the *partnership* that pagans were thought to experience in their sacrificial rituals: "Consider the people of Israel; are not those who eat the sacrifices *partners* in the altar?" (v. 18). He strictly forbids participation in idol worship banquets, even for those whose strong belief in Christ leads to a denial of any real existence of the gods the idols represent because "I do not want you to become partners with demons" (v. 20). He further explains the point by showing that the Christians' celebration of the Eucharist concretizes their relationship one to another "as one body" when they are nourished by "the body of Christ" in their solemn remembrance of the saving act of Christ: "The bread that we break, is it not a sharing in the body of Christ? Because there is one bread, we who are many are one body, for we all partake of the one bread" (vv. 16–17).

2) *Inequality in Participation in the Lord's Supper (1 Corinthians 11)*

Paul brings the words of the Lord at the Last Supper to the fore in chapter 11 in order to address an intolerable lack of respect and concern by some Corinthians for the less fortunate members of their community. The scenario related in verses 17-22 is well known: when they came together to celebrate the eucharistic meal, some of the more prosperous members regularly showed up early, eating and drinking to satiety, and not providing for those who could only arrive late because of their evidently menial employment: "Do you show contempt for the church of God and humiliate those who have nothing?" (v. 22). At this point he recounts the tradition of the Last Supper (vv. 23-25) to show how the behavior of these Corinthians was very improper. Then he says, "For as often as you eat this bread and drink the cup, you proclaim the Lord's death until he comes" (v. 26). With these words he points out their hypocrisy while practicing the ritual that recalls the selfless death of Jesus Christ. As Paul had so often taught, Jesus underwent death precisely to do away with the oppressive social distinctions between rich and poor, slave and free, the very discrimination that they were practicing at their eucharistic gatherings.

Taking up the image of the assembly as one body from 10:17, Paul identifies it with the body of Christ as the image of the death of Jesus for all, making two conclusions: 1) "Whoever, therefore, eats the bread and drinks the cup of the Lord in an unworthy manner will be answerable for the body and blood of the Lord" (11:27). Here he connects the unworthy behavior of the Corinthians negatively with the very saving event that it commemorates. 2) "For all who eat and drink without discerning the body, eat and drink judgment against themselves" (v. 29). In this statement, he cleverly changes the metaphor to name their mistaken behavior as not "discerning the body," that is, the "one body" formed by those "who partake of the one bread." Their behavior must change, he says, "so that when you come together, it will not be for your condemnation" (v. 34).

3) *Supposed Inequality of Spiritual Gifts (1 Corinthians 12)*

In chapter 12 Paul answers the problem of some members lording it over others because of the supposed superiority of their spiritual gifts. To counter this, he again uses the metaphor of the body of Christ (vv. 12-31), this time explaining how the unity of Christians is constituted by their baptism into Christ. "We were all baptized into the one body" (1 Cor 12:13), Paul states. In the artful allegory that follows, he shows that the diversity of members is necessary for its proper functioning: "Indeed the body does not consist of one member but of many" (v. 14). He concludes that this unity in diversity was ordained by God: "God arranged the members in the body, each one of them, as he chose" (v. 18). Indeed, their solidarity comes from their mutual interdependence: "If all were a single member, where would the body be?" (v. 19).

Furthermore, there is no ranking of one member as higher than another, for Paul insists on the indispensability of the weak: "On the contrary, the members of the body that seem to be weaker are indispensable, and those members of the body that we think less honorable we clothe with greater honor. . . . But God has so arranged the body, giving the greater honor to the inferior member, that there may be no dissention within the body" (vv. 22-25). For Paul, the wholeness that results from this interdependence is the hallmark of the body of Christ (see also Rom 12:3-8).

Far from being a hindrance to its operation as the body of Christ, the diversity of believers and the unevenness of their gifts are necessary to its proper function. All are considered equal, "for all of you are one in Christ Jesus" (Gal 3:28), but the different needs of each member provide the occasion for the exercise of Christlike love for the other members. In this way they participate in God's plan in every aspect of their lives. The community grows in visible form into the ideal fellowship (*koinonia*) that transcends all dichotomies and becomes the concrete model of God's will for humanity.

4) *Improper Sexual Behavior (1 Corinthians 6)*

Finally, although he does not use the phrase "body of Christ" in the discussion, we find that Paul had been thinking of it earlier in the letter in the context of another errant practice of some community members: the procurement of sexual intercourse with prostitutes. We can imagine that certain believers' hearing had been impaired by the cacophony of popular philosophers who railed their contempt for the human body. Confused by their dichotomy between law and morality, it seems that the unthinkable had happened: some members of the community somehow came to consider illicit sexual intercourse as part of their Christian freedom from the law! We can tell how they justified their actions from their self-serving proverbs that Paul quotes with great patience here in order to neutralize them.

First, they evidently had mistaken Paul's teaching on freedom from the law by their generalizing quip, "All things are lawful for me."

Paul quotes it back to them twice in verse 12. Although he cannot contradict the saying, he qualifies it twice: "but not all things are beneficial"; and "but I will not be dominated by anything." Second, they gravely misunderstood Paul's teaching on the importance of the spiritual, filtering it through their own Hellenistic anthropology with its contempt for the body as belonging to the inferior material realm. In their former lives as pagans in this wide-open imperial city, they had thought nothing of sexual intercourse with prostitutes, considering it to be as normal a human activity as having a meal. Paul quotes their self-justifying proverb, "Food is meant for the stomach and the stomach for food" (v. 13a).

On the offensive now, Paul first corrects the notion that the body only exists for sexual intercourse, especially the illicit kind with a prostitute: "The body is not meant for fornication, but for the Lord, and the Lord for the body" (v. 13b). He denies the crassness of their anthropology by reminding them of the creation narrative where God intentionally created the corporality of humans, saying that a man and a woman become intimately united in their sexual relationship, "For it is said [in Gen 2:24], 'The two shall become one flesh'" (v. 16). Quickly pointing out that as part of the body of Christ "your bodies are members of (the body of) Christ," he shows the falseness of their actions with a question, "Should I therefore take the members of Christ and make them the members of a prostitute?" (v. 15).

Scholars differ considerably in their opinions on the reality of the unity that body of Christ expresses. Opinions range from seeing it as merely metaphorical, claiming "Paul knows nothing of a 'mystical body of Christ' to which believers are joined" (Fee, 1994, 74, n. 5), to the other extreme of calling the church "really and ontologically the body of Christ" (Son 2001, 109). The truth lies somewhere in the middle. The attentive reader knows that Paul can consider the body of Christ as the individual, discrete existence of Jesus Christ, as in Romans 7:4 and Philippians 3:21, cited above. Yet in 1 Corinthians 12, Paul can also say that believers are baptized into one body (v. 13), that "all the members of the body, though many, are one body; so it is with Christ" (v. 12), and finally, "Now you are the body of Christ and individually members of it" (v. 27). We must remember, as the wise scholar Gerard Sloyan once told me, that the ancients knew more kinds of real than we do.

In order to more fully grasp the meaning of the body of Christ in Paul, we must be aware that it is symbolic language. As we have pointed out above in chapter 1, symbolic thinking is the key to much ancient understanding. Instead of a discursive, conceptual description of an abstract reality, biblical authors often adduce a known, concrete reality to describe something difficult to understand by itself. What is known about the symbol points to what can be known about the abstract reality in question without fully identifying it or exhausting the complexity of its nature. We may conclude in our discursive, conceptual language that the image of "body" here conveys in a special way the unity, equality, integrity (wholeness), interdependence, and sacredness of believers in union with Christ. They, as community, participate in the very existence of the risen Christ whose Spirit dwells in them as the single source of that life in both. More simply put, they are "the body of Christ."

Dying and Rising with Christ

The focal point of Paul's Christology is that Jesus Christ participated in the suffering and death that is the lot of sinful humanity, that God raised him from the dead, and transferred him into a new mode of being in the resurrection. Because of Christ's participation in our sinful humanity, God makes it possible for us to participate in Christ's glorified humanity now in this life, sharing in his saving death, with the firm hope of our similar resurrection in the future. Paul says, "We know that our old self was crucified with him so that the body of sin (= "our sinful existence") might be destroyed, and we might no longer be enslaved to sin" (Rom 6:6). As we have seen above, the phrases "in Christ" and especially "through Christ" are used in connection with these saving acts of Jesus Christ in history. Paul names nearly every image he uses to evoke the effects of the Christ event (those discussed in chapters 3 and 4) in the context of unity "in" or "through" Christ. We have also seen that the phrase "with Christ," along with the compound verbs that designate activity "with Christ," bring out the essential relation of the Christian community to those deeds: believers "have been crucified with Christ" (Gal 2:19), and they "have been buried with him into death" (Rom 6:4).

The goal of Christ's selfless obedience to God's plan was to bring about a complete transformation in believers so that they might return to the original union with God they were created to have. Thus

Christ, raised from the dead, is the first fruits of our human destiny after death (1 Cor 15:20). Christians are brought into a new sphere of life in union with Christ as individuals and also in community as church. They embark together in a new mode of being, sharing the effects of the cruciform life of Christ in their own lives now, from the beginning of salvation in their coming to faith and baptism to its consummation at the End when they too will be raised.

This is the most intuitive way that Paul expresses salvation in Christ: that the believer is united with him in his historical death and resurrection. More than an intellectual assimilation of doctrine about Christ, it speaks of a radical change in the individual's personal life and in the manner of existence of the whole community that lives in hope by a real participation Christ's saving actions. Thus believers can internalize and participate in Christ's own faithfulness (*pistis Christou*), so that such faith leads to a shared justification in which God accepts sinners based on Christ's righteousness (Cobb and Lull 2005, 19).

Just how Paul understands this participation of the community of believers in the death and resurrection of Christ is a question that has had limited discussion among scholars for a variety of reasons that we need not go into here. Readers of Paul notice that he says very little in his letters about the public ministry of Jesus. He almost never repeats the Lord's exemplary teaching that we find in the gospels or mentions one of Jesus' many miracles. Paul's theology is concerned mainly with Christ's death and resurrection, I think, because Paul saw the early years of Jesus' life as preparation for what was to become the pivotal point for the salvation of fallen humanity. His sinless life-for-others and his announcement of the kingdom of God were put to the proof only when he went to Jerusalem to announce the priority of God's kingdom and confront the evil of religious and political society at their roots. Only after his tragic death and God's full vindication and exaltation of him in the resurrection could people begin to understand the truth about what God could do with fallen humanity.

The reason that God "sent his Son in the likeness of sinful flesh, to deal with sin" (Rom 8:3) was to set up an exchange between the graced state of God's Son ("righteousness") and sinful humanity: "For our sake he made him to be sin who knew no sin, so that in him we might become the righteousness of God" (2 Cor 5:21). Raymond

Tannehill puts it very well when he sees this "exchange of attributes between Christ and Christ's people" as based on the "self-renouncing identification of the divine with humans in their need, enabling a reciprocal identification of needy humanity with God's Son, his death, and his victory over sin and death" (2007, 225).

In this expiatory process God mandates that Christ participate in the human catastrophe of sin "by sending his own son in the likeness of sinful flesh" (literally "in the likeness (*homoiōma*) of the flesh of sin" [= "our human sinfulness"]; Rom 8:3). As the (probably pre-Pauline) Philippians hymn most graphically points out, "[Christ], though he was in the form (*morphē*) of God . . . emptied himself, taking the form (*morphē*) of a slave, coming in human likeness (*homoiōma*), and being found in outward appearance (*schēma*) as a human" (Phil 2:7-8). This is no merely metaphorical transference of Christ from sinlessness to the present human condition, but as Fitzmyer boldly asserts, "[Christ] came in a form like us in that he became a member of the sin-oriented human race; he experienced the effects of sin and suffered death, the result of sin, as one 'cursed' by the law (Gal 3:13). Thus in his own self he coped with the power of sin" (1993, 485).

As a result of this exchange, our union with Christ enables us to partake in God's salvation of the world. We suffer in our lives for the good of others and "know Christ and the power of his resurrection and the sharing of his sufferings by becoming like him in his death" (Phil 3:10).

Our exchange or identification with Christ can only be understood if we accept as real the possibility that who we are as humans is greatly influenced by our relation to other human beings whom we know, love, and respect. Anyone can see the newness of being that occurs in the generous sharing of a life together by lovers. So also, what we do and how we think under God's grace in Christ can be understood as our "mystical" participation in the life of Christ. By this we do not mean that somehow our individuality is swallowed up in the greatness of the glorified Lord, but that our very being is *enabled* by the same transcendent power of God that transformed Christ's humanity (what later theology would call his "human nature").

Tannehill's example of the life of Martin Luther King Jr. is quite helpful here. Some persons, especially some African Americans, are not only moved by the selflessness of Dr. King, but they are clearly *empowered* by his solidarity with the marginalized against the oppression of segregated society. In their identification with him, they are actually *changed* by the reality of his dedication to the truth of God's will and the payment with his life for his conviction. That story "both invites others to live in the freedom that he made possible and provides a guiding image of what their life is meant to be" (Tannehill 2007, 237). How much more, then, is the gift of life from Jesus Christ able to lift humanity out of its slavery to sin and death to transform our lives—using Paul's symbol of metamorphosis—as a creeping caterpillar becomes a beautiful, soaring butterfly. Thus as we "walk in newness of life" (Rom 6:4), "all of us, seeing the glory of the Lord as though reflected in a mirror, are being transformed into the same image from one degree of glory to another" (2 Cor 3:18).

Chapter 8

The Nature of Unity "in Christ"

Now that we have examined in some detail the language Paul uses, we can appreciate the centrality in Paul's teaching of the unity of Christians with Christ and with each other. We may now make some general comments on the nature of this unity as Paul sees it.

Baptism: Our Entrance into Union "in Christ"

By accepting the gift of faith from God, Christians enter this new realm of existence when they are baptized. Faith, however—the beginning of the process of salvation—involves intellectual assent to the lordship of Christ and an affective confidence that one will share in the same resurrection as Christ. Faith starts out with a "hearing" (*akoē*; Rom 10:17; Gal 3:2; 1 Thess 4:14) of the gospel about Christ, but is complete only with a faith-filled "submission" (*hypakoē*), literally a "hearing-under," meaning that the hearer is *under* the power/authority of someone (Rom 1:5; 16:26). Thus faith is the *commitment* of the whole person to God in Christ that negates all reliance on self and any kind of self-conceit (Fitzmyer 1990, 1407). True, the obedience required is to a way of living (Rom 6:17), but more than that, it is a putting of one's person at the disposal of God as "God's servant," literally "enslaved to God" (Rom 6:22). Now God wishes all to be led by God's Son, Jesus Christ.

Paul describes his own experience of coming to faith in a series of questions: "Everyone who calls on the name of the Lord shall be saved [citing Joel 2:32]. But how are they to call on one in whom they have not believed? And how are they to believe in one of whom they have never heard? And how are they to hear without someone to proclaim him? And how are they to proclaim him unless they are sent? . . . So faith comes from what is heard, and what is heard comes through the word of Christ" (Rom 10:13-15, 17).

Before his conversion, Paul was certainly not looking to learn anything from the Christians he was persecuting, but that is just the way that God's call can work sometimes. "Proclaiming the word" does not happen through the *preaching* of believers only. No, we can imagine that Paul, like a policeman on the vice squad trying to identify and punish offenders, had learned quite a bit about what the Christians believed and how they acted. It was undoubtedly their behavior that first puzzled Paul and caused him to wonder. They were exhibiting a kind of love for each other and even for outsiders (including Paul!) that caught Paul by surprise. He first heard what they were proclaiming about "this Jesus" with disgust, but when he encountered them personally, he couldn't miss the depth of the humanity that is the hallmark of a community of love.

Fortunately for us, Paul was an authentic enough religious man to finally admit to himself that his life was a pale and empty imitation of righteousness, his existence filled with constant stress. His struggle to be perfect in all lawful activity gave him a life that was "rubbish" (Phil 3:8), not at all like the rich and creative lives of the stories in the scriptures he knew so well. We can see Paul's coming to belief in the Nazorean he once so hated if we reverse the questions in his rhetorical description cited above (Rom 10:13-17). Paul's faith came as a gift of God through what he "heard through the word of Christ," for God had "sent" those Jewish Christian believers to provoke Paul, and their very lives "proclaimed" Christ so that Paul was able to be open to belief in Christ himself. I believe that Paul "called on God" in hopeful "half belief" to show him this Christ—and God did!

The commitment to God in faith is very specific, however, because it rests on the faithfulness of Christ himself, "we have come to believe in (literally, "into") Christ so that we might be justified *by the faith of Christ*" (Gal 2:16). Note that Paul has said that we "believe *into* Christ" (Gal 2:16), that we have somehow moved inside the new eschatological age that the Christ event has brought about. The result is a personal unity. Christ lives in me in a relationship of faithful love with the One "who loved me and gave himself for me" (Gal 2:20). This is how the death and resurrection of Christ act redemptively. Believers who are now one with Christ are free to reorder their entire existence to imitate their Lord and be "guided by the Spirit" (Gal 5:24-25) in a life where "the only thing that counts is faith working through love" (Gal 5:6).

This coming to faith in Christ with interior conviction is not the whole story of how Christians enter into unity with Christ. Union with Christ means union with all others who are united to him in faith. In baptism believers are brought into the sphere of God's saving grace with others who have accepted the call to faithful living. The progressive sanctification of the individual believer requires the context of community, for it is that community that God is shaping by the Spirit to become the model for all of humanity. James Howard puts it clearly: "God's normal method of moving his people to righteous living is through the catalytic effect of believers relating to one another in authentic ways" (2007, 184).

Paul's conversion to Christ had rendered him alien to his former manner of believing and from the society that gave him his identity. He must have been both unsettled and terribly isolated (for three whole years?) until he went up to Jerusalem to visit Peter (Gal 1:18) and connect with the Christ-believing community there (Bond 2001, 104). He doesn't speak of his own baptism when he relates the beginning of his life as a believer, but this is probably for polemical reasons. In Galatians 1, he is trying to show his independence as an apostle. His acceptance of the absolute importance of baptism, however, is clear from his teaching. The movement of faith is completed only when believers join the community of all believers by means of the rite of baptism. The idea of entering "into Christ" is stated three times as the result of "believing" (Gal 2:16; Phil 1:29; Rom 10:14), but it also occurs another three times in conjunction with baptism "into Christ" (Gal 3:27; Rom 6:3; 1 Cor 12:13). The individual's belief and his or her entrance into the community of believers are so united in Paul's mind that Murphy-O'Connor can say, "Faith and baptism are two moments of a single act; neither is complete without the other. Faith, for Paul, *is* the choice of a mode of being that is essentially social. Faith is a new way of being with others" (2009, 174–75).

We are fairly sure that Christians entered the community by means of a ceremony in which they were dunked in a pond or stream of water or soaked by a pouring of water over their head and down all over their bodies. Paul did not record for us the exact ritual of baptism in his churches, but the *purpose* of baptism, on the other hand, he spells out clearly.

Paul was acquainted with the earlier Christian tradition of baptism as being a ritual washing away of past sins, as he says, "You were washed . . . in the name of the Lord Jesus Christ" (1 Cor 6:11). But Paul is not content with baptism's import merely as an initiatory rite. When the Corinthians were regarding baptism individualistically and broke into factions based on their different sponsors (1:12), he explains that they are missing the explicitly social, unifying dimension of the action. With a flash of insight, he sees a parallel with the initiation of the Israelites into God's plan: "All were baptized into Moses in the cloud and in the sea. . . . Nevertheless, God was not pleased with most of them, and they were struck down in the wilderness" (10:2, 5). The Israelites, too, underwent initiation, but that was far from the end of their sad tale. Paul knows that, similarly, mere membership in the new Christian movement hardly explains the reality that baptism should convey. The effects of the ritual are much more profound, for believers accept the saving moment of baptism in order to participate communally in the saving work of none other than Christ himself (Pastor Ramos 1991, 146).

Paul writes a fuller theology of baptism in his Letter to the Romans: "Do you not know that all of us who have been baptized into Christ Jesus were baptized into his death? . . . so that, just as Christ was raised from the dead by the glory of the Father, so we too might walk in newness of life" (Rom 6:3-4). Taking his cue from the tradition that Jesus spoke of his death as a "baptism" (see Mark 10:38), Paul interprets the ritual envelopment in the baptismal water as a symbolic burial with Christ. This means that believers are united with Christ and, as we have seen, undergo his death and resurrection (2 Cor 5:14-15). When believers rise out of the watery tomb of baptism, they rise—not yet to final resurrection (which can only happen on the Last Day)—but to "newness of life." In baptism, believers die to the former age of salvation history, where sin and death prevailed. It was a merely carnal existence, with opposing social differences and segregation of classes. They now enter into the new unity where people are "dead to sin and alive to God in Christ Jesus" (Rom 6:11), where no person or group may claim advantage over another.

The Equality of All "in Christ"

Perhaps the most radical tenet of Paul's ecclesiology is the equality before God of all Christians. Paul sees this principle as absolutely necessary for unity "in Christ." Such a belief stands in stark opposition to the importance of status in both the legal system of Judaism and the patronage of the Roman Empire. Paul experienced the mercy of God after his painful realization that he had sinned gravely in opposing God's own movement of salvation. He had persecuted the followers of Jesus Christ, even to the point of participating in the execution of Stephen, a man he must have known to be just. On that long journey to Damascus he experienced total forgiveness of his transgression and was reconciled to a most loving God, who not only accepted him but called him to play a great role in spreading the Gospel he once hated. All of this grace, however, could not erase the haunting memory of his past conduct that he painfully remembers and shares with his churches in his letters (Gal 1:13-14; 5:11; Phil 3:7-9; and to some extent Rom 7:5-25). If *even he* could be accepted into God's loving community, then there was no factor that could allow discrimination of any sort, any privileged status or lesser esteem for any member in good standing who was trying to follow Christ. Thus he says, "There is no longer Jew or Greek, there is no longer slave or free, there is no longer male and female; for all of you are one in Christ Jesus" (Gal 3:28; see 1 Cor 12:13). Let us examine Paul's teaching on the equality each of these pairs.

A. *"Neither Jew nor Greek"*

Paul maintains that all men and women, whether Jew or Gentile, can participate equally in the new eschatological phase of God's plan for the salvation of the world. He does this without either blurring the ethnic identity of Jews or diminishing the importance of Judaism in God's plan. We have seen that Paul knows (and respects) the differences between those of Jewish descent and religious background (whether Christian or not), and all the rest of humanity who are not Jewish. He represents all the Gentiles here by the figurative use of the adjective "Greek," meaning "under the influence of Greek, that is, pagan culture."

Paul's basic argument is that all human beings are justified now by God's grace given in the faithful death and resurrection of Jesus Christ, the fulfillment of God's earlier covenant with the Jews and a new opportunity for the Gentiles. As such, all believers are invited to membership in the Body of Christ in a new covenant empowered by the Spirit. Since they have "put on Christ" in baptism (Gal 3:27), they are all Abraham's offspring and heirs to God's promises through Christ, to whom they belong as the new "Israel of God" (Gal 6:16). When Paul says "not all who are of Israel are Israel, nor are they all children of Abraham because they are his descendants" (Rom 9:6-7), he means that God has created a new people by adding Gentiles to the remnant of Israel who have embraced Christ. Thus Jews have no higher rank in Christianity than Gentiles, even though their religious pedigree is superior to those with no faith background. (On this whole question of "Israel and the Church" see Matera 2012, 147–51.)

As for those Jews who did not respond to covenant with Christ, God has not rejected them, "for the gifts and the call of God are irrevocable" (Rom 11:29). Furthermore, there is to be no reverse discrimination of Gentile against Jew for whatever reason. As for those Jewish Christians who maintain their ethnic and religious traditions, Paul advocates their equal standing in the community, even though their pious devotions may appear "weak" in comparison to the freedom of those unencumbered by the law. Paul's reason for this is as blunt as it is simple, "For God has welcomed them. Who are you to pass judgment on the servants of another?" (Rom 14:3-4).

B. *Slavery in Paul's Works*

In the Letter to Philemon, Paul strongly suggests (compels in love) to his Christian friend Philemon not only to receive back the fugitive slave Onesimus without punishment, but to free him. "Welcome him as you would welcome me," says Paul, and receive him back into the household "no longer as a slave but more than a slave, a brother, beloved especially to me, but even more so to you, both in the flesh and in the Lord" (Phlm 15-16). Note those last two qualifiers. Philemon is not just to make some "religious" show of Onesimus' equality with himself, but he is to believe it as a reality, both in his own human relationship with Onesimus and in his conscience before Christ.

Paul's general advice to slaves is recorded in only one text, and it is notoriously difficult to translate. Here he seems to be telling slaves to take advantage of any chance for their freedom via manumission. "Were you a slave when you were called? Never mind. But if you are really able to be free, take advantage" (1 Cor 7:21). Paul knows the truth of the matter: "For whoever was called in the Lord as a slave is a freed person belonging to the Lord, just as whoever was free when called is a slave of Christ" (1 Cor 7:22). Thus in spite of the apparent acceptance of slavery in the later, disputed letters (Eph 6:5-8; Col 3:22–4:1; 1 Tim 6:2), Paul himself is strongly against the inequality of the institution of slavery. The fact that the later letters had to give such counsel shows that some slaves of Christian masters in later, post-Pauline communities were questioning their obligations, very likely based on the very information they had from the authentic teaching of Paul when they became Christians.

C. *Paul and the Women of His Churches*

Perhaps the most disingenuous dislike of the great apostle today stems from a complete misunderstanding of his beliefs on the equality of women with men. Because of the importance of Paul's acceptance of the equality of women, we give a more lengthy explanation of this Pauline principle here. For those who want to delve even more deeply into the texts, we give in an appendix a full exegesis of the only two texts in the authentic letters that might raise a problem with this opinion.

1) Paul's Own Attitude

Let us now examine Paul's own attitude and teaching (in the seven undisputed letters) on the women of his churches. Is he, in fact, demeaning to them? Or if not, does he not at least follow the conventions of the Roman Empire (and the Jewish Law!) and consider them to be an inferior part of the human race, and thus second-class members of the Christian community? The surprising answer is: Absolutely not! In fact, the opposite is true. Paul's own words not only *never* subordinate any woman to any man because of her gender, they even make a special point of equality of the sexes. He really meant what he said in Gal 3:28, "there is no longer male and female . . . for all of you are one in Christ Jesus."

Paul's esteem for the women who worked with him is clear in a number of his letters. He demonstrates touching concern for Euodia and Syntyche, urging them "to be of the same mind in the Lord." He asks other members of the church at Philippi to help them, "for they have struggled beside me in the work of the gospel, together with

Clement and the rest of my co-workers" (Phil 4:2-3). Another example is his trust in, and response to, the information brought to him by emissaries sent by Chloe, an important woman whose name was obviously also respected by the Corinthians (1 Cor 1:11).

Chapter 16 of the Letter to the Romans reveals that Paul entrusted the delivery (and probably the reading) of that letter to Phoebe, a woman patron whom he calls a "minister," (*diakonos* in Greek; Rom 16:1), the exact same title he gives to Timothy, to Apollos, and even to himself. There, he goes on to underline the importance to him of other women in his large ministerial network and presumes their notoriety among Romans by naming eight of them. Here we see the designations of some of them as co-workers (*synergoi*), the same appellation he gives to male colleagues like Timothy and Titus. He uses the quasi-technical verb, "work to exhaustion; labor earnestly" (*kopiaō*) for their service in community, the same verb he uses of his own work and that of his close apostolic associates, as in 1 Thess 5:12, where he parallels "those who labor earnestly (*kopiōntas*) among you" with "those who have charge of you" (*proistamenous*, literally "those who stand before you, who rule you"). He even says of Junia and her husband Andronicus that "they are prominent among the apostles" (Rom 16:7). With regard to "the household of Stephanas . . . [who] have devoted themselves to the service (*diakonia*) of the holy ones," Paul admonishes the Corinthians to "be subject (*hypotassō*) to such people, and to everyone who works and toils with them" (1 Cor 16:15-16). With such language it is almost certain that Paul includes the women of the household as well as the men.

Now that we have discussed those gifted women leaders and teachers who assisted Paul personally in his apostolic ministry, what about the common women, the rank and file members of his churches? Here again Paul shows great respect and affirms their equality with men. When he gives his lengthy teaching on marriage and virginity in 1 Corinthians 7, he takes care to make sure everything he says applies equally to males and to females. Paul repeats the entire counsel (both duties and rights) that he gives for men to women. For example, when he speaks of the married state of life, he proclaims that "each man should have his own wife and each woman her own husband" (v. 2). Notice how he doesn't just say, "and vice versa," or the like. He repeats his teaching for men each time in the same words for women. And he doesn't do this just once, but seven more times he repeats the exact same requirements for husbands (vv. 3, 4, 10-11, 12-13, 14, 15, 16). Thus Paul was very strict on the equality of women in marriage and thus "gave to Christian women a stability and even a degree of freedom that were otherwise not available to them" (Harrington and Keenan 2010, 201).

How different in attitude are the deutero-Pauline Colossians and Ephesians! There we have the explicit subordination of wives to their husbands: "Wives, be subject (*hypotassō*) to your husbands as is fitting in the Lord" (Col 3:18 paralleled in Eph 5:22). Authentic Paul does use this word (*hypotassō*, "be subject/subordinate to; obey"), but he uses it for proper subordination of believers to Christ, to civil authorities and to church leaders, as we saw above in 1 Corinthians 16:16— never of women to men. Authentic Paul doesn't anywhere subject a woman to any man because of her gender. In fact, he says, "The wife does not have *authority* over her own body, but the husband does; likewise the husband does not have *authority* over his own body, but the wife does" (1 Cor 7:4). If Paul had actually written "Wives, be subject to your husbands," he wouldn't have done it without adding, "And likewise, husbands, be subject to your wives"!

2) The Question of Proper Attire for Communal Prayer (1 Cor 11:2-16)

Now there are two texts in the undisputed letters that may seem to contradict what we have just said, namely 1 Corinthians 11:2-16 and 15:34-35. Let us examine the first of these texts, in which Paul tackles a delicate problem of gender difference in the behavior of one of his churches (1 Cor 11:2-16). This is the only text where authentic Paul counsels divergent action based on the differences between men and women, so we must not allow our understanding of it to be prejudiced by reading it in the light of some later non-authentic Pauline text that subordinates women. This text neither advocates women's inferiority to men nor does it subject women to men. What it does advocate is that men should not, in literal translation, "pray or prophesy having [something] down from the head" (v. 4) and that women should not "pray or prophesy with their head uncovered" (v. 5). There is a great deal of scholarly discussion on the text's several ambiguities, but its importance to our whole understanding of Paul requires that we examine it here in some detail. We intend to give the most plausible interpretation of it, embedded as it is in first-century culture.

It seems that certain women in liturgical assemblies at Corinth were participating in public worship with a freedom of expression that crossed the normal boundaries of decency in dress when they appeared "with their head uncovered." This is the problem as noted by almost all Pauline scholars. The normal manner for a woman to present herself, in a Roman colony like Corinth, was with her hair done up and covered with a veil or head scarf. We are all familiar with the Roman portrait busts of prominent women with their braided hair coiled up and around the top of their heads. Women of the more common folk probably just gathered their hair up in a more simple fashion and then covered it with a head scarf or a part of their mantle that they pulled up over it. This custom was not merely a matter of hairstyle, for women's hair was considered to be part of their sexual attraction in the ancient world. To be perfectly frank in this matter, let me quote noted Scripture scholar Sandra Hack Polaski, "Women were viewed as inherently more sexually charged than men; . . . a connection was held to exist between the genitals and the head" (Polaski, 54–55). Thus women normally undid their hairdo only in the privacy of their own homes at night or for bathing. Untressed hair would have been considered to be very improper in public. Indeed, prostitutes commonly wore their hair down to advertise their intentions, and women devotees of the god Dionysius were known to worship in such a state of "undress" in their orgies, legitimated by their possession by the god.

There is ambiguity in what Paul says about the men's appearance, too, for the descriptive phrase "having down from the head" could also refer to a veil that a man might wear in pagan worship, like the famous statue of the Emperor Augustus with a shawl-like garment covering his head and hanging down over his shoulders. There are even scholars who opine that Paul is here speaking of the curling and styling of long hair (hair that "hangs down from the head") that was commonly attributed to homosexuals at the time. In fact, in verse 14 Paul explicitly mentions that "if a man wears long hair, it is degrading."

It is obvious to us moderns that the acceptable attire of women (and men) throughout the world varies greatly from culture to culture, from the topless native dress in many tribes indigenous to the tropics, to the scanty halter tops worn on the beaches in many communities, to the headscarves requisite in the Middle East, the partial and full veils used in some cultures, and even the mandatory full body covering of the *burqa*. In all of these cultures, men and women presume that such a dress code is the proper and "decent" way for women to appear in public. Thus we might compare the kind of shock the sight of untressed hair would produce in Corinth to how many Americans might feel if people arrived for Sunday Mass in bikinis!

The great apostle maintains some composure throughout this controversy, and follows his usual manner of thoroughly explaining the reasons for any recommendations he gives. But we can see that he is rather flustered by this neglect of what we would today call "common decency." It is obvious to him that some of the Corinthian Christians have really twisted his preaching on religious freedom, but just what to say in correcting them proved to be a very difficult task! In fact, his first argument comes dangerously close to implying some kind of separation or antipathy between men and women, but he is very quick to correct any hint of that in verse 11.

Whatever the exact hairstyles in question might have been, the point of Paul's argument is that it was necessary for men and women in that part of the world to present themselves in public with proper manner of dress, and that the custom of differing, gender appropriate, dress should be the case also for Christian men and women. Thus when Christians gathered for prayer, the proper decorum would be maintained and public scandal avoided. We can see that Paul is very concerned with the outward appearance of his assemblies in another context when he explains at length the propriety of speaking in tongues later in the letter (14:20-24). Exactly what the head dress Paul was talking about may be debated, but that is not really the important point here. It is in what Paul offers as the reasons for the difference in what is required for men and women that the problem arises.

Before we tackle the interpretation of the text, let us be clear that Paul is talking about public prayer here. His concluding argument from the custom of the other "churches of God" (v. 16) would make no sense if he were talking about private prayer in the home, as some have argued. Secondly, he clearly takes for granted that both women and men are free to speak in the assembly, since he begins his statement with his typical repetition of the exact same words for men as for women: "Any man who prays or prophesies" (v. 4), "any woman who prays or prophesies" (v. 5). Thirdly, true to form, Paul spells out the proper headdress both for men as well as women, whether or not some of the men were actually offending common custom. (He may just be mentioning men's fashion only as a foil for his argument.) From all this we can see that Paul is only trying to regulate the manner of a woman's vocal sharing in the worship of the assembled church, not stifle it. He is obviously very much in favor of women taking part if he goes to such lengths to make sure they participate properly and in an edifying manner.

The whole problem boils down to the meaning of three of Paul's statements that all have to do with the creation stories in Genesis 1–2:

1) "The husband is the head of his wife" (v. 3). The key word here is "head" which normally means "source" or "origin." In only an extremely few texts in the vast amount of Greek literature that we know of does it ever refer to "authority." Thus, for Paul, the biblical story in Genesis 2 has God as the source for the man, while Adam (actually, his rib) is the source of the woman.

2) "For a man ought not to have his head veiled, since he is the image and reflection (Greek *doxa*, literally "glory") of God, but woman is the reflection (*doxa*) of man." Here Paul is claiming that woman is the reflection of man, who is her source, just as man is the reflection of God, who is his source in creation, for *doxa* here is the "reflection" of what is praiseworthy in someone.

3) "Man was not created for the sake of woman, but woman for the sake of man" (v. 9). In the second Genesis creation story (Gen 2:4b-25) God created the man first, and then, because "it is not good that the man should be alone, I will make him a suitable partner" (Gen 2:18).

In all three of these texts Paul is citing the Genesis story to justify gender differences on the basis of the difference in the creation of the man from that of the women. By it Paul means to answer the question: Why should women dress differently in public? His answer: Because they were created differently by God! Lest anyone see in this a diminishment of the status of women, at the center of the argument Paul clarifies, "Nevertheless, in the Lord woman is not independent of man or man independent of woman. For just as woman came from man, so man comes through woman; but all things come from God" (vv. 11-12).

We conclude that Paul's tortured arguments here show the tension that occurs sometimes when the master has to point out the obvious to the neophyte. It is not always easy to show how theology translates into practical action. For Paul, all men and all women are equal in the Lord, even though there are true and important differences between them. Paul could not let a woman's right to lead the congregation in prayer or prophecy be denied because of how she wore her hair. In this passage he explicitly defends that right by cautioning against any behavior offensive to her womanliness. How to maintain equality in difference is always difficult. What is clear here is that Paul insists on the equal opportunity for women and men to be vocal in prayer and prophecy in the liturgical assembly.

3) The Mandate of Silence for Women in the Churches

"Women should be silent in the churches. For they are not permitted to speak, but should be subordinate, as the law also says. If there is anything they desire to know, let them ask their husbands at home. For it is shameful for a woman to speak in church" (1 Cor 14:34-35). This certainly doesn't sound like Paul, especially when only two verses before he says, "You can *all* prophesy one by one, so that all may learn and be encouraged." And what would be the meaning of his teaching in 11:2-16 that we have just considered, if women weren't allowed to pray or prophesy out loud? No, this must be an interpolation, a small text added by an editor or copyist, reacting with the opinion of a later, non-Pauline teaching like 1 Tim 2:11-12, "Let a woman learn in silence with full submission. I permit no woman to teach or have authority over a man; she is to keep silent."

In fact, verses 34-35 are an interruption to the flow of 14:26-40, and an important manuscript tradition has them in a different place (at the end of the discourse), often a telltale sign of the later intrusion of a text. It may also be that Paul is citing here the argument of his opponents as he does elsewhere in the letter (6:12a, 12b, 13; 7:1; 8:1; 10:23). Whatever the case, these words make no sense as Paul's own.

Conclusion

Paul does not think that women are subordinate to men when it comes to their participation in the Christian community, and these texts proffer no exception. A growing number of scholars are strongly challenging the fiction that Paul thought of women as inferior to men. Recently, Tim Milinovich has argued that Paul composed the entire First Letter to the Corinthians as a series of chiasms (a repetition of similar ideas in the reverse sequence: *a b c b' a'*) that in turn are made up of smaller chiasms. He has made a very strong case for this conclusion by pointing out the repetition of both grammatical and lexical (vocabulary) items that form the chiasms. According to this study, both the texts we have just studied (1 Cor 11:3-15 and 14:34-35) break this firm chiastic pattern and thus seem to have been interpolated into Paul's original letter (2012, 144–52). For the readers who want a more detailed interpretation of these two texts, we invite you to look at the more complete exegesis of them in the Appendix.

An Eschatological Continuum

There is a kind of temporal continuum behind Paul's understanding of Christian unity "in Christ," a framework in which we may "sketch in" several areas of Paul's rich ideas. When we consider the experience of time for Paul and his contemporaries in the ancient world, we must realize that they did not perceive the temporal in the same way we do today. We moderns tend to think in terms of equal units of time, of days and months and years lined up and stretched out like a ribbon from the past to the future. For the ancients, the experience of time was as one long and enduring "now," a lingering "present" with attention paid to the past and the future only when they should affect the present in some pressing manner. The vividness of past or future events in the present consciousness of a writer like Paul makes us modern readers think that in his early letters he considered the parousia to be closer to him in time than in the later ones. In fact, Paul understood the actual course of future events to be knowable only by God. Paul was quite convinced that there would be a parousia, but it was God's domain alone to actually bring about such a change in history (for more on this ancient experience of time see Maloney 2004, 81–87).

While in his earlier letters the parousia figures very prominently, Paul never thought in terms of stages of growth for the church. In his later (undisputed) letters, after his brush with death in prison at Ephesus, he became even more convinced that the ultimate future in the kingdom of God was assured, although hidden in God's will. He would, however, have to turn to more pressing concerns, dealing with them in the overlap between the Old Age and the New, but always in light of the resurrection and the coming fullness of the New Age.

The saving events of Jesus' death and resurrection were not simply the completed actions of a separate past epoch, but the founding events of the present "now" in which the believers' own time participates, the constant of its *present* reality. Their lives correspond to the New Age that will be fully revealed only at the parousia (Rom 6:4-5). But now, in the overlap of the ages, they are to remain blameless, for the parousia will be a day of judgment for all. Christians live in this "newness" in the present world, albeit still "in the flesh," that is, in mortal life that still belies its perishability, dishonor, and weakness (1 Cor 15:42-43). But even so, they live differently from nonbelievers, in an altogether new relationship to God and to their fellow humans, "by faith in the Son of God" (Gal 1:20). This is the "power of the resurrection" (Phil 3:10) already effective in the present life, and it enables Paul to live differently in hope, free from the grip of sinful society, "living for God" (Gal 2:19; Rom 6:10).

Believers celebrate their new life in which they are nourished and empowered by the "faithfulness of Christ," when they participate in the Eucharist, "for as often as you eat this bread and drink the cup, you proclaim the Lord's death until he comes" (1 Cor 11:26). The Christian community has died with Christ, and shares now as one body in the newness of a communal life free from slavery to sin and the law. For in the Eucharist they "enjoy a communion with the risen Lord that excludes being in communion with other lords" (Matera 2012, 170). This bond is the living inner resource of Christ's love that sustains them and bonds them as one (Dunn 1998, 400–401). Community members grow in conformity to Christ and look forward to complete transformation in their personal resurrection at the parousia. Even this future aspect is experienced in the "present," as if it was already happening, because it is guaranteed by God: "For in hope we are saved" (Rom 8:24).

The Cruciform Reality of Union "in Christ"

In their day-to-day living, believers assume as their own the experiences of the Lord. They re-present them and re-live them as "united with him in a death like his" (Rom 6:5) and "conformed to the image of [God's] Son" (Rom 8:29). This is what Paul means by "knowing Christ" when he says, "I want to know Christ and the power of his resurrection and the sharing of his sufferings by becoming like him in his death" (Phil 3:10). The power of his resurrection is the change of life that hope brings about in a person who believes in God's power already manifest in the resurrection of Jesus Christ. Such knowledge comes to one only through the "sharing of his sufferings," that is, when one experiences the radical freedom that follows the surrender of the will to God in the cruciform manner of Christ: "For I decided to know nothing among you except Jesus Christ, and him crucified" (1 Cor 2:2).

Thus Christ is the context of all we are and all we do, our constant source of strength. We die and rise with Christ, "always carrying in the body the dying of Jesus, so that the life of Jesus may also be made visible in our bodies" (2 Cor 4:10). The sacrifices we make and the sufferings we bear in living lives that witness to the Gospel are but the cost of true union with Christ. Paul can even say, "For God has graciously granted (literally "gifted") you the privilege not only of believing in Christ, but of suffering for him as well" (Phil 1:29). We take as our model the *kenotic* (self-emptying) life of Christ (Phil 2:6-8), and pattern our lives on his cruciform life. In all of this, however, believers are empowered in their task not by imitation, even imitation of the great saint Paul, but by the very real gift of the indwelling of the Spirit of Christ.

On the cruciform life of the Christian, Michael Gorman is a most eloquent spokesperson. He notes that Paul's most powerful language of conformity to Christ highlights our sharing in his death. Since in baptism we have "died to sin" (Rom 6:2), we "have been co-crucified with Christ" (Gal 2:19), that is, "our old self was crucified with him" (Rom 6:6; see Gal 5:24). One still lives "*in* the flesh," that is, in the neutral sense of "flesh" as human frailty and mortality, but one has escaped the total dominance of sin and death, that is, of living "*according* to the flesh," in the negative sense. Believers "in Christ" are no longer ruled by the old aeon with its law that could not bring life (see Gal 3:21), but are controlled by the working of the Holy Spirit (Rom 7:6; see Gorman 2004, 120–24).

Gorgulho and Anderson point out that this self-emptying action brings about a joyful and loving attitude (2006, 85). Indeed, in the Letter to the Philippians, where Paul speaks of Christ's *kenosis* and his own near-death experience, the words "joy" and "rejoice" are used twelve times. Conforming to Christ's death enables one to leave behind self-centered desires in a generous and creative manner, freeing the person of all responsibility that is not completely from God. Believers are totally dependent on God's assistance, not their own power. Paul can say, "Do not worry about anything, but in everything by prayer and supplication with thanksgiving let your requests be made known to God" (Phil 4:6). The result is in no way a cold detachment from or relinquishing of interest in human affairs, but a true peace, "the peace of God which surpasses all understanding" (4:7).

The Mission to Reconcile the World with God

We can say that the church is the community formed by God to make present to the world the salvific work of God in Christ (Pastor Ramos 1991, 136). Paul says that "in Christ God was reconciling the world to himself . . . entrusting the message of reconciliation to us. So we are ambassadors for Christ, since God is making his appeal through us" (2 Cor 5:19-20). Note Paul's confidence that "all things work together for good for those who love God" (Rom 8:28). As Murphy-O'Connor explains: "What Christ did in and for the world of his day through his physical presence, the community does in and for its world" (2009, 186).

Believers can carry on the salvific function of the risen Christ only within the context of authentic existence that is modeled on Christ's, namely, to act always out of love. For this reason Paul says, "Let all that you do be done in love" (1 Cor 16:14). In this way we form an organic unity that mirrors human life the way God intended it to be, a life of freedom oriented toward the other in deepest love. This is authentic human life as restored by the death and resurrection of Jesus Christ. Such an attitude of love and regard is to be shared also with those outside the community: "Let us work for the good of all" (Gal 6:10; also 1 Thess 3:12; 5:15). This will manifest to the world the true, loving nature of God, who wants nothing more than the end of all evil and oppression on Earth. God's true will is not to condemn and judge, but to grace with newness of life all who seek it. The faithful response of Christ shows humanity how God truly loves all human beings, for "while we were still sinners, Christ died for us" (Rom 5:8).

Summary and Conclusion to Chapters 7 and 8: Christian Unity "in Christ"

Scholars have tried various approaches to provide a synthesis of Paul's many-layered vision of the union of believers with Christ and each other. Unfortunately for us, Paul never wrote anything like a systematic theological treatise on the nature of Christian unity. It is probably not wise, then, to attempt an overall synthesis of Paul's thought here. We agree with the sage advice of James Dunn, who allows the great diversity of Paul's language on this Christian unity "in Christ" to speak for itself: "Better to let the richness of the vision, its poetry and harmonies, capture heart and spirit, even if conceptual clarity remains elusive" (1998, 410).

Paul's overall vision is that Christian believers now live in a realm that is no longer dominated by sin and death, a world ruled by the desires of the flesh. They are part of a new epoch of truly human living, life in a communal "habitat" that is under the lordship of the risen and glorious Jesus Christ. Christ leads the new community both by the example of his selfless life-for-others and his powerful presence.

"In Christ" identifies the sphere of being believers live in. They begin their life in it at their first encounter with God's salvation. They live in it now, and will continue to live in it until its consummation. The power of Christ's resurrection is already in their lives. This new life does not physically separate believers from the rest of the world, but it is radically different from any way of living or mode of action that is not "in Christ." It is comprised of an international communion of *ekklēsiai*, or special assemblies, that understand themselves uniquely in terms of the saving deeds of Jesus Christ. The term *ekklēsia*, usually translated as "church," shows the continuity of the individual Christian congregations, as well as the whole Jesus movement, with the Old Testament people of God. Moreover, it has a definite political dimension that is countercultural to the reigning imperial propaganda of the emperor cult and its elitist patronage system. The whole Church draws its power from the constant presence of Christ in its midst and in its shared experience of Christ's triumph over evil in spite of affliction.

Paul extends the idea of the close unity of believers with the image of a corporate group, or "body," that is "in Christ." This means first of all that the unity of Christians with each other and with Christ is grounded in the historical, bodily existence of Christ. The Spirit of the risen Christ is so present in this protective sphere of living that Paul can even say, "Now you are the body of Christ and individually members of it" (1 Cor 12:27). Its unity actually requires the diversity of believers and the unevenness of their gifts to function. Their differing needs give the opportunity for each member to exercise the love patterned for them by Christ so that they participate and bring about the newness of the eschatological age desired by the Father and inaugurated by Christ.

We can now see that Paul's praise of the women who aided him as "co-workers" precludes any indication that a woman's judgment or performance is inferior to a man's. We can also understand how Paul had to correct the self-presentation of some women in Corinth in public gatherings in order to uphold their freedom to lead the community in prayer. We also see that 1 Corinthians 14:34-35 ("Women should be silent") contradicts Paul's teaching for and about women, and that there is good textual evidence of its un-Pauline nature. Later "Pauline" texts regarding women began a perhaps necessary compromise with the *mores* of the empire.

Believers actually participate in the dying and rising of Jesus Christ by their faithful incorporation "into" him in baptism. The result is that their present life of human suffering takes on new meaning as a participation in Christ's suffering, turning their ordinary lives into a unity with the glorified Lord that actually transforms them into a "new creation." This is accomplished by means of an exchange granted by God. We may now participate in Christ's sinless existence because he took on our sinful condition and died to it on the cross. Believers receive the God-given freedom of Adam's original creation and union with God the Father, for now they are "sons and daughters" with Christ. They anticipate the full transformation of their humanity after their death into the resurrection form that Christ himself now enjoys. In this way, the strangulating effects of sin and death are severely curtailed, and believers, as individuals and as community, are invited to live lives of great virtue. Thus in baptism one seals and confirms one's self-identity with Christ by "putting on Christ," being adopted into and becoming part of the community of salvation (Pastor Ramos, 1991, 145).

The present state of Christian unity may be seen in terms of an eschatological timeline known fully only to God. The past saving events of Christ's life and death, as well as our glorious future, are present in time and, in a real way, shape the life of the church now. This ongoing life of the church requires our lives to be cruciform, based not on our own efforts in imitation of Paul, or even of Christ himself, but as the result of the Spirit of Christ dwelling within us.

The mission of the church is to make present to the world the salvific work of God in Christ. Believers are to portray in their own communities the kind of life that God has always meant for human beings, a life of freedom oriented toward the other in deepest love. In this way, Christians carry on the ministry of reconciliation of the world to God as "ambassadors for Christ."

Suffering in a world that is not yet fully a new creation is part of the ongoing conformity to the death of Jesus. Believers suffer both in their own transition to full holiness and in their care for the needs of others. On this journey, they rely completely upon God and live in peace in a new era of which the resurrected Christ is the first fruits (1 Cor 15:23). In this way they participate in a new, eschatological future in which they are reoriented from self-centered lives. In relation to Christ they find their true selves and allow their connection to their fellows to be transformed. In their new community, God's will determines every aspect of being and action (Schnelle 482).

Believers still "see dimly as in a mirror" (1 Cor 13:12) and still "do not know how to pray as we ought" and "groan inwardly while we wait for adoption, the redemption of our bodies" (Rom 8:26, 23). This is because "we are caught in the overlap of the ages . . . called to produce, in a thousand different ways, signs of God's new world within the apparently unpromising landscape of the old one" (Wright 2005, 150).

In this atmosphere the baptized may bond as one family as each local church grows and takes on a more public, visible form, as it is transformed into the image of Christ (see 2 Cor 3:18). This glory produces joy that thrives within a "habitat" protected by the life-giving love of Christ and shared among all who know the support of many brothers and sisters. They are to struggle side by side now, but as participating in the faithfulness of Christ. In their eucharistic gatherings they "proclaim the Lord's death until he comes" (1 Cor 11:26), when in a final parousia, Christ will come again to bring God's plan of salvation of the whole world to completion. Such closeness to God and to each other brings about a new kind of security, a sense that an eminently approachable God is in charge.

Paul's language of the indwelling of the Spirit overlaps considerably with his understanding of the presence of the risen Lord. This is because the Spirit of Christ has been completely identified with the Spirit of the Father. Christians experience new life with Christ because as members of Christ they share his Spirit. We may say then that Paul's use of "in Christ" language identifies the personal aspects of living in a new way—we might even call it a mystical relationship that the community has with Christ, while Paul's language of "Spirit" connotes the very dynamic quality of that life as a result of God's grace.

We have delineated the main themes that Paul lays out as the "indicative," that is, the given nature of this new state of being in Christ, from the believer's entrance into it in baptism to its guarantee of life after death. What is left for us to explore in our final chapter, then, is the "imperative," that is, Paul's practical opinions and recommendations on how believers are to live together and carry out their God-given mission to the world.

Chapter 9

The Praxis of Christian Life "in Christ" (The Pauline Imperative)

We have laid out Paul's theology of what has happened in the Christ event for the benefit of men and women who believe "in Christ" (Paul's "indicative"). Let us now examine the advice (Paul's "imperative") that this master of the spiritual life gave his communities on living out their commitment to the Gospel. Our methodology will be to consider every command, every prayer and every wish (some four hundred thirty-five items) that Paul makes in the seven undisputed letters. We shall present this data with *some* detail because it has not been done in this way before, but we shall try to keep from redundancy and too much quotation of the texts. As expected, we shall give a summary of these admonitions and prayers, and then make our conclusions as the last section of the book.

Because we are aware that Paul's ideas developed as his ministry progressed, we shall start with the recommendations of his earliest letter, 1 Thessalonians, move on to 1 Corinthians, and continue until we have looked at the entire spectrum of Paul's opinions on Christian living, tracing them through to his last uncontested words in Romans.

First Thessalonians

In his earliest letter Paul gives the greeting that became the standard opening of all the subsequent letters that we know he himself wrote (or dictated): "grace and peace" (1:1). For Paul, *charis* is above all the grace of living in full union with Christ in freedom from sin and in authentic union with other believers. The result of such favor is "peace," the second part of Paul's greeting. What Paul wants for his communities is real peace, the inner calm and lack of anxiety that comes from being filled up with God. Such is the composure that God's favor, in the gift of the Holy Spirit, brings to those who know they are justified in Christ and have been reconciled to God to live in hope of a glorious end to all their afflictions.

Paul greets the Thessalonian Christians as *ekklēsia*, "assembly" or what we would call the local church. He declares his happy memories of them and his longing to see them some eight times (1 Thess 1:3; 2:17, 18; 3:1, 5, 6, 10, 11). Such a close connection with a group, of course, is a common experience of a good pastor or teacher who has labored to share fully the "message of the Gospel." They will often say that they received far more from their parishioners and students than they ever could have imagined. Paul notes his share in their joy in the Spirit (1:6; 3:9), and he thanks God that he has had some part to play in their authentic reception of God's word (2:13). With his beloved Thessalonians he has shared his very self (2:8); they are his "glory and joy" (2:20), his "hope or joy or crown of boasting before our Lord Jesus at his coming" (2:19). Paul had indeed grown close to this group!

In his thanksgiving, Paul thanks God "constantly remembering before God your work of faith and labor of love and steadfastness of hope in our Lord Jesus Christ" (1:2). These images of faith, love, and hope, called the theological virtues in later theology, sum up the Christian response to grace. Their practical employment is the basis of Paul's directives for the strength of the covenant connection to the divine sphere (faith), the motive for its other-centered living (love), and the resoluteness with which that life is carried out (hope).

Although Paul congratulates them on their progress, he knows that the Christian life is an ongoing process. That is why he wanted to see them, "to restore (or better "to further adjust") what is lacking in your faith" (3:10). He prays that "the Lord make you increase and abound in love for one another and for all" (3:12), for this is the way that the Lord "may strengthen your hearts in holiness that you may be blameless . . . at the parousia of our Lord Jesus" (3:13). In what follows we see what he means by the ongoing need for spiritual direction of a community.

In chapters 4 and 5 of this letter, Paul gives a long list of imperatives for Christian living, starting with his sincere wish "that, as you learned from us how you ought to live and to please God (as, in fact, you are doing), you should do so more and more" (4:1). It is interesting that Paul's first recorded imperative, an "instruction" that he calls "the will of God," is about the sexual lives of believers: "Abstain from sexual immorality" (4:3). His admonition does not end with negative prescriptions on sexual behavior, however, but with the positive reminder of God's call to holiness and deeper "love of the brothers and sisters" (4:7, 10). We should not fail to see the inverse connection in Paul's mind here between the call to selfless love and the squandering of one's affect in promiscuity.

Paul follows these concerns with an admonition to quiet living and hard work, "so that you may behave properly toward outsiders and be dependent on no one" (4:12). Paul has radicalized the Christian work ethic with this statement. He affirms that "working with your hands" is not the miserable plight of slaves, but the backbone of an honorable life in light of the Gospel "taught by God" (4:9). For doing one's own work, making one's own living, hard as that may be, frees one from dependence on the dole of the wealthy that inevitably subjects its recipients to outside control of their lives. He contradicts society's lie that only a privileged few can reach the full and honorable life that only wealth and power can provide, and that work is the province only of slaves (Mesters 2009, 17–20). His paradoxical claim is that, for the sake of the Gospel, "though I am free with respect to all, I have made myself a slave to all" (1 Cor 9:19). Indeed, it was the grace of God that kept him "working night and day, that we not burden any of you while we proclaimed to you the gospel of God" (1 Thess 2:9). But what could be nobler in life than proclaiming the Gospel?

Next Paul fills out his instruction on the resurrection of Christ by imagining, for those who are mourning for their beloved dead, a grand reunion at the parousia in the resurrection. It is by the recital of our firm beliefs and hopes that believers are always to encourage one another so that God "may strengthen your hearts in holiness . . . in the coming (*parousia*) of our Lord Jesus" (3:13; see 5:11). In this vein, then, Paul reassures the community that they have all the knowledge they need to be ready for the parousia (5:1-11). They are to be vigilant by their holy lives, armed as they are with the virtues of faith, hope, and love (v. 8).

As to that life in community, Paul urges love and respect for those who are leading them, and sketches an outline of what that life should be (5:13-22): believers must assist each other and always "be at peace." They are to strengthen the weak, always avoid revenge; they are to rejoice and pray, "giving thanks in all circumstances." They must not "quench" the working of the Spirit as it beckons them forward, since it is always the power of "the God of peace [who will] sanctify you . . . and keep you sound" (5:12-23). Paul's final wishes are for their peace and holiness as conveyed by a warm and well-meaning greeting ("a holy kiss").

Excursus: Paul's Understanding of "Love"

Since Paul's most frequent and profound imperative to believers is to love, this would be a good place to examine the great apostle's understanding of this expression that occurs in both noun (*agapē*) and verb (*agapaō*) forms. First, we note that this word names God's own love for us ten times in Paul, the Son's love four times, and the love of the Spirit once. We remember from our discussion of "grace" (chap. 3) that Paul includes the actual love of God for humankind in every use of that word, along with its Old Testament emphasis on "favor." Paul explicitly connects the "love of God" to God's favor on us in the Christ event (1 Thess 1:4; 2 Cor 13:11, 13; Rom 5:5, 8; 8:39) and twice, in citations from the Old Testament, to God's favor on the chosen people (Rom 9:13, 25). The one mention of the Spirit's love is placed in parallel with "our Lord Jesus Christ" (Rom 15:30) to highlight the dynamism of Christ's spiritual presence. While considering "the love of the Spirit," we should also remember that love is the first-mentioned "fruit of the Spirit" (Gal 5:22; see Rom 5:5), and the "greatest" of all the virtues (1 Cor 13:13).

We have also seen that, in the frequent image of "the grace of Christ," Paul includes both Christ's love and favor. His explicit emphasis on Christ's love for us grounds our faith in living like Christ, and is our source of hope and solace in suffering (Rom 8:35, 37; Gal 2:20). Christ's love is the source of courage in Paul's pastoral leadership, "For the love of Christ urges us on" (2 Cor 5:14). This is because the Gospel of Christ is love, and the way of the cross alone can overcome evil by absorbing it in an even more powerful blanket of love. The "power of God for salvation" (Rom 1:16) "is the power of *agape*, whether in God or in the believer" (Spicq 1965, 2:339).

Not surprisingly, Paul's most frequent uses of *agapē* and *agapaō* refer to human love. The believers' love of God is mentioned a few times (1 Cor 2:9; 8:3; 2 Cor 9:7; Rom 8:28), but Paul's regular use of love is of the "God-taught" love of believers for other human beings (1 Thess 4:9). Paul speaks frequently and freely of his own love for his communities (1 Cor 4:21; 16:24; 2 Cor 2:4; 6:6; 8:7; 11:11; 12:15; Phlm 9), because personal concern is so central a part of his ministry. He says, "So deeply do we care for you that we are determined to share with you not only the Gospel of God but also our own selves, because you have become very beloved to us" (1 Thess 2:8), "like a nurse tenderly caring for her own children" (2:7), "like a father with his children" (2:11). He even felt "orphaned by being separated from you" (2:17).

Love is the greatest of all virtues (1 Cor 12:31; 13:13) and the only true operation of faith (Gal 5:6). Love is selfless benevolence, the putting aside of one's own needs and desires for the good of the other person. This is strikingly described by Paul in two places: in his request that the Corinthians forgive the man who had falsely accused him, "I urge you to reaffirm your love for him" (2 Cor 2:8), and when he asks the slave owner Philemon to take back his slave "as a beloved brother . . . both in the flesh and in the Lord" (Phlm 16). Love is service to others, freely given, in every conceivable aspect of human interaction (1 Cor 16:14). It replaces the law but fulfills it at the same time (1 Cor 13:10; Gal 5:14; Rom 13:8-10) as the absolute norm of one's conscience (Pastor Ramos 1991, 159). Moreover, Paul takes up Jesus' command to love one's enemy by positive action: "Do not repay evil for evil . . . if your enemies are hungry, feed them" (Rom 12:17, 20).

Love is the link between all members of the Body of Christ and the only fuel of its growth and edification (1 Cor 8:1; 10:23; 14:17; 2 Cor 12:19; Rom 15:2). Love alone can overcome all ideological differences, all quirks of temperament, all self-oriented and therefore wrongheaded action (1 Cor 13:4-7). It must always increase and abound (1 Thess 3:12; Phil 1:9). It is often hard work, but it is also joy, encouragement, and consolation (1 Thess 1:3; Phlm 7; Phil 2:1). When it is genuine, it hates what is evil (Rom 12:9), but is deeply generous (2 Cor 8:8, 24) and obedient (Gal 5:13; Phlm 9). Love is always given both freely and cheerfully (2 Cor 9:7).

Life is worthless without love (1 Cor 13:1-3), but the life created in a community of love is the original goal of God's creation. It is the only deterrent to sin, and so only when love is complete will humanity have arrived at its fullness (Salas 1994, 138). Love is "the eschato-logical power of God at work" (Collins 1999, 443), the "essence of Christian life . . . infused by God into the hearts of Christians" (Spicq 1965, 2:338). Love is the affective way of speaking about what happens to someone "in Christ"; it is the very "mind of Christ" (Phil 2:2).

The First Letter to the Corinthians

We may now move on to Paul's First Letter to the Corinthians, written a bit more than a year after the composition of 1 Thessalonians. Paul had spent that year with the fledgling community at Corinth. It was a year in which he learned a lot about the practicality of Christian living. Paul's time in Corinth stretched him—he grew exponentially in his application of gospel principles in order to serve that community. Called by new possibilities, he moved on to Ephesus to establish a beachhead in Asia Minor, thinking that the time he had spent with his Corinthians and the leadership he had left behind was sufficient for the community to flourish in its enthusiastic reception of the gospel. However, very quickly after he departed from Corinth, the influence of pagan culture insinuated itself back into what he had hoped was a safe habitat. It is impossible to know the exact details of the Corinthians' thinking, but we get some idea from a mirror reading of what Paul tries to correct in their praxis.

The basic problem seems to have been the idea that their personal appropriation of the Spirit created a recognizable superiority of certain individuals, who saw themselves as exceptional because of their use of extraordinary spiritual gifts. In fact, these were probably the community members of higher social status. They likely mistook their superior education and skill in self-presentation in public for a God-given preeminence of character. Such individuals must have gravitated together to form a faction that tried to dominate the others by their superiority—a superiority they attributed to the Spirit. This was little more than a new manifestation of the age-old desire to appear to be better than the rest. It was a trait that mistakenly built on Paul's early emphasis on the holiness and specialness granted by the Spirit to *all* the members of a community. The high-status members of the community overlooked Paul's emphasis on the fraternal love that should have underlined their holiness and the fact that the power of the Spirit lifted them up in equality.

In his opening words to the Corinthians, Paul reminds them of his teaching on holiness: *all* those who invoke Jesus Christ as their Lord share in holiness, "called to be saints, together with all those who in every place call on the name of our Lord Jesus Christ" (1:12-13). After his standard greeting of "grace and peace" and a quick *Deo gratias* (1:4), he goes on to acknowledge the reality of the spiritual gifts among them (1:5). He makes his initial appeal "that all of you be in agreement . . . united in the same mind and the same purpose" (1:10). He then appeals to the cross of Christ to show them that the true way to greatness seems to be foolishness and weakness to the worldly-wise, "those who are perishing" (1:18). He shows them that the paradox of the cross applies to them since at their own call to faith, "not many were wise by human standards, not many powerful, not many of noble birth" (1:26). No one, then, has any reason of his or her own to boast, and so he gives them the age-old, sage-old advice: "Let the one who boasts, boast in the Lord" (1:31, alluding to Jer 9:24).

He goes on to sum up his disapproval of the divisions caused by their allegiance to different leaders (seemingly a "wise" instinct even in our own day!): "Let no one boast about human (leaders)" (3:21-22). In Paul's mind the only true leader, the one who *wholly* belongs to God, is Christ himself. Putting it another way, human leaders—Paul included—are only "servants of Christ and stewards of God's mystery" (4:1). No one should make a final judgment upon them without looking first at their own motives and keeping God's final judgment upon themselves in mind (4:5). Convinced that his behavior in leadership was correct, Paul makes his frequent request: "Be imitators of me, . . . of my ways in Christ Jesus" (4:16-17).

In chapter 5, Paul responds to the case of the incestuous man with more indignation toward the community as a whole than toward the perpetrator. The church must mourn a sinner, not coddle one, much less brag about some kind of freedom in wrongdoing (v. 2). As for the public sinner himself, he must be excommunicated, cut off from the common table (vv. 9, 11), like old leaven. But this does not mean that the sinner is to be hated or cursed to damnation. Paul evinces a strong hope that the sinner's re-immersion into the sinful world outside the protection of the body of Christ will sober him up to the futility of life without Christ (v. 5).

He next shows in his teaching that their holiness differentiates them from non-believers, not from each other: "When any of you has a grievance against another, do you dare to take it to court before the unrighteous, instead of taking it before the saints?" (6:1-2). In fact, he says, the truly holy person should be ready to suffer wrong, realizing that they themselves are not perfect (6:7) and that the truly just person can absorb injustice.

Again and again Paul must confront head-on the ordinariness of sexual promiscuity in the ancient world. He does it not with prudish superiority but with a solid theology of the body: the members of the body of Christ express that relationship bodily (Gorman 2004, 251). After all, their unity with Christ will culminate in their bodily resurrection. Moreover, they are a temple of the Holy Spirit (6:15, 19—the whole community is the temple in 3:17). Rather than for casual sex, the body, one's whole being (in Paul, "body" is always one's whole life, as lived in the concrete), has been redeemed for God's glory in honor and freedom (6:20).

With regard to the sexual relationship of marriage, Paul shows an egalitarianism quite remarkable for his day. This teaching is a good example of the effect of Christlike, other-centered living: when all in community show concern for the other, the result is that they treat each other as equals. Here every admonition for the husband is repeated exactly—in full—for the wife (7:2-16). It is important to note that Paul is not giving a theology of marriage here, but is dealing with some ideas and concrete practices that arose at Corinth from a mistaken application of Hellenistic dualism to the Christian emphasis on the spiritual. Denying this opposition, Paul evaluates the states of life by a very different criterion. Whether one should be married, single, or remain betrothed or widowed depends on the openness that that state of life lends to each individual for service in the community (Vidal 2005, 318). Paul wants to show his support for the proper relationships of community members and to encourage "care for what the Lord wants" as opposed to "the affairs of the world" (7:34).

In his discussion of the conjugal activity of spouses, Paul shows himself to be a realist. This lends credibility to the common assumption that he had at one time been married, although his wife was no longer with him (deceased? separated?) when he wrote the letter (7:8). He understands that for some people marriage is the most natural, and even necessary, state for their spiritual development, and that only a self-serving and wrong-headed super-asceticism would deny value to conjugal love. Rather than legislate their choice of marriage or celibacy, he says that "each has a particular gift from

God" (7:7), and so commands only the will of God, "Let each of you lead the life that the Lord has assigned" (7:17, see also 7:20).

Paul advocates for a celibate life, so that one might not "experience distress in this life" (literally "in the flesh")" and that one "be free from anxieties" (7:28, 32). This might say something about his own, earlier marriage, for here he seems to overlook the unquestioned success of the various married couples he has worked with in the mission. At any rate, he advocates that widows and the unmarried should remain without a spouse, but only according to their temperament—and God's will (7:38, 40). This state is "better" for virgins, and for a widow to remain unmarried in Paul's judgment means that "she is more blessed if she remains as she is" (7:40). Given the lopsided arrangements of marriage and its low ranking of women in Paul's day, he was probably right in most cases!

In his discussion of food sacrificed to idols, Paul is aware that almost all the meat available in Corinth would have been dedicated to the gods by the guild of butchers who prepared it. "We know," he concedes, "that no idol in the world really exists" (8:4), but again, correct action is to be judged by its effect on the community, not, as we might say today, "on principle" or on one's "personal rights." Believers may have to forego some of their freedom of action because of the weakness of other members of the community, lest their liberty "somehow become a stumbling block to the weak" (8:9). He illustrates this principle with his own renunciation of any payment for his apostolic work (9:1-12a), and is quite adamant that the conduct of his own life never "put an obstacle in the way of the gospel of Christ" (9:12b). It is "for the sake of the Gospel" that he denies himself and accommodates his style of living to the needs of those he is with (9:24). Moreover, he advocates that all live in this manner with all the sacrifice and intensity that an athlete utilizes for a competition: "Run in such a way that you may win" (9:24).

When it comes to participation in a banquet at a pagan temple, however, his directives are quite strict. Just as Christians become one with the body of Christ in their eucharistic banquet, so their presence at a temple banquet unavoidably compromises their integrity and makes them, in some way, "partners (*koinonoi*, "community members") with demons" (10:20). The case is different, however, if the banquet is in a private home. Paul is aware of the public obligations of those of a certain social ranking within the community. He knows that important business is often conducted at table along with some very necessary social and political intercourse. On these occasions there should be no problem with eating "meat sold in the market" even though it has undoubtedly been "dedicated" to the gods, for one's own conscience should be one's guide (10:25). No problem, unless of course someone makes a point of the meat being a sacrificial offering (10:28). By partaking in that banquet, one might disturb another believer's conscience, even though in reality no kind of idolatry is in play. Paul's rule of thumb is to avoid giving offense in these matters of social nicety. The reason one is to avoid giving offense is selflessness. The believer should live a life "not seeking my own advantage, but that of the many" (10:33). On matters of table fellowship, Paul admonishes, "Be imitators of me, as I am of Christ" (11:1).

In chapter 7, we discussed Paul's teachings on the manner of dress for women at worship in the community. Paul presents his case strongly that gender differences ought to be preserved in propriety, and thus that women present themselves as properly dressed. From his point of view, the whole church would suffer from such an egregious flaunting of decorum.

Paul's only disquisition on the Eucharist is a reaction to a grave misuse of their leisure by the more affluent members of the community. They have brought the pagan atmosphere of privilege and status into the very sacrament of equality, so that Paul says that their celebration is anything *but* "the Lord's Supper" (11:20). He censures their humiliation of the less influential brothers and sisters (11:22) and reminds them of the Lord's injunction at the original Supper to "Do this in remembrance of me" (11:23; repeated in 25). The imperatives "Examine yourselves, and only then eat of the bread and drink of the cup," follow the indicative, "For as often as you eat this bread and drink this cup, you proclaim the death of the Lord until he comes" (11:28, 26). As Gorman puts it, their dining together is an *"event of memory"* that makes present the death of the Lord, an act of love for all believing members, an *"experience of solidarity"* (Gorman 2004, 268–69). Not "discerning the body" of Christ present at the supper, they leave the less independent members out of account, and so they "eat and drink judgment against themselves" (11:29). They are turning the Lord's Supper into an all-too-common pagan dinner party of the elite, where the stratification of different social levels is affirmed (ibid., 268). Paul commands the common courtesy that they "wait for one another" until all can gather together, and then, tersely, "If you are hungry, eat at home, so that when you come together, it will not be for your condemnation" (11:34).

Paul addresses the conduct of the Corinthians with regard to spiritual gifts (*charismata*) in his typical fashion: he presents a theology of the reality and meaning of the subject followed by his advice and admonitions on how the gifts are to be employed. He starts out in chapter 12 with an admonition in his most serious language, "I do not want you to be uninformed" (v. 1; also 10:1; 1 Thess 4:13; 2 Cor 1:8; Rom 1:13; 6:3; 7:1; 11:25) and then follows with his polite "I want you to understand" (12:3; also 15:1; 2 Cor 8:1; Gal 1:11). What he needs to tell them in chapter 12 about spiritual gifts is very important: all true charisms are from the Spirit, they are all for service (*diakonia*), and they share a consistent goal because they are all brought about by God (12:4-6). They are not badges of individual greatness, but gifts given in conformity with the "weakness" of the Messiah Jesus. They are therefore directed toward the building up of the community, the diverse "body of Christ," the "new humanity . . . where every one of its members exists for the service of the others" (Vidal 2005, 307).

In 12:31 he announces that there is a still more excellent way to build up the community. There follows perhaps the most beautiful and poetic exposition of Christian love, Paul's "love command" in the indicative, his description of how love ought to be (13:1-13). It is impossible to reduce the depth of his intuition here to a few maxims. We must simply read it—again and again.

It is in chapter 14 that he draws his practical conclusions on how to show love properly in using spiritual gifts, with no less than eighteen directives! His first command is no surprise: "Pursue love." This he follows with the charge, "Strive for the spiritual gifts, especially that you may prophesy" (v. 1), made with a heavily weighted comparison favoring prophecy over the gift of tongues. The difference between the two is that when one prophesies, the language is clearly understandable and meant for the edification of others. Speaking in tongues seems only to enhance one's own prayer experience. He admonishes that there be order in the Christian assembly, and prohibits any imitation of pagan rituals, where all the chaos of individualism and emotionalism reign. Above all, he orders that all be done for the "building up of the church" (vv. 3, 4, 5, 12, 17, 26).

With regard to the reality of the resurrection, he first reminds the Corinthians of the Gospel he first proclaimed to them, "in which you also stand and through which you are being saved" (15:1). He concludes the first half of his dissertation by discussing the reality of the resurrection, saying that those who deny the resurrection are like the pagan philosophers who deny the afterlife. They have no understanding of the power of God to raise the dead and are left with a hedonism that corrupts the mind like excessive alcohol. Thus Paul reproves them, "Come to a sober and right mind, and sin no more" (15:34). In the second half of this discourse, Paul tells of the manner of the resurrection and raises the triumphal cry, "Death has been swallowed up in victory" (15:54). With this great hope, he can urge them to live greatly as believers "because you know that in the Lord your labor is not in vain" (15:58).

Paul ends the letter with a few details in chapter 16. First, he gives orders for what he evidently considers an accepted routine for the weekly saving of money for the Jerusalem collection (vv. 1-2). He asks for the proper reception and send-off for Timothy, who "is doing the work of the Lord just as I [Paul] am" (vv. 10-11), and gives a final wrap-up of the advice he gave throughout the letter, "Let all that you do be done in love" (v. 14). He reminds them of the cooperation he expects them to give to Stephanas' people on their return from their mission with Paul in Ephesus. Such leaders should be obeyed and given the recognition they deserve as people who "have devoted themselves to the service of the saints" (vv. 16-18). He starts off his final greeting in the usual way, but after all he has said about love in the letter, his use of a curse seems a bit harsh: "Let anyone be accursed who has no love for the Lord." Its un-Pauline language (Paul never uses *phileō* instead *agapaō* for "love") is apparently a well-known formula that he uses to underline his seriousness about love. This is unusually harsh for Paul, but he deflects its negative energy with a prayer, "Our Lord, come," a hopeful wish, "The grace of the Lord Jesus be with you" and a heartfelt goodbye, "My love be with all of you in Christ Jesus" (vv. 22-24).

The Letter to the Galatians

We next consider the Letter to the Galatians. It is likely Paul's first response to community difficulties brought on by outsider Christians who found his teaching on freedom from Jewish law excessive. His reaction was quite strong, for in the usual self-identification at the top of the letter, he already bursts into strong polemic about his identity as an apostle. He does give his special greeting of "grace and peace," but omits any thanksgiving for their progress in grace, descending immediately into a diatribe on their lack of fidelity to the Gospel—and to himself. In his first imperative, he takes dead aim at anyone who contests his gospel of freedom from the law: *"Anathema"* (1:8, 9). This curse results from Paul's conviction of the heavenly origin of his gospel, as he says, "I received it through a revelation of Jesus Christ" (1:12).

He then recounts the events of his call to apostleship and his subsequent dealings with those called before him in the Gospel, concluding with Peter's shameful vacillation at Antioch. With high rhetoric he recalls the Galatians' own call to faith in the Spirit and assures them that as believers in Christ they have become "heirs according to the promise to Abraham" (3:29). The Mosaic law cannot separate humanity into two parts, with those outside the law being unacceptable to God. Paul asks them to "become as I am" (4:12), namely, free from slavery to anything that is not the Lord Jesus Christ.

As we should expect, the bulk of Paul's directives come in chapters 5–6, rightly named the hortatory part of the letter. He first calls on them to "stand firm, then, and do not submit again to a yoke of slavery" (5:1). Going from the slavery of their pagan superstition to slavery to an outdated law does not bring freedom! On those who would reintroduce them to such slavery, especially in the foreign and useless practice of circumcision, Paul recommends an even more drastic surgery (5:12)!

Paul cleverly combines his explanation on the proper use of freedom with an instruction on the new principle for right action, the Spirit. He starts off with a positive note, "You were called to freedom, brothers and sisters," and then wisely cautions, "only do not use your freedom as an opportunity for self-indulgence" (5:13). The only way to be sure of your behavior is to make sure that it is oriented in love for the good of others. Two points are made here: righteous living always *serves*, and acting justly is always done *not* for the sake of being "right," but out of authentic love. Those who continue to gratify the flesh, that is, those who look to their own advancement (as if there were nothing else to guarantee their own survival), will in fact perish. They "will not inherit the kingdom of God" (5:21), since they do not live as its heirs. Paul contrasts life in the flesh to the fruit of the Spirit (5:22-23), the various facets of behaving with the good of the community in mind. Believers should never "become conceited, competing against one another, envying one another" (5:26). Paul's solution to any risks that might come from freedom from the law is very clear: "If we live by the Spirit, let us also be guided by the Spirit" (5:25).

Next, Paul delves into the nitty-gritty of community living with imperfect members. One doesn't jump on another's mistake, but tries to "restore such a one in a spirit of gentleness," ever aware of one's own fragility (6:1). For those who worship the one, true God, the real value of the law ("the whole law") "is summed up in a single commandment, 'You shall love your neighbor as yourself'" (5:14). Again, Paul admonishes, "Bear one another's burdens, and in this way you will fulfill the law of Christ" (6:2). Paul's spiritual advice turns practical with frank imperatives: "All must test their own work . . . all must carry their own loads . . . those who are taught the word must share in all good things with their teacher (that is, with financial support!) . . . let us not grow weary in doing what is right" (6:4-9).

We note that the believers' goodness is to extend beyond the confines of the Christian community when Paul says, "Let us work for the good of all, and especially for those of the family of faith" (6:10). He concludes that the only thing worth boasting about is "the cross of our Lord Jesus Christ." He prays for "peace and mercy" upon them and upon all who have become "a new creation," for all Christians are "the Israel of God." He pleads for no more trouble from the anti-Paul "teachers" in the community, yet with all this he concludes with a prayer for the Lord's favor to touch their inmost spirit (6:18).

The Letter to Philemon

We turn next to the only undisputed letter of Paul to an individual, although its greeting includes the whole church that met in Philemon's house. Paul is in prison now, probably during his long stay in Ephesus where he had written 1 Corinthians and Galatians (and would later dictate Philippians). Paul starts off with his customary greeting "grace and peace" and mentions that he always thanks God in prayer for "your [Philemon's] love for all the saints and your faith toward the Lord Jesus." He prays that Philemon's "faith become effective" when he considers the proposal Paul is about to make. His humble approach (his imprisonment is mentioned three times and he calls himself "an old man") is a counterweight to his powerful authority, "though I am bold enough in Christ to command you to do your duty, yet I would rather appeal to you on the basis of love."

In a rhetorical tour de force, Paul puts forward his request to Philemon for Onesimus, a (runaway?) slave of Philemon, "that you might have him back for ever, no longer as a slave but as more than a slave, a beloved brother . . . both in the flesh and in the Lord." No wiggle-room here! Paul then protests that he himself will make up for anything that Onesimus owes (as if Philemon would not be far too embarrassed to take money from Paul!), but not without mentioning that "you owe me even your own self." Outrageous! He pleads that this would be "a benefit from you in the Lord" and begs him, "Refresh my heart in Christ." In a veiled command Paul says, "Confident of your obedience, I am writing to you, knowing that you will do even more than I say." And if this is not enough, sly old Paul makes a cheerfully veiled threat: "One thing more—prepare a guest room for me, for I am hoping through your prayers to be restored to you." Oh yes, Paul promises check up on the situation and closes with a prayer. What a lesson in the right way to use authority in charity!

The Letter to the Philippians

A good candidate for his next missive, the Letter to the Philippians shows that Paul, still in his Ephesus imprisonment, has found out that the Judaizing "reform movement" has moved westward from Galatia to darken his first European community, Philippi, with the troublesome question of circumcision. After a warm opening with thanks to God for that community's openness in "sharing the gospel" (1:5), Paul prays for them with eschatological fervor, "that your love may overflow more and more . . . so that on the day of Christ you may be pure and blameless" (1:9-10).

Paul is thinking about the parousia, and no wonder, he has just had a very close encounter with death. He knows that what got him through that episode was love, his assuredness of the love of God and "the help of the Spirit of Jesus Christ," along with the prayerful support of the Philippians (1:19). He has thought it through, and although "my desire is to depart and be with Christ, for that is far better," he decides "but to remain in the flesh is more necessary for you" (1:22-23). There he goes again, once more putting the welfare of others before his own wishes.

Paul is hopeful that in the decision to suffer more for the Gospel, he "will not be put to shame in any way, but that by my speaking with all boldness, Christ will be exalted now as always in my body, whether by life or by death" (1:20). High rhetoric? Surely. But for Paul, "to live is Christ." To his friends, he states, "because you hold me in your heart . . . I want to share abundantly in your boasting in Christ Jesus when I come to you again" (1:7, 26). Here is Paul's classic recipe for Christian suffering: share and prayer. He prays in union with the suffering of Christ (a "privilege" in 1:29) and shares his pain with his beloved fellow believers "who share in God's grace with me in my imprisonment" and in all his suffering (1:7). He has only one request. It is, as so often, directed away from himself and toward those he loves: "Only, live your life in a manner worthy of the gospel of Christ, so that . . . you are standing firm in one spirit" (1:27).

At the beginning of chapter 2, Paul rehearses the benefits of community life: "encouragement in Christ, consolation from love, fellowship in the Spirit, compassion and sympathy." His plea that the community "be in full accord and of one mind" will "make my joy complete" (v. 2). This call to concord in community is a perfect definition of a grateful response to Christ's saving deeds, the very heart of a countercultural life that seeks to do God's will as Christ did (vv. 3-5).

Such other-centeredness can only occur in those who imitate the self-emptying life of Jesus Christ that is described in such a stately way in the famous hymn that follows (vv. 6-11). This "being of the same mind" does not just mean sharing a similar point of view, but demands real imitation of the humility and service of Christ (see also Gal 5:10; Phil 3:15; 4:2; 2 Cor 13:11; Rom 8:5; 15:5). Such is the program of Christian living, to "work out your own salvation with fear and trembling" (v. 12) and to do it "without murmuring and arguing" (v. 14), so that "in the midst of a crooked and perverse generation, you shine like stars in the world" (v. 15).

Paul speaks sacramentally of his "labor and pain" as a sacrificial offering for their faith, and paradoxically says that he rejoices in all of this (v. 18). He concludes this section with a recommendation that they heartily welcome a co-worker of Paul's and honor him because of his great sacrifice in helping Paul (v. 30). Then he says it again: "Rejoice!"

There follows a brief interlude whose stark change of subject makes many scholars consider it a fragment of another letter edited here into the text. In it Paul cautions the Philippians to beware of those "reformers" who insist on circumcision for all male believers, calling them "dogs" (unwanted scavengers in the ancient world!), "evil-doers" who want to "mutilate the flesh" (3:2). He uses his former self as an example of a completely observant Jew, setting out his impeccable credentials and zealous accomplishments only to repudiate them as mere loss of time and energy. His perfection was "garbage," a poor imitation and a distraction to the true righteousness (3:9). The genuine desire of the believer should be only "to know Christ and the power of his resurrection" which we receive only in the "sharing of his sufferings by becoming like him in his death" (3:10). Those who suffer in Christ are stripped of self-delusion when they honestly confront their hurt by prayer and sharing it in community. Freed from the burden of hiding or repressing their pain, they become a great witness to the community of faith in Christ. Their affliction can give them great power for the consolation of anyone in community who must experience a similar difficulty. This positive manner of dealing with affliction is a great gift to the world at large (3:17).

The goal of such a life is "resurrection from the dead" (3:10): progress toward this "prize of the heavenly call of God in Christ Jesus" (3:14) comes about in faithful imitation of the *kenosis*, the self-emptying of Christ spelled out so beautifully in the chapter 2 hymn. This is the mindset that all are to share (3:16). By this Paul means that although they are far from perfect, they are on the path of true righteousness, of living as God wants them to in Christ. They don't need any "new" old pious practices! They should just observe the "example" of the lives of Paul and those who live like him: "Stand firm in the Lord in this way" (4:1).

A certain situation in Philippi was troublesome to Paul. Two women co-workers of his apparently did not fully buy into this kenotic mindset. The details are known to Paul and to the Philippians, but are not fully explained for us. Their names, Euodia (literally, "good road," = "Success") and Syntyche ("Lucky") indicate that they are probably slaves or freed slaves. Perhaps their (former) lowly state precludes their spontaneous embrace of such self-emptying as Paul is advocating. Whatever the case may be, Paul obviously holds them in high regard and begs help from the community for them to come around to this position, "to be of the same mind in the Lord" (4:2), who "emptied himself, taking the form of a slave" (2:7).

Now Paul returns to his earlier theme: "Rejoice in the Lord always; again I will say, Rejoice" (4:4). Remember that Paul is in jail, having had a close call with death. He has seen the gnawing specter of legalism raise its ugly head in his most beloved community. How is it that he can advocate a joyful attitude, obviously radiating from his own joy at this dark moment? The next two commands tell the tale. First, he says "Let your gentleness be known to everyone" (4:5). "Gentleness" is a word of many meanings, deriving from the Greek idea of what is right or fitting. Here it seems to mean "forbearance" or even "leniency" in dealing with problems, whether internal (like the situation with Euodia and Syntyche) or external (like the present threat against freedom from the law). A non-defensive, gentle response to whatever the difficulty may be is surely a great witness to an interior life. This kind of detachment comes only from great trust in the Lord and is a prerequisite for joy.

The reason for this gentleness is that "the Lord is near" (4:5). Paul speaks with a different eschatological accent now that he has had a brush with death, no longer concerned with the span of time until the parousia, for the Lord is *always* very near to the one suffering in his name. So in the next breath he can give his second directive, "Do not worry about anything." Absence of anxiety is the genuine effect of the Lord's peace. The Hebrew root of *shalom* means being filled (with God), and so there is no room for selfish pity here—one is not alone! Only in suffering do we really know how much we need to trust in the Lord and in our fellow believers. Only in suffering do we really give them a chance to prove that love for us. For this we can rejoice in suffering!

A faith-filled attitude does not always take away the emotion of fear, but for that there is prayer. In fact, "in everything by prayer and supplication with thanksgiving let your requests be known to God" (4:6). God knows we need to talk out our fears with others, but the deepest ones can only be aired in prayer. And don't forget to be thankful once in a while amongst all your petitions! For then, "the peace of God, which surpasses all understanding, will guard your hearts and your minds in Christ Jesus" (4:7).

Finally, Paul asks in deepest love that his flock mull over all he has said about the benefits of trusting in God. This is the guide for the daily life of those who know the loving concern of the community. They rely on Christ's saving power, "for I can do all things through him who strengthens me" (4:13). Paul reciprocates by praying for their needs (4:19), and concludes the letter with praise to God and greetings to his beloved both with him and afar.

The Second Letter to the Corinthians

Whether the canonical edition of Paul's later correspondence to Corinth is a single letter or as many as five separate missives redacted into one text (with several rough seams!), it seems that most of it belongs to the year or so after he left Ephesus for Macedonia and Illyricum, and before he visited Corinth for the last time (where he wrote Romans). Alas, the "Judaizing" reformers have finally reached his westernmost community, Corinth.

After his usual greeting of "grace and peace," Paul prays that he will "be able to console those who are in any affliction" (1:4). He expresses solidarity with the Corinthians, "for we know that as you share in our sufferings, so also you share in our consolation" (1:7). Then he declares his hope that God will rescue him again, and notes the thanks one ought to give for the prayers of the community in hard times (1:8-11). He further hopes that they and he will be able to be proud of one another "on the day of the Lord" because of the way they have interacted in the many difficulties they have had (1:14). A very interesting approach during the heat of conflict! And, as an example of how to act when wronged, Paul shows great mercy for the person who had caused him no little pain. Toward this wrongdoer he urges the community to "forgive and console him, so that he may not be overwhelmed by excessive sorrow. So I urge you to reaffirm your love for him" (2:7-8).

This spirit of detachment empowers in Paul the ability to pardon any wrong done to him, since any harm received is deflected by, or absorbed by, the whole community, as Paul says, "If anyone has caused me pain, he has caused it not to me, but to some extent—not to exaggerate—to all of you" (2:5). One does not compromise the truth in absorbing evil, but hopes for the reconciliation of the offender. Believers should not react in anger at an oppressor, lest they succumb to a similar evil. Rather, they respect human dignity everywhere and the possibility of change for all. One chooses this optimism freely, believing that God's grace can liberate any person's will. Much more than a mere sacrifice of self, this hopeful openness is a radical transformation to the same viewpoint as God's, a participation in the very power of God. This is the true love in which Christians participate in God's own wish for others to *become more* in freedom (Gorgulho and Anderson, 2006, 85–86). Paul concludes these biographical notes with a prayer of thanks for success in the mission (2:14).

In the following three chapters, Paul makes no prayers, wishes, or commands, but explains calmly how all should act in their apostolate, speaking "as persons of sincerity, as persons sent from God and standing in his presence" (2:17). Paul has said quite sincerely, "Be imitators of me as I am of Christ" (1 Cor 11:1; also 4:16; 1 Thess 1:6), and so we may take as instructional for his followers all that he now commends himself for in his ministry. As Tom Stegman points out, "Paul's strategy is to help the Corinthians understand that his comportment embodies the gospel" (2009, 221). Thus he recommends the following: have confidence through Christ and only claim competence as from God (3:4-5); have hope and act with great boldness (3:12), as being transformed into the image of the Lord (3:18). Do not lose heart; renounce shameful hidden things; refuse to practice cunning, but state the truth openly (4:1-2, 16). Do not proclaim yourself but proclaim Jesus Christ as Lord and yourself as the slave of others "for Jesus' sake" (4:5). The extraordinary "treasure" of the Gospel resides in us as in fragile clay jars so that it is clear that all comes from God (4:7). In every adversity, "the life of Jesus [should] be made visible in our mortal flesh" (4:11). Believe what you say and say what you believe in preaching (4:13-15); look beyond "what can be seen" to "what cannot be seen . . . the eternal" (4:18).

In chapter 5 Paul continues his catalogue of right attitudes and convictions: he is "always confident" because of belief in the afterlife: "we make it our aim to please [the Lord]," aware of "the judgment seat of Christ" and the promise of "recompense for what has been done in the body, whether for good or evil" (vv. 9-10). All apostolic endeavors are other-centered, "For the *love of Christ* urges us on (that is, Christ's own love for us), because . . . one has died for all" (v. 14). Therefore, "we regard no one from a human point of view" (v. 16), that is to say, human standards do not enter into his dealings with people.

What then is the proper way of knowing, of regarding others, for the believer? If it is not to know them "according to the flesh," is it to know them in the Spirit, from a divine point of view? No, says Louis Martyn, for we are not yet completely a part of the age to come, the future, when Paul says, "we will see [God] face to face," and "know fully, even as I am known [by God]" (1 Cor 13:12). Rather, since we still exist in the overlap of the Old Age and the New, we still know "only in part . . . we see as in a mirror, dimly" (ibid.). For now, "knowing by the Spirit can occur only in the form of knowing by the power of the cross . . . which is precisely to know and to serve the neighbor who is in need" (Martyn 1997, 108–109). Using the Old Testament metaphor of walking for all human activity, Paul explains, "for we walk by faith not by sight" (2 Cor 5:7), faith learned from the love of Christ on the cross.

Paul turns back now to his instructions for believers: "We entreat you on behalf of Christ, be reconciled to God" (5:20). Anything less than complete reconciliation with God and with one's fellows would be "to accept the grace of God in vain" (6:1). Paul candidly completes his recommendations based on his own missionary practice, cataloguing his exploits and virtues in 6:3-10. In fatherly fashion he pleads with them, "In return—I speak as to children—open wide your hearts also" (6:13). Paul's appeal here, rather than some command, shows that he trusts the power of "truthful speech and the power of God" to win out (6:7). After a vehement digression (6:14–7:1), Paul concludes his appeal, "Make room in your hearts for us," assuring them of his powerful bond with them and great pride in his association with them (7:2-5).

Paul's digression in 6:14–7:1 appears to be aimed at the undue influence of nonbelievers on the community, although many see it as Paul's invective against his Christian rivals at Corinth. Although he is a realist about their pagan environment (1 Cor 5:9-10), he is quite clear that Christians are not to compromise their faith by any adaptation of immoral pagan practices. Using the images of righteousness, light, Beliar (the devil), and their being the temple of God, he clarifies that full separation from sinful, worldly ways is the only course open to believers (7:1).

Chapters 8 and 9 begin a new topic, the rather sensitive issue of sharing with the needy. He will not order them to give, but asks for their generosity in response to the self-impoverishment of our Lord Jesus Christ, who "became poor, so that by his poverty you might become rich" (8:9). This is nothing less than a test of their authenticity and of their imitation of Christ's love for the poor (8:24). It is appropriate to give "according to what one has—not according to what one does not have" (8:12), so that one does not give because of any perceived coercion. Paul envisions a new economy where one balances the abundance of present circumstances with the need of others (8:13-14), since the goal in the New Age of Christ is not the amassing of wealth, but sharing it (Hoppe 2004, 161). Paul calls this "fair balance" (8:14), and provides a helpful equation: "God is able to provide you with every blessing in abundance . . . so that you may share abundantly in every good work" (9:8). The virtue of generosity not only provides for the needy, but glorifies God in obedience to the Gospel (9:13).

Paul thanks God for the willingness of Titus to work in this apostolate, and then acknowledges as proper the oversight even of someone not of Paul's own people, a brother "who has also been appointed by the churches to travel with us while we are administering this generous undertaking" (8:19-20). Yes, Paul has accepted oversight from outside in the matter of a financial collection so that it be carried out "openly before the churches" (8:24). Paul's maxim in giving to the needy is good for all time: "God loves a cheerful giver" (9:7). He assures their reward "for your great generosity" (9:11), and reminds them to pay it forward by his prayer of thanks for God's grace (9:15).

In the final portion of the letter (chaps. 10–13), one that many scholars consider an originally separate letter, Paul changes his mood considerably, starting off with sarcasm, mocking their opinion of his last visit: "I who am humble when face to face with you, but bold toward you when I am away!" (10:1). Even so he hopes "that when I am present I need not show boldness," for he has no small weapons in his arsenal, "for the weapons of our warfare are not merely human, but they have divine power to destroy strongholds" (10:4). In language that would hardly be fashionable in our world, Paul reminds them that he and they are on the same side. He is not trying to frighten them, but only to make clear that his attitude is constant whether he is writing or in person (10:7, 9, 11). This is an honor/shame culture, and so he says flatly that they will listen to him "when your faith increases," so that he can get on with his mission to "proclaim the gospel in lands beyond *you*" (10:15-16).

Now he goes into high gear, forced to "play the fool"—sly fox that he was!—in order to out-boast some "super-apostles" who evidently want to take over leadership of the community because of their imagined superiority to Paul. Paul will have none of this nonsense! His strategy is to shame them for boasting (10:17). Paul teaches on boasting almost thirty times, but here he matches all their boasts by attributing only weakness to himself and true power to the Lord. To their claims, he retorts: 1) his knowledge is based on the reality of experience of Christ in him and proven by "signs and wonders and mighty works" (12:12). 2) He did not ask for or receive remuneration because of awareness that donors can declare themselves the equal of those they support (11:12). 3) He shows that his ministry came at a much higher personal cost in suffering than theirs, but what he really boasts of are those things that show his weakness and can be attributed only to the Lord who rescued him again and again (11:30-33). 4) His mystical experience has been of "paradise" and "things that are ineffable, that no mortal is permitted to repeat" (12:4), but he sees no need to boast about his own heightened religious experiences since they do not do much to build up the community. In fact, truth be told, his mystical experience only resulted in a denial of his request to be rid of his "thorn in the flesh" (12:7-8). Evidently for Paul, listening in prayer was far more important than unusual occurrences in it, for in listening Paul was able to make his own the most profound knowledge of the Lord: "Power is made perfect in weakness" (12:9; see Stegman 2009, 273).

Paul ends his distraught comments with the warning that if their disruptive and unrepentant behavior necessitates another—this time disciplinary—visit, "I will not be lenient—since you desire proof that Christ is speaking in me" (13:2-3). Again, the imperative follows the indicative, what should be done follows what is in fact supposed to be the case for believers: "Examine yourselves to see whether you are living in the faith. Test yourselves. Do you not realize that Jesus Christ is in you?" (13:5). What Paul wants is only "that you may do what is right" (13:7), indeed "that you may become perfect" (13:9). His final greeting is "Rejoice," because if they listen to his appeal and put things in order they will "live in peace" (13:11). He reaffirms his unity with them, wishing that "the fellowship (*koinōnia*, "communion") of the holy Spirit be with all of you" (13:13).

The Letter to the Romans

After his greeting of grace and peace, Paul composes a flattering thanksgiving for this community of Christians he himself did not found. He proclaims his gratitude for their renowned faith and tells them of his frequent prayer for them. He prays for the grace to visit them in person (1:8-10). His wish is "to share some spiritual gift" with them, and in a long stretch of indicatives in the next four and a half chapters of the letter, he lays out his gospel, "the power of God for salvation for everyone who has faith, to the Jew first, and also to the Greek" (1:16).

In chapter 6 Paul must answer the objection that without the law, Christians would have no basis for moral behavior. Should they just continue a life of sin only to ask repeatedly for the grace of forgiveness? Paul begins his answer with a reminder that Christians are now dead to sin since they died with Christ in baptism. The result is that "we might too walk in newness of life" (v. 4), and "no longer be enslaved to sin" (v. 6). From this follows a set of Christian imperatives: being "alive to God in Christ Jesus," which means they must act as free from the dominion of sin over the passions of the *mortal* body, that is, human passions oriented to the sole purpose of self-preservation and self-indulgence (vv. 11-12). Rather "present yourselves to God as those who have been brought from death to life, and present your members to God as instruments of righteousness" (v. 13). The new servanthood is to righteousness that reorients one's life to accept God's grace (v. 14). "The advantage you get is sanctification. The end is eternal life" (v. 22).

After Paul explains the subterfuge of sin seizing control of the law and its paralyzing effect for those still locked in a life of slavery to sin, "this body of death" (7:24), he sings the glory of the life according to the Spirit (chap. 8). Instead of using the imperative mood to encourage proper living, Paul presumes that the baptized have been changed and uses the indicative to delineate their spiritual life. Those who "have the Spirit of Christ" and therefore "belong to him" (v. 9), "live according to the Spirit (and) set their minds on the things of the Spirit" (v. 5). Thus they "walk not according to the flesh but according to the Spirit" (v. 4). He shows how believers are empowered for good by the indwelling of the Spirit (v. 11), and how the Spirit also aids in prayer (v. 26).

In the next section of the letter, Paul opens his disquisition on the fate of nonbelieving Israel, with the impossible wish that "I myself were accursed and cut off from Christ for the sake of my own people" (9:3). He restates this positively in his prayer, "my heart's desire and prayer to God for them is that they may be saved" (10:1). Only after he gives a reason for their temporary failure, with the hope that they might still be saved, does he give a protocol for the proper Christian attitude toward their forbears in salvation: "Do not boast over the (cut off) branches," remembering that it is their "root that supports you" (11:18). There is no room for pride here but only awe at "God's kindness toward you" (11:20, 22). The section ends with a doxology that glorifies God's inscrutable ways (11:33-36).

At this point in the letter Paul begins a long catalogue of imperatives on Christian living. This is the moral stance that is derived from their union in Christ with a righteous God, the theme of the whole Letter to the Romans. Often pairing a positive demand with a negative counterpart, Paul lays out in chapter 12 the basics of Christian life as a "living sacrifice, your spiritual worship" of God (12:1), the opposite of conformity to this world's closed system of power and status. It requires a total "transformation by the renewal of the mind" (12:2) that can only result from Christlike living. This means that all worldly wisdom, secular ethics, and even Jewish law are not to be discarded, but that Christians are to bring them to bear in their deliberations. In communal discernment, Paul assures, they will receive a new kind of understanding that is completely controlled by the transforming power of the Spirit in their Christlike life.

Believers must have a sober assessment of themselves that can only occur in an open and concerned community where love is genuine and the good of others is paramount (12:3, 10). Such an ambience requires the virtuous behavior of all. To demonstrate proper actions, Paul gives some thirty imperatives (12:9-21) in which he highlights the inner attitudes of mutual honor and affection: zeal, hope, patience, and prayer, coupled with the outgoing actions of deep empathy with others and a noble life of peace that excludes revenge. The reader must meditate on them personally to do them justice.

Paul next turns to a knotty problem and gives a command that is surprising at first: "Let every person be subject to the governing authorities" (13:1). The burning question here seems to be the payment of taxes, a matter quite strictly enforced in Rome, the capital of the empire. How is it that Christians, whose real Lord is the Son of the almighty God, can freely obey pagan civil authorities? Paul's answer is brilliant. The authority secular rulers have is from God—not from the emperor! Believers may obey, then, not only out of fear of reprisal, but may accept taxation as the right thing insofar as "the authorities are God's servants" (13:6). This gives them a way to comply "because of conscience" (13:5). Perhaps reminded of Jesus' word on tribute to Caesar (Mark 12:17), Paul says that in this way, taxes, revenue, and even polite honor may be paid to civil authority (13:7), since their legitimate function is to serve God. While talking about paying what you owe, however, Paul brings to the fore the only debt a Christian should incur: "Owe no one anything except to love one another" (13:8). Such an attitude is not only legal, but it is the fulfillment of the law, for the godly command of the Jewish law is to "Love your neighbor as yourself" (13:9).

With all this discussion on temporal matters, Paul brings us back to the eschatological reality that "now is the moment for you to wake from sleep; for salvation is nearer to us now than when we became believers" (13:11). God's plan is unfolding for salvation and our personal clock is ticking. Combining metaphors of light and battle, Paul urges that we "put on the armor of light" to "live honorably" and eschew all worldly pursuits and distractions (13:13). "Instead," remembering our baptism, we are to "put on the Lord Jesus Christ, and make no provision for the flesh, to gratify its desires" (13:14).

Practical observances in religion are always difficult! It seems that everyone has an opinion on what type of food and how much should be eaten, how to celebrate religious feasts, and on which days. Everyone always has good reasons to think that everyone should observe as they do. I know a Benedictine monk of forty-five years who will verify that the celebration of the Eucharist, the symbol of unity of a community, is often also one of their most divisive concerns. He would agree with Paul's timeless advice. First of all, it is not always clear just who are the strong and why the others are "weak." When Paul speaks of the weak in faith, he is talking about anyone who wants to "quarrel over opinions" (14:1), and cautions that those "who are strong ought to put up with the failings of the weak, and not please themselves" (15:1). True, he does mention "the weak [who] only eat vegetables" (14:2), but the *really* weak in faith are those who "eat meat or drink wine or do anything that makes your brother or sister stumble" (14:21). The truly strong are those who would never "let what you eat cause the ruin of one *for whom Christ died*" (14:15; see 14:20). Always thinking about the good of the community, Paul shifts the discussion out of the realm of what we often call "the principle of the thing," to a primary concern for others. Motivation must come from true commitment, "your own conviction before God" (14:22). The axis of any discussion should be the faith shown by Jesus Christ and our willingness to follow his lead, to "put up with the failings of the weak," and to "please our neighbor for the good purpose of building them up" (15:1, 2). Only in this way may "all be fully convinced in their own minds," in all things "in honor of the Lord and giving thanks to God" (14:5-6; cf. 15:5-6).

Paul then returns to his desire to come to Rome to spend time with the community and to be "sent on" by them, that is, to receive their help in his mission. He speaks of the gratitude that all believers ought to have for their predecessors in the faith and that "they ought also to be of service to them in material things" (15:27). He asks unabashedly for prayers for himself and for success in his ministry (15:30), that he might have a joyful visit with them, wishing them God's peace (15:33).

In an attachment to the letter he commends a fellow worker, Phoebe, and hopes that they will welcome her and help her in her duties. His list of greetings shows that he really has been preparing for this trip. His knowledge of and friendship with many of their number will hopefully serve as an introduction and proof of his authority, as he mentioned earlier, to "share some spiritual gift to strengthen you" (1:11). With that, he urges the Romans to be wary of "those who cause dissentions and offenses to the teaching that you have learned" (16:17). Such "smooth-talkers" must be avoided since they "deceive the hearts of the innocent" (16:18). On the contrary Paul wants all believers "to be wise in what is good and guileless in what is evil" (16:19). With a final wish for the Lord's grace, he concludes with praise for God's revelation disclosed in Jesus Christ.

Conclusion

Paul's constant refrain for his communities is that they continue to live in grace and peace of the Lord. He is personally moved by their holiness, and is thrilled to be a part of bringing them to authentic life in Christ. To attempt a summary of all Paul's admonishments, prayers, and wishes would produce only a caricature of their anxious concern. The sense of immediacy present in the letters as Paul deals with real situations would be eclipsed, along with the hope and love expressed in them. Instead, in the conclusion to our study that follows, we give only a rough sketch of Paul's wishes as today's communities might carry them out.

Conclusion
The Ideal Pauline Community

To complete our study, let us attempt to portray a Christian community whose members follow the teaching of St. Paul, the great spiritual master, to carry out their mission to live according to the Spirit of Christ, entrusted as they are with God's appeal to all of humanity in the Gospel. I will not make these remarks with the words "Believers *would* do such and such," or the prognostic "they *will* do such and such." For I have already seen these faith realities in action, at least in a partial way, in my own Benedictine community, in many a parish setting, and with other religious groups, in base communities and Bible studies in Latin America and in the village churches and among the vowed religious in Africa, to recall just a few places in my own experience.

The Gift of the Cross

Members of Christian community believe that, contrary to so many naysayers, the "human condition" is not irreparable. From their own experience as a community of faith, they know the goodness and joy of people who are secure in their place in God's plan and dedicated to serve others as their main task in life. They believe that human nature is truly good because God created it but that it has been wounded by sin. These faith-filled people believe that God is pledged to humanity's success and is in real partnership with communities that are profoundly related to God and in fellowship with one another "in Christ."

Communities of faith see how Paul is firmly connected with the earlier Christian tradition's proclamation of the Gospel. He has taken up the idea of Christ's expiating death for our sins in God's gift of redemption (Rom 3:24-25), but he brilliantly recasts this sacrificial action as the solution to humanity's most profound question, the problem of evil. Only the believer can understand the wisdom of the cross and its power in weakness. Christ showed us on the cross, to use our graphic metaphor, how to nullify evil by relying on God's power to *absorb* evil, *neutralize* its poison, and then harness its energy to empower action for the good in a kind of spiritual *metabolism* of evil, that bane of human existence. This is the glory of God shining on the face of Christ, glory that transforms church members in the power of the Spirit, people who work in this Christlike manner to finally put an end to the reign of sin and evil over the world.

Pauline Christians know that they have been sanctified by Christ's expiating sacrifice, made "special" in God's love. Since God's Spirit makes all believers God's own children, there can be no undeserved privilege or discrimination against anyone in community. Thus they are all members of the covenant ratified by the blood of Christ, having received their justification as a pure gift of God. However, rather than merely "paying off" their debt of sin to God, Christ's saving deed makes it possible to actually become "just" as freely forgiven by God. We are now able to live a righteous life as we share in Christ's death and resurrection and "work out our own salvation" (Phil 2:12).

The cross paradoxically embraces both the goodness of God and the horrible perfidy of humanity. It highlights real institutional evil of the kind that put Christ to death in the first place. At the same time, it shows the love of God that saves us from such evil. Though we cannot fully comprehend its truth, we take the cross as a revelation from God that unmasks all human pretensions to wisdom, not pitting faith against reason but manifesting truth that is *as beyond* human reason as it is *evident* to those who believe. In its crossing meet the human and the divine, in its outreach are believers and nonbelievers, by its power is evil resisted, and in it the exaltation of the Son by the Father has its origin (França 2010, 53).

Community

In baptism, believers "put on Christ" to enter into a new community that lives for God. They turn away from "the old self," slaves no more to the bonds of sin. Their redemption has freed them from the shackles of the law and of their own egos. No longer is life to be the duty of proper comportment, but an adventure in engendering others to join in the communal project of building up the Body of Christ. They become a new creation, constantly being cleansed of defilement from sin, a veritable temple of God's Spirit. There the members, as slaves of God, "through love become slaves to one another" (Gal 5:13b), providing a loving space for all to grow in freedom. Since all the many members function as "one body of Christ, and individually as members of one another," they never stand alone in their actions, but work together in harmony. Each must live the cruciform life of Christ, basing all they do in faith, ever keeping "the judgment seat of Christ" in mind.

A striking aspect of such communities is their intolerance of prejudice. Believers pay due honor to those in leadership roles, understand the social limitations of others, and respect gender differences. However, any discrimination because of religious beliefs ("Jew or Greek"), social or economic status ("slave or free"), or gender ("male or female") is strictly avoided, "for all are one in Christ Jesus" (Gal 3:28). Paul understood well and taught most forcefully that it takes every member of the community, from the noblest (in human terms) to the most lowly, to make up and operate fully as the Body of Christ. Indeed, every member contributes to the opportunity for Christlike living at the same time with their strength *and* with their neediness. For this reason believers celebrate their diversity, assured that the newness created in difference is a "new creation," empowered by the Spirit with a new identity and purpose as the kernel of a new civilization. Equality is not real until all actually serve one another because they regard the other as *completely worthy* of it.

Internal strife is dealt with head-on with prayer, as well as a realistic recognition of the suffering that causes it. With hope, the community builds on past resolution of difficulties through forgiveness and consolation. Leaders address failings not so much as "evil," but as inferior to the exercise of freedom. Those in the wrong are not indulged but confronted simultaneously with the strong demands of the Gospel and a loving attitude with sincerity, humility, and the promise of open-hearted assistance. Correct action is not so much what is "right" as what bears fruit in the Spirit. Thus believers are ready even to suffer wrong for their brothers and sisters, as Christ did, to give up their "personal rights" for the sake of the weak. This is the valid and true asceticism for Christ's body, its authentic holiness. Community leaders must never frighten, must never be responsible for any less than Christlike action, but act as "vessels of clay" who work confidently and in hope for the weak. They must strive to turn every situation into an opportunity for God's powerful action through their love and concern.

Authentic Living

The self-renunciation required for true growth is not self-disparagement or some kind of Stoic asceticism. It is self-*acceptance* according to God's plan. In place of the absolute "I," believers achieve authentic self-realization that comes only in relationship (Grilli 2012, 69). They live in real freedom, choosing the greatness of God's plan over any fleeting imitation. Believers understand that being "flesh" is not bad unless they let it be, if they deny their dependence upon God and turn away from Christ as their unique model. Keeping Christ as its model leads to a transformation of the community, the ongoing process of each member becoming what later theology calls a "sacrament" of Christ.

Believers also are aware that one is not perfect at the beginning of the journey with Christ. They learn from Paul's mistakes and from their own in the self-knowledge that comes from the sharing of Christ's sufferings. They know "that suffering produces endurance, endurance character and character hope" (Rom 5:3-4). The hope of Christians is grounded in the joy that they experience in loving fellowship, where the Spirit sustains them in affliction and turns evil into an occasion for good, misfortune into an outpouring of compassion. When believers experience the radical freedom that follows the surrender of the will to God, they know peace and are confident that together they are pleasing God.

As the Body of Christ, believers share the experience of Christ's affliction in his triumph over evil. They know that God's response to evil is compassion for its victims, and that love is evil's only antidote. Evil is *never* to be "accepted" as without remedy, never consented to as one's lot in life. Suffering and affliction are not good, but they can be dealt with as a graced opportunity from God. Paul's recipe for suffering Christians demands both a horizontal and a vertical response: sharing with the community and praying to God. Confiding the truth of one's fears and weaknesses to another brings realistic self-acceptance. The loving response of community builds the self-esteem necessary for growth. Their prayers build a unity in suffering with Christ that pushes the sting of suffering outward, turns it around, and makes it an effective weapon for the redemption of the world, bringing joy and peace, blessing, witness, and the power of the resurrection to ministry.

Paul is pragmatic. He deals very directly in practical matters from hard work to paying taxes. He understands that ultimately these are not the most important considerations in life for believers, "For the present form of this world is passing away" (1 Cor 7:31). At the same time he never negates the importance of this world, and shows how it can be better if people live together in peace and equality as children of God. Thus Christians are always aware of their witness to the world and their ambassadorship of reconciliation. They treat outsiders kindly, doing good to all.

Paul is a realist when it comes to human sexuality. One's sexual life is an integral part of one's holiness and love. Any illicit affair demeans one's own body, that is, one's own person, as it dishonors the community that is, after all, the body of Christ and the temple of the Holy Spirit. By contrast, a true marriage of equals is an indissoluble gift from God that leads to mutual sanctification, both for the individuals and the community. There are also good reasons for celibacy, not the least of which are the detachment and freedom that it can bring about. That life, however, simply will not work in healthy fashion without a special vocation from God, usually for some kind of communal service.

The lives of believers are fully realized by their dedicated work. By it they show up the self-centeredness and counterfeit humanity of those who live only for the pursuit of wealth or status. Believers can "aspire to live quietly and mind [their] own affairs," (1 Thess 4:11), making honest work their honor. By and by they will be relieved of the endless desire for more material goods so that they may live in peace and find a realistic way to rise out of abject poverty by their own labor (see Mesters 2009, 63–70).

Prayer is "the hallmark of true piety . . . the lifeblood of every Christian and the wellspring of all Christian ministry" (Longenecker 2001, 226). All of our prayer is through Jesus Christ because we exist "in Christ." In prayer we do not just make plans in hope; we carry them through with God's help. United to Christ in prayer, we are strengthened in our inner selves by his power and wisdom (see Hays 2008, 345–48). We learn from Paul something about prayer we don't often admit: Paul spends a great deal of time and energy remembering those he loves, as well as others who are making a difference in his life. He wraps them all up in prayer, the good and the bad, in God's love and care. He meditates on all the good that has happened in the past and counsels others to do the same in awareness of the presence of the God of peace. He prays that his mission plans succeed and thanks God when they do. He believes he sees what God wants him to do, and then prays for the strength and good fortune for it to happen.

Eucharistic celebrations recommit believers to the death and resurrection of the Lord and to their role in the unfolding of salvation (Pastor Ramos 1991, 148). These celebrations are open to a wide range of form and style, always orderly and dignified, but never encrusted in outmoded mannerisms that deter meaningful participation. In the Eucharist the worshipers discern the body of their fellowship in the Lord as they are spiritually nourished by the bread and wine, the sacramental Body and Blood of Christ, his whole selfless life and the sacrifice of his death.

The Gift of the Spirit

The Pauline community is quite familiar with the presence of the Spirit in their midst. They recognize it as the powerful presence of God, the ongoing revelation of Christ's self-denying openness to every situation meant to build up a new and liberated world. This joyful experience comes when needed to intensify their commitment to manifest Christ's saving presence in their deliberations, to facilitate their reception of new people and events, and to comfort and guide them in their afflictions and decision-making. The Spirit is at the core of honest self-esteem. It is both the orientation and the empowerment to do what is right, what is edifying for the community, and what is positive for change in the world. We might say that the Spirit is the affective component of religious experience. Believers name it, enjoy it, and allow it to guide them in firm and confident action to absorb evil and spread the freedom of God's kingdom—never by violence or coercion, but in the "weakness" of the offer of genuine and Christlike love.

For believers, this eschatological outpouring of the Spirit is the real presence of God that the prophets of old promised to the people of

God. They recognize the Spirit in the intimacy they have with their loving Father in prayer, allowing themselves to be moved in their inner depths to own what is the real situation of their lives and to beg for the help they need to do God's will. Their joyful peace is remarkable and known to all. They perform charismatic acts, knowing that even the lowliest among them have been chosen by God to carry on the work of Christ in building community.

Spiritual gifts, especially extraordinary ability, are all for the same goal: the building up of community. There can be no spiritual elite since all honors and accomplishments are mere rubbish when compared to the true righteousness gifted by God. The whole of Christian life is to be seen as a spiritual liturgy for all to partake in: all should meditate on the work of the Spirit in the community's progress. Aware of the frailty of the "innocent," Paul warns against those who cause dissention by self-serving rhetoric and deceptive flattery.

The presence of the Spirit intensifies at special times like baptism, marriage, and the death of a beloved member, but it is not limited to those sacramental occasions only. Believers know the Spirit in their loving relationships with other Christians, as Paul did in the welcome and generosity of his communities. The Spirit endows community members with a deep love for one another and the righteous orientation to act in behalf of others. The rule-bound life of the spiritual novice has been replaced by the Spirit of Jesus himself that opposes all selfish pettiness ("the flesh") and beckons to greatness. The Spirit-filled receive holiness in a new life of obedience in community, enrichment in knowledge, and boldness of speech.

The Moral Life of the Community

The Christian community decides the direction of their actions in open dialogue with Sacred Scripture, their past traditions, and contemporary wisdom, but do this with a "renewal of [their] minds" (Rom 12:2). They see that service forms conscience and that love engenders knowledge of the worth of every creature—even difficult personalities and perpetrators of evil deeds. The Christian imagination is transformed by the interaction of Spirit-guided community discernment where the moral *imperative* is always based on the reality (the *indicative*) of the actors being chosen by God. They know that when moral theory can't solve a question, as in the idol and meat controversy at Corinth, love must. One's personal rights must sometimes be put second to the welfare of others, in loving forbearance, for right action does not flow from principle or from individual rights, but from the will of God and the desire to build up the Body of Christ.

Since even believers do not yet "know fully even as they are fully known," the present manner of knowledge for right action remains "dim, as in a mirror" as cruciform love, self-giving but at a cost. Making the right decision is difficult because it must still be based on the faithfulness of Christ and the faith and trust of those who believe in this perfect model. Since they still live in this overlap of the Old Age of sin and the fulfillment of the New Age (at the parousia), Christians continue to suffer as they deny sin's power in their lives. This is the reason for the (sometimes even morbid!) recognition by some great saints of sin in their lives. It wasn't that they were committing great sins, but they still felt the pull of evil. One often has to learn the same lesson over and over again in humility and with prayer.

Pauline believers understand the value and dignity of hard work. Their goal is not a life of leisure, of having others perform for them the menial tasks that life requires. Nor do they live to amass wealth. On the contrary, they see that the real value of work is to provide for the human needs of all. Thus giving to those in need is a routine and anticipated part of Christian ministry that focuses on the balance between the need of some and the abundance of others. Wealth, when it accrues from honest work, provides the possibility of generosity in sharing, always out of love and with the joy of serving a brother or sister. Believers try always to work at their level of competence, but never refrain from getting their hands dirty when the community is in need. The modern possibility of retirement is often the opportunity for them to take on even more charitable work, using skills won in a busy life for the benefit of those less practiced.

Eschatology

Pauline Christians understand that they now belong to the life sphere of the risen Christ, a new stage of humanity that transcends history and all previous religiosity (Saunders 2002, 162). Moreover, with Christ comes the new kingdom of God, so that Paul can say, "The Lord is near" (Phil 4:5) in both a temporal and a spatial sense. Thus Christians live in a new eschatological present, and with this alternative view of reality they form an international communion of *ekklēsiai,* special assemblies that understand themselves in terms of the saving deeds of Jesus Christ. Believers thus reject all compromise with worldly standards of status and power, "the law of sin and death."

Pauline Christians understand that what Paul calls the "cosmic powers" of evil refers to the malevolence inherent in so many human institutions today: the will to dominate, the pursuit of privilege, the reckoning of value by status, the morbid cult of physical beauty, the cultivated fear of death. These forces of malice have not yet been overcome, but, as Paul predicts of the parousia, "Then comes the end, when [Christ] hands over the kingdom to the Father . . . after he has put all his enemies under his feet" (1 Cor 15:24-25).

But what of the future of the world? If Paul seems to be detached from world politics, it is because his movement was so tiny within the giant Roman Empire. Under his tutelage, however, Christians of all ages have known their mandate to "change their world toward the values of God" (Osiek 2000, 109). Paul's driven activity in founding one community after another proves that he was concerned to spread an international movement to the borders of the known world. We moderns finally have the telecommunications to learn from and know about the whole world, and we have a community of believers large enough to bring about significant change by our witness and benevolent influence. The eschatological orientation of Pauline Christians was never an escape from the here and now into some utopian dream where God does all the work. The parousia remains "an act of God rather than the culmination of a historical process" (Matera 2012, 212). But now we can act with even more hope in this alternate view of reality for the potential of our world to become what God intended it to be.

Believers thus make the church countercultural: it abides in, influences, but is not itself an integral part of any single nation. Pauline Christians abide by the rule of law and execute their civic duties as citizens, but their true ruler is Jesus Christ. They participate in the political process, yet their major concern is not the political advancement of their nation or the narrow agenda of any political party or religious sect. Their focus is the discernment and execution of God's will. They remain within society but challenge it to become more humane as God intended it to be. They strive to bring on "a new creation" that provides peace and equal rights for all, that is, a world where value does not depend on status. Their holiness makes them separate from worldly ways in thinking and action, as they live fully in the present but act in hope with God's future in mind.

The Mission

Christians know that evil cannot be explained, but that to people who have been overcome by evil, God's response is loving concern. They understand that when people sin they are acting in a hopeless manner, reacting defensively to their finitude, bereft of any power to live greatly as God created them to do. In response, Christians work for God to invite them to become a new humanity, to walk with God's people and share in the transcendent life they always knew they were capable of. They join Paul in his sorrow and hope for the Jews, for without them there would be no Christian dispensation, no grafting of Gentiles into the plan of salvation in Christ.

Pauline Christians have an affective relationship with their Lord Jesus that is both emboldening and consoling. They grow in fellowship with one another as they carry out their mission in joyful peace. Their debt to Christ is seen as a debt to all those Christ wishes to save as they respond to God's grace with a ministry and service (*diakonia*) owed to their savior but now given for the salvation of many (Minear 2002, 240). They know that their being "body," the Body of Christ, means that their organic and active relationship to others is the actual presence of the risen Jesus in history now. They work to reconcile the world to God and lead the way in the life of freedom that God has ever planned for humankind: truly authentic living, loving service, joy that overflows, and peace in a secure and untroubled heart.

We conclude with this hopeful yet difficult advice from Paul, the great spiritual leader and practitioner of Christlike love: "Rejoice in the Lord always; again I will say, Rejoice. Let your gentleness be known to everyone. The Lord is near. Do not worry about anything, but in everything by prayer and supplication with thanksgiving let your requests be made known to God. And the peace of God, which surpasses all understanding, will guard your hearts and your minds in Christ Jesus" (Phil 4:4-7).

Appendix:
Exegesis of Two Controversial Texts

Exegesis of 1 Corinthians 11:2-16

We may outline St. Paul's overall argument as a chiasm (crisscross construction) with the center point being equality:

a) verse 2 – The Corinthians follow church traditions.

b) verses 3-10 – The biblical evidence shows that gender distinctions are extremely important. Paul says that they are rooted in the different ways the two genders came about in creation story of Genesis 2.

c) verses 11-12 – This is a statement of equality, overall gender equality, "in the Lord." The equality with which Christians are to regard one another is rooted in the present reality of the life cycle.

b') verses 13-15 – For Paul, "natural" law dictates common sense comportment. As Paul's society sees them, gender distinctions are rooted in the very nature of things.

a') verse 16 – In this matter the Corinthians ought to follow church tradition.

Paul first commends the Corinthians' thoughtfulness and care in maintaining the Christian traditions that he taught them (v. 2). This is a rhetorical setup for his concluding argument which appeals to just such a church custom (v. 16). Note that this proves that Paul is talking about public church prayer.

Paul launches into his argument before he names the particular problem he has in mind (v. 5): "I want you to understand that Christ is the head of every man, and the man is the head of the woman and God the head of Christ" (v. 3). Such a rhetorical pre-positioning sometimes obscures the logic of the following argument, but heightens the interest of the audience: "Now where is he going to go with this idea?" However, the statement itself sets up the meaning of the whole line of reasoning up to verse 10 and so is very important to understand. Paul probably chose this argument using the word "head" as a rhetorical flourish as well, since the focus of his instruction is about the attire of the "head" of Christian men and women. The question is: What did Paul mean by saying that man is the "head" of woman?

Some commentators maintain that verse 3 clearly identifies a hierarchy of authority: God is over Christ (who does God's will), Christ is over man (for whom he is Lord), and man is over woman (who should "be subject to your husbands" as in Col 3:18 and Eph 5:21-24). But there are two big problems here: 1) *Kephalē*, the Greek word for "head," almost never refers to "authority" in first-century Greek. In fact, Paul does use the word for "authority" (Greek *exousia*), later in verse 10 about the woman's "authority." When he used the verb form "having authority" (*exousisiazō*) earlier in his instructions for married people, he is completely egalitarian: "For the wife does not have authority over her own body, but the husband does; likewise the husband does not have authority over his own body, but the wife does" (7:4). As to the command for women to be subject in Colossians and Ephesians, these letters were not written by Paul. They interpret Paul's teachings for a later time, and are answering a different question there. (In fact, we may have something to learn about Christ as "head of the body, the church" in Colossians and Ephesians from the present text!)

It is useless to compare verse 3 ("Christ is the head of every man," etc.) to the similar series in 1 Corinthians 3:23 ("you belong to Christ and Christ belongs to God") because the word "head" is not used there, and the plural "you" addresses the whole community, both men and women. In this text Paul is referring to the quarrels among the Corinthians who were saying "I belong to Paul, I belong to Apollos, I belong to Cephas, I belong to Christ," (1:12) where the implication is similar to the allegiance of individuals to a leader of a political group, as is made clear in 3:21, "So let no one boast about human leaders." The full text states "For all things are yours, whether Paul or Apollos or Cephas or the world or life or death or the present or the future—all things belong to you, and you belong to Christ and Christ belongs to God" (3:21-23). There is no distinction between man and woman here!

Kephalē, the Greek word for "head" in our text (1 Cor 11:3) is the key term, and its connotation is widely (and hotly!) disputed. Paul's other (authentic) letters do not settle the matter, because other than here he only uses the word "head" twice, both times in the literal sense, meaning the physical head of the human body (Rom 12:20 and 1 Cor 12:21). In contemporaneous secular Greek the word *kephalē* first of all means the "head" in a physical sense, whether of a human or animal body, or figuratively of the top part of a thing such as a mountain. In a metaphorical sense it may refer to the "source" of something, like the "head" of a river where it begins, or a god or a man as the "head" or progenitor of his clan. It is true that in Paul's Bible, the Septuagint translation of the Old Testament, *kephalē* is the most frequent rendition of the biblical Hebrew word for "head" (*rosh*), usually referring to a physical "head." However, when *rosh* refers to "head" in the sense of the top person in authority, another Greek word like *archē*, "ruler," is generally used for translation!

Thus the most natural understanding of the word *kephalē* here for a first-century Greek speaker would be "head" as "source," the first in a series in the sense of the origin of something or someone. This is corroborated by what Paul says in verses 8-9, where he explicitly cites the creation stories in Genesis 2 in an attempt to anchor the gender differences between man and woman in the different manner of their creation. Thus God is the head of Christ because Christ is God's Son. That Christ is the "head/source" of man is more difficult to explain, but we know that Paul says earlier in 8:6 that there is "one Lord, Jesus Christ, through whom are all things and through whom we exist." Such a statement refers to Christ as the embodiment of God's wisdom, present at the time of creation in such texts as Proverbs 8:22. Thus Christ, as the embodiment of God's creative wisdom at creation, is the "head" or origin of Adam at his creation "from the dust of the ground" (Gen 2:7).

In this understanding we have to suppose that Paul is thinking of the first story of creation in Genesis (1:1–2:4), and reads 1:26 "Then God said, 'Let us make a human being (*anthrōpos* in the Greek text that Paul would have known) in our image, according to our likeness.'" Paul takes the inclusive term *anthrōpos*, however, in the sense of *anēr*, "a male," and then ignores the following verse, Genesis 1:27, "So God created humankind in his image . . . male and female he created them." He then skips to the second story of creation in Gen 2:4-25 where God creates the woman from Adam's rib.

The ancients did not read the Bible with the critical sense that we have today, but saw the second creation story (Gen 2) as an overlay, or further elaboration of the first (Gen 1), and not as we do, namely as a narrative with a much earlier origin and a different theology. This is how Paul could see the man as created by God (through God's wisdom embodied in Christ), and thus that Christ is the head of man. The man is then the "head" of woman, because he (his rib) is the "source" of the woman. As Adam says "This at last is bone of my bones and flesh of my flesh" (Gen 2:23), so Paul confirms it in our text, "Indeed, man was not made from woman, but woman from man" (1 Cor 11:8). This part of the argument, then, highlights the different ways God created the man and the woman. The point would be: If God created them differently they are really different and should identify themselves as different in their manner of dress.

Verses 5b and 6 intensify Paul's argument against a woman not covering her head, likening it to having her hair cut off, or even having her head shaved. This symbolic denudation was quite shameful even up to modern times, for example, when as a public humiliation, some French citizens shaved the heads of women who had befriended their German occupiers in the Second World War.

In verse 7 Paul continues the biblical argument, saying that "a man should not have his head covered (with a veil or long hair?), since he is the image and glory (*doxa*) of God; but woman is the glory of man." The allusion to Christ in the opening statement of verse 3 has been dropped, probably as too hard to fit into this part of the argument, which also alludes to the text of Genesis 1–2. But in order to make this argument work Paul must further accommodate the Genesis text. We have already seen how he refers to the text of Genesis 1:26 as saying, "Let us make man in our image, according to our likeness." Next he must refer to that text as if it spoke of God's "image and glory" instead of "image and likeness"! He has to do this because it is the *difference* between man and woman, not the likeness that makes Paul's point. "Glory" here, as in the Old Testament and elsewhere in Paul, indicates "that which exhibits one's inner worth and demands respect of others" (McKenzie 1965, 313). Thus here Paul is claiming that woman is the glory of man, who is her source, just as man is the glory of God, who is his source in creation, for "glory" here is the "reflection" of what is praiseworthy in someone. This is proved by what Paul says about "glory" when he says to the Thessalonians "You are our glory and joy!" (1 Thess 2:20). They are his glory because they are the reflection of his work for God as an apostle, his "crown of boasting before our Lord Jesus at his coming" (1 Thess 2:19).

From this tortured interpretation of the Genesis stories Paul deduces that a man should not cover his head since it is as a man that he is the immediate and direct reflection of God on earth, God's glory as the first human creation. Thus he must appear as manly, without any hint of femininity (long hair or a veil, in that culture). Of course, the modern reader will note the circular reasoning here: a man should wear his hair short/not cover his head because it is as man that he is the glory of God, and men do not wear their hair long/use a veil. Woman, the source of whose creation was from the man, and thus whose glory she represented, should appear with appropriate gender difference and thus glorious in her own right. As Paul states in verse 15, "if a woman has long hair, it is her glory." Thus both the man and the woman are glorious, but in different ways because of the difference in their creation by God, as verse 15 continues, "Long hair has been given to her for a covering." Remember that the "covering" is strictly required as appropriate to her nature according to the ancient concept of feminine sexuality as mentioned above. It is the sign of her femininity.

Later on in the Genesis text God says to the woman "your desire shall be for your husband, and he shall rule over you" (Gen 3:16). This text is sometimes adduced as contributing to Paul's thinking, since it clearly subordinates woman to man—but this is what God says is the result of original sin! It is clearly not what God wanted to happen to humanity any more than what God notes at the beginning of that same verse, "I will greatly increase your pangs in childbearing; in pain you shall bring forth children." It is unlikely that Paul would advocate this result of the sinfulness of humanity for the new family of the Body of Christ that does not live in slavery to sin.

In God's original creation community woman's role was to be the glory of her man, not his chattel. For Paul the Gospel of Jesus Christ restores this original complementarity of the sexes. Thus we would expect Paul to conclude the argument here by saying something like "if men and women do not live out their gender differences in demeanor and dress, then they no longer reflect God's glory in the way they were created." Instead Paul makes this conclusion, "Wherefore [because of what the creation narrative thus says], a woman ought to have authority (*exousia*) over (*epi*) her (own) head (v. 10 – neither the words "symbol" nor "sign" occur in the original Greek text, as in some translations: "a woman ought to have a symbol/sign of authority")." Paul's teaching on equality in Christ gave women the authority to lead the congregation by prayer or prophesy as woman, something forbidden by Jewish custom at the time. Thus she ought to have authority/control over what she wears on her head in order to exercise that authority properly.

To put the finishing touch on this part of his argument, Paul completes verse 10 with an unusual reference, "because of the angels." No one is sure of the exact meaning of the phrase, but "angels" are probably mentioned here because they symbolize God's presence at the sacred assembly, as they do also at Qumran, the Dead Sea Scrolls community of Jewish Essenes. So Paul is likely reminding the Corinthians of the solemnity of their liturgies, where no offense should be given to God (or God's representative angels), a theme that he takes up at length in a discussion of decorum at the liturgical assembly in chapter 14, "for God is a God not of disorder but of peace" (1 Cor 14:33).

Now we come to the third part of the argument (vv. 11-12). As a corrective to any hint of subordination of woman to man, the strong adversative *plēn*, "nevertheless, in any case; however," signals a reversal of any such thinking. Paul clarifies with his typical repetition of language for each gender: "in the Lord woman is not independent of man nor is man independent of woman" (v. 11). By this he means that in the redeemed world of baptized Christians there is equality of the sexes, even though the natural process of birth shows that there are obvious differences between the genders: "For just as woman came from man, so man comes through woman (at birth); but all things come from God" (v. 12).

Next, in verses 13-15 (part b') Paul shows again here that he shares the cultural context of his day in thinking that customs representing sexual distinctions are rooted in nature: "Does not nature itself teach you that if a man wears long hair, it is degrading to him, but if a woman has long hair, it is her glory?" (vv. 14-15). This kind of thinking about "nature" is common in first-century writers, as, for example, in the Stoic teacher Epictetus who states that a woman has no beard and a lighter voice in order that the gender of the person whom one approaches is immediately clear. His conclusion on the matter is, "Therefore, it behooves us to uphold these God-given signs; we ought . . . not, insofar as we are able, to confuse the sexes since they are thus determined" (Discourses 1.16.9-14; my translation). Paul knows that his arguments won't convince everyone, and so his final appeal in the matter is to the customs of other churches (v. 16), thus finishing up (as part a') where he began the discourse.

Silence for Women in Paul's Churches? (1 Cor 14:34-35)

Finally, we must deal with the only text that appears in an undisputed Pauline letter that indeed does subordinate women to men: "Women should be silent in the churches, for it is not permitted to them to speak, but they should be subordinate just as the Law also says. If they wish to learn anything, let them ask their own husbands at home. For it is shameful for a woman to speak in church" (1 Cor 14:34-35).

Here we have words attributed to Paul that absolutely contradict his teaching on the public praying and prophesying of women in 1 Corinthians 11 that we have just discussed. How could he prohibit their speaking in church if he has just regulated how they were to do it? And are we to imagine that Paul would invoke the teaching of the law ("just as the law also says" = the Jewish Torah) to reinforce this dictum? Something here is not what it seems to be! These blatant contradictions cause a growing majority of Pauline scholars to insist that Paul himself is not responsible for verses 34-35. There are, in fact, two ways to explain the presence in the letter of this passage that Paul himself did not write.

Some text sensitive commentators explain the non-Pauline command as an "interpolation," an insertion of a later text into the original text. This well-known scribal practice consists of the addition, in the production of a new copy of a text, of some words that were in the margin of the manuscript that was being copied. It certainly appears that verses 34-35 address a different topic: they appear to have been intruded into the middle of a discussion of prophecy (vv. 31-40). The rest of the text surrounding verses 34-35 makes more sense without the subject change of verses 34-35. Just look at the continuous teaching on prophecy that results when we omit these verses:

For you can all prophesy one by one so that all may learn and all be encouraged. And the spirits of the prophets are subject to the prophets, for God is a God not of disorder but of peace, as in all the churches of the holy ones. [vv. 34-36 omitted] Or did the word of God originate from you, or did it come to you alone? Anyone who claims to be a prophet, or to have spiritual powers, must acknowledge that what I am writing here is a command of the Lord. (vv. 31-33, 36-38)

When scholars argue that a text is an "interpolation," they look for the manuscript tradition to show evidence of some tampering with the more original text. (Remember: none of the original letters that Paul himself or his secretary wrote have survived. We only have copies of them from the third century and later.) Such evidence does indeed exist here: several important early manuscripts have the text exactly as we have above, that is, *without* verses 34-35 in the discussion of prophecy, although they place those verses after what our modern bibles call verse 40. We can imagine that, early in the Church's process of editing and copying Paul's letters some twenty years after his death, some scribe made a note in the margin here of the kind of teaching he knew of elsewhere in the "Pauline" writings. The next copyists decided to put the "gloss," as this type of notation is called, *into* the text itself, but the different positions of verses 34-35 (after v. 33 in some manuscripts and after v. 40 in others) are the result of the choice of different copyists.

Gordon Fee has pointed out something that has gone unnoticed by many commentators: the manuscripts that place verses 34-35 after verse 40 represent the entire Western manuscript tradition before St. Jerome's Vulgate translation (Fee, 1994, 274). This means that before 400 CE, the text read in Rome and in most of western Christendom was different from the one we read today, where verses 34-35 occur after verse 33. Thus, since verses 34-35 are so contradictory to what Paul himself presumes and regulates in chapter 11, and since they occur at different places in the manuscript tradition, they may well be an incorporated gloss that echoes the post-Pauline dictum, "Let a woman learn in silence with full submission. I permit no woman to teach or have authority over a man; she is to keep silent" (1 Tim 2:11-12).

Many commentators have a different explanation of why verses 34-35 should not be accepted as genuinely Pauline. They maintain that here Paul is citing the argument of his opponents at Corinth, but without giving us any literary indication that it belonged to the opponents. This is a common rhetorical practice of the time. Paul does it earlier in this letter when he quotes the opponents' argument, "All things are lawful for me," to which he himself retorts "but not all things are beneficial" (1 Cor 6:12a; see other quotations of his opponents' arguments in 6:12b, 13; 7:1; 8:1 and 10:23, as the quotation marks around these words in modern editions of the Bible indicate). The original hearers of the discourse would have known full well that these were the arguments of the opposition and how Paul was contradicting them, and that he was doing it with a fine rhetorical flourish that could be indicated by the letter reader's voice.

The placement, if authentic, of verses 34-35 just after Paul affirms that everyone has the right to prophesy in verse 31 ("For you can all prophesy one by one") surely must indicate that they are the opinion of someone opposed to the usual practice of prophecy by men and women in the Pauline churches, whether a contemporary Corinthian or a later redactor. Whatever one may make of this text that orders the silence of women in church, it is most unlikely that these are Paul's words!

Bibliography

Anderson, Ana Flora. "Paulo, apóstolo dos povos." In *A história da palavra*. São Paulo: Paulinas, 2005.

———. "O Evangelho da Liberdade." *Estudos Bíblicos* 2 (1987): 38–49.

Arias, Javier Velasco. "La alegría del Evangelio no es cómplice de la injusticia." *Eseña bíblica* 38 (2003): 53–62.

Asoanya, Chiedozie. *Global Environmental and Ecological Crises in the Light of the Holy Scriptures*. Enugu, Nigeria: Snaap, 2007.

Baillie, Gil. *Violence Unveiled: Humanity at the Crossroads*. New York: Crossroad, 1995.

Barbaglio, Giuseppe. *Il pensare dell'apostolo Paolo*. Bologna: Dehoniane, 2004.

Barrett, Charles K. *A Commentary on the Epistle to the Romans*. Harper's New Testament Commentaries. New York: Harper & Row, 1957.

Bassler, Jouette M. *Navigating Paul: An Introduction to Key Theological Concepts*. Louisville, KY: Westminster John Knox, 2007.

Bird, Michael F. *Introducing Paul: The Man, His Mission and His Message*. Downers Grove, IL: Intervarsity Press, 2008.

Bond, Gilbert I. *Paul and the Religious Experience of Reconciliation: Diasporic Community and Creole Consciousness*. Louisville, KY: Westminster John Knox, 2001.

Borg, Marcus, and John Dominic Crossan. *The First Paul: Reclaiming the Radical Visionary Behind the Church's Conservative Icon*. New York: HarperOne, 2009.

Bultmann, Rudolf. "Das problem der Ethik bei Paulus." *Zeitschrift für die neutestamentliche Wissenschaft* 23 (1924): 123–40.

Byrne, Brendan. *Reckoning with Romans: A Contemporary Reading of Paul's Gospel*. Good News Studies 18. Wilmington, DE: Michael Glazier, 1986.

———. *Romans*. Sacra Pagina 6. Collegeville, MN: Liturgical Press, 1996.

Byrnes, Michael. *Conformation to the Death of Christ and the Hope of Resurrection.* Tesi Gregoriani S.T. 99. Rome: Gregorian University, 2003.

Callan, Terrance. *Dying and Rising with Christ: The Theology of Paul the Apostle.* New York: Paulist, 2006.

Campbell, Constantine R. *Paul and Union with Christ: An Exegetical and Theological Study.* Grand Rapids, MI: Zondervan, 2012.

Casalegno, Alberto. *Paulo: o evangelho do amor fiel de Deus.* São Paulo: Loyola, 2001.

Cobb, John B., and David J. Lull. *Romans.* Chalice Commentaries for Today. St. Louis: Chalice Press, 2005.

Colijn, Brenda B. *Images of Salvation in the New Testament.* Downers Grove, IL: IVP Academic, 2010.

Collins, Raymond F. *First Corinthians.* Sacra Pagina 7. Collegeville, MN: Liturgical Press, 1999.

Crossan, John Dominic, and Jonathan L. Reed. *In Search of Paul: How Jesus' Apostle Opposed Rome's Empire with God's Kingdom.* San Francisco: HarperSanFrancisco, 2004.

Dunn, James D. G. *The Theology of Paul the Apostle.* Grand Rapids, MI: Eerdmans, 1998.

Fee, Gordon. D. *God's Empowering Presence: The Holy Spirit in the Letters of Paul.* Peabody, MA: Hendrickson, 1994.

————. *Pauline Christology: An Exegetical-Theological Study.* Peabody, MA: Hendrickson, 2007.

Fitzmyer, Joseph A. *First Corinthians. A New Translation with Introduction and Commentary.* Yale Anchor Bible 32. New Haven, CT: Yale University, 2008.

————. "Pauline Theology." In *New Jerome Biblical Commentary.* Englewood Cliffs, NJ: Prentice Hall, 1990. 1382–1416. Published separately as *Paul and His Theology: A Brief Sketch.* Second Edition. Englewood Cliffs, NJ: Prentice Hall, 1989.

————. *Romans. A New Translation with Introduction and Commentary.* Anchor Bible 33. New York: Doubleday, 1993.

França, Ágda. *A cruz em Paulo: Um sentido para o sofrimento.* São Paulo: Paulinas, 2010.

Gaventa, Beverly Roberts. *Our Mother Saint Paul.* Louisville, KY: Westminster John Knox, 2007.

Gorgulho, Gilberto, and Ana Flora Anderson. *A Origem e o Mistério do Mal.* São Paulo: 2006.

Gorman, Michael. J. *Apostle of the Crucified Lord: A Theological Introduction to Paul and His Letters.* Grand Rapids, MI: Eerdmans, 2004.

———. *Inhabiting the Cruciform God: Kenosis, Justification, and Theosis in Paul's Narrative Soteriology.* Grand Rapids, MI: Eerdmans, 2009.

Greenman, Jeffrey, and George Kalantzis, eds. *Life in the Spirit: Spiritual Formation in Theological Perspective.* Downers Grove, IL: IVP Academic, 2010.

Grilli, Massimo. *"Paradosso" e "mistero." Il Vangelo di Marco.* Bolgna: Dehoniane, 2012.

Harrington, Daniel J. *Meeting St. Paul Today: Understanding the Man, His Mission and His Message.* Chicago: Loyola, 2009.

Harrington, Daniel J., and James F. Keenan. *Paul and Virtue Ethics: Building Bridges between New Testament Studies and Moral Theology.* Lanham, MD: Rowman & Littlefield, 2010.

Hays, Richard. "What Is 'Real Participation in Christ'? A Dialogue with E. P. Sanders on Pauline Soteriology." In *Redefining First-Century Jewish and Christian Identities: Essays in Honor of Ed Parish Sanders.* Fabian E. Udoh, et al. eds. Christianity and Judaism in Antiquity 16. Notre Dame, IN: University of Notre Dame Press, 2008. 336–51.

Horsley, Richard A., ed. *Paul and Empire: Religion and Power in Roman Imperial Society.* Harrisburg, PA: Trinity, 2000.

Howard, James M. *Paul, the Community, and Progressive Sanctification: An Exploration into Community-Based Transformation within Pauline Theology.* Studies in Biblical Literature 90. New York: Peter Lang, 2007.

Izejie, Luke. "God's Presence in the Created World: Its Implications for Theology and Evangelization for Today." In CATHAN [Catholic Theological Association of Nigeria]: *A Searchlight of Saint Paul.* Eds. Obanure, Cyril and Mary Silvia Nwachukwu. Makurdi, Nigeria: Aboki Publishers, 2010. 117–35.

Jennings, Theodore W. *Transforming Atonement: A Political Theology of the Cross.* Minneapolis, MN: Fortress, 2009.

Johnson, Luke Timothy. "Pauline Traditions." In *The Writings of the New Testament.* Rev. ed. Minneapolis, MN: Fortress, 1999. 239–456.

Käsemann, Ernst. *On Being a Disciple of the Crucified Nazarene.* Grand Rapids, MI: Eerdmans, 2010.

Keener, Craig. *1–2 Corinthians.* New Cambridge Bible Commentary. Cambridge, UK: Cambridge University Press, 2005.

Kim, Yung Suk. *Christ's Body in Corinth: The Politics of a Metaphor.* Paul in Critical Contexts. Minneapolis, MN: Fortress, 2008.

Konings, Johan. *Liturgia dominical: mistério de Cristo e formação dos fiéis.* Petrópolis: Vozes, 2003.

Koperski, Veronica. *What Are They Saying about Paul and the Law?* Mahwah, NJ: Paulist, 2001.

Levison, John R. *The Spirit in First-Century Judaism.* Leiden: Brill, 2002.

Lopez, Davina C. *Apostle to the Conquered: Reimagining Paul's Mission.* Paul in Critical Contexts. Minneapolis, MN: Fortress, 2008.

Malina, Bruce J., and John J. Pilch. *Social-Science Commentary on the Letters of Paul.* Minneapolis, MN: Fortress, 2006.

Maloney, Elliott C. *Jesus' Urgent Message for Today: The Kingdom of God in Mark's Gospel.* New York: Continuum, 2004.

Martyn, J. Louis. *Theological Issues in the Letters of Paul.* Nashville: Abingdon, 1997.

Masi, Nicolau. "A lei do Espirito de Vida (Rm 8,2)." *Estudos Bíblicos* 45 (1995): 67–75.

Matera, Frank. *God's Saving Grace: A Pauline Theology.* Grand Rapids, MI: Eerdmans, 2012.

McKenzie, John L., *Dictionary of the Bible.* New York: Macmillan, 1965.

Mesters, Carlos. *Entrevista com Paulo Apóstolo: Uma porta de entrada para sua vida e missão.* São Paulo: Paulinas, 2009.

Minear, Paul. *The Bible and the Historian: Breaking Silence about God in Biblical Studies.* Nashville, TN: Abingdon, 2002.

Milinovich, Timothy. *Beyond What Is Written: The Performative Structure of 1 Corinthians.* Eugene, OR: Pickwick, 2013.

Munzinger, André. *Discerning the Spirits: Theological and Ethical Hermeneutics in Paul.* SNTSMS 140. Cambridge, UK: Cambridge University Press, 2007.

Murphy-O'Connor, Jerome. *Becoming Human Together: The Pastoral Anthropology of St. Paul.* Third Edition. Atlanta, GA: Society of Biblical Literature, 2009.

Obanure, Cyril, and Mary Silvia Nwachukwu, eds. CATHAN [Catholic Theological Association of Nigeria]: *A Searchlight of Saint Paul.* Makurdi, Nigeria: Aboki Publishers, 2010.

Osiek, Carolyn. *Philippians, Philemon.* Abingdon NT Commentaries. Nashville, TN: Abingdon, 2000.

Parra Sánchez, Tomás. *Paulo: aventura entre os pagãos.* Conhecer a Bíblia 6. São Paulo: Paulinas, 1996.

Pastor Ramos, Federico. *Corpus Paulino*. 2 Volumes. Comentarios a la Nueva Biblia de Jerusalén. Bilbao, Spain: Desclée De Brouwer, 2005.

———. *Pablo, un seducido por Cristo*. Navarra: Verbo Divino, 1991.

Penna, Romano. *Paul the Apostle: A Theological and Exegetical Study*. 2 Volumes. Collegeville, MN: Liturgical Press, 1996.

Pesce, Mauro. *As duas fases da pregaçao de Paulo*. Coleçao Bíblica Loyola 20. São Paulo: Ed. Loyola, 1996.

Polaski, Sandra Hack. *A Feminist Introduction to Paul*. St. Louis, MO: Chalice, 2005.

Pontifical Biblical Commission. *The Interpretation of the Bible in the Church*. 1993.

Rainbow, Paul A. *The Way of Salvation: The Role of Christian Obedience in Justification*. Milton Keynes, UK: Paternoster, 2005.

Reasoner, Mark. *Romans in Full Circle: A History of Interpretation*. Louisville, KY: Westminster John Knox, 2005.

Roetzel, Calvin J. *The Letters of Paul. Conversations in Context*. Fourth Edition. Louisville, KY: Westminster, 1998.

Salas, Antonio. *Pablo de Tarso*. Madrid: San Pablo, 1994.

Santos, Amanda. *Facing the Apostle: Paul's Image in Art*. Boston: Pauline Books & Media, 2009.

Saunders, Stanley P. "Learning Christ: Eschatology and Spiritual Formation in New Testament Christianity." *Interpretation* 56 (2002): 155–67.

Schnelle, Ugo. *Apostle Paul: His Life and Theology*. Grand Rapids: Eerdmans, 2005.

Son, Sang-Won. *Corporate Elements in Pauline Anthropology*. Analecta Biblica 148. Rome: Biblical Institute Press, 2001.

Spicq, Ceslaus. *Agape in the New Testament*. 2 volumes. St. Louis, MO: Herder, 1965.

Spitaler, Peter, ed. *Celebrating Paul: Festschrift in Honor of Jerome Murphy-O'Connor and Joseph A. Fitzmyer, SJ*. Catholic Biblical Quarterly Monograph Series 48. Washington, DC: CBA, 2011.

Stowers, Stanley. "What Is 'Pauline Participation in Christ'?" In *Redefining First-Century Jewish and Christian Identities: Essays in Honor of Ed Parish Sanders*. Fabian E. Udoh et al. eds. Christianity and Judaism in Antiquity 16. Notre Dame, IN: University of Notre Dame Press, 2008. 352–71.

Tambasco, Anthony. *A Theology of Atonement and Paul's Vision of Christianity*. Zaccheus Studies. Collegeville, MN: Liturgical Press, 1991.

Tannehill, Robert C. *Dying and Rising with Christ: A Study in Pauline Theology.* BZNW 32. Berlin: Töpelmann, 1967.

———. "Participation in Christ: A Central Theme in Pauline Soteriology." In *The Shape of the Gospel: New Testament Essays.* Eugene, OR: Cascade Books, 2007. 223–37.

Thiselton, Anthony C. *The Living Paul: An Introduction to the Apostle's Life and Thought.* Downers Grove, IL: Intervarsity Press, 2009.

Thompson, James W. *Pastoral Ministry according to Paul: A Biblical Vision.* Grand Rapids, MI: Baker Academic, 2006.

———. *Moral Formation according to Paul: A Biblical Vision.* Grand Rapids, MI: Baker Academic, 2011.

Tobin, Thomas H. *The Spirituality of Paul.* Eugene, OR: Wipf & Stock, 1987.

Vahrenhorst, Martin. *Kultische Sprache in den Paulusbriefen.* Wissenschaftliche Untersuchungen zum Neuen Testament 230. Tübingen: Mohr Siebeck, 2008.

Vidal, Senén. *El proyecto mesiánico de Pablo.* Biblioteca des Estudios Biblicos 116. Salamanca: Sígueme, 2005.

Ware, James P. *Paul and the Mission of the Church: Philippians in Ancient Jewish Context.* Grand Rapids, MI: Baker Academic, 2011.

White, Ernest. *Christian Life and the Unconscious.* New York: Harper, 1955.

Wright, N. T. *Paul: In Fresh Perspective.* Minneapolis, MN: Fortress, 2005.

———. *What Saint Paul Really Said: Was Paul of Tarsus the Real Founder of Christianity?* Grand Rapids, MN: Eerdmans, 1997.

Index of Scripture Citations

Subject Index